BEYOND MEASURE

Rescuing an Overscheduled, Overtested,
Underestimated Generation

VICKI ABELES

WITH GRACE RUBENSTEIN

SIMON & SCHUSTER

New York London Toronto Sydney New Delhi

Simon & Schuster
1230 Avenue of the Americas
New York, NY 10020

First Simon & Schuster hardcover edition October 2015

SIMON & SCHUSTER and colophon are
registered trademarks of Simon & Schuster, Inc.

For information about special discounts for bulk purchases,
please contact Simon & Schuster Special Sales at
1-866-506-1949 or business@simonandschuster.com.

The Simon & Schuster Speakers Bureau can bring
authors to your live event. For more information or to book
an event contact the Simon & Schuster Speakers Bureau at
1-866-248-3049 or visit our website at www.simonspeakers.com.

Manufactured in the United States of America

1 3 5 7 9 10 8 6 4 2

Library of Congress Cataloging-in-Publication Data

Abeles, Vicki.
Beyond measure : rescuing an overscheduled, overtested, underestimated
generation / by Vicki Abeles.
pages   cm
1. Educational change—United States.   2. Overpressure
(Education)   3. Motivation in education—United States.
4. Academic achievement—United States.   5. Students—
Academic workload—United States.   I. Title.
LA217.2.A24   2015
370.973—dc23   2015022235

ISBN 978-1-4516-9923-4
ISBN 978-1-4516-9925-8 (ebook)

To my children—Shelby, Jamey, and Zak—
who are my greatest teachers

Contents

Foreword

Lynda Weinman, founder of Lynda.com

I AM A POSTER child for someone who was failed by standardized education but who found personal and professional success despite the experience.

I started out as a happy student who thrived in and loved school. But when my parents went through an acrimonious divorce, sending my siblings and me back and forth to and from unwanting guardians in whose homes I suffered neglect and abuse, my life took a terrible turn. No longer thrilled just to please teachers and parents, I struggled to find meaning in my lessons. School felt impersonal and irrelevant. No one really knew me there. I went from getting straight A's to becoming more and more depressed, disenfranchised, and disengaged. By middle school I was getting C's and D's. I dreamed of dropping out.

What saved me was a chance at a wholly different kind of learning. I found a high school that afforded students two rare gifts—choice and trust—allowing me to hew my studies to my own curiosity, with teachers' support. At this pivotal time in my life, when I could have easily given up and been drawn down a darker path, I instead learned to believe in myself beyond how school defined me. My new education connected me with my passions and motivated me to work for something more than a grade.

My story is not unique. Today, millions of young people are checking out, alienated by an educational culture that obsesses over products—transcripts, test scores, top-ranked college admissions—while missing the diverse potential and passions of individual people. At the same time, millions of others are swept up in the rush to rank and measure each student. These beleaguered young people spend their whole childhoods racing for perfection, or giving up altogether like I almost did, driving themselves to hollow exhaustion to meet an impossible ideal. This kind of high-stakes childhood is an experience that, as a parent, I know all too well.

My exposure to divergent forms of education was still with me when, in 1995, I cofounded an online learning company called Lynda.com, offering online video lessons in design, computer, and business skills to learners inside and outside the classroom. The company recently sold to LinkedIn for a record-breaking sum and now serves hundreds of millions of people around the world, a testament to the hunger for new ways of learning.

As a hiring manager for the past twenty years, I have seen firsthand how hard it is to find employees who are self-motivated, creative thinkers, and contributors versus followers. Job seekers emerging from a school system and a culture at large that place the most value on what can be measured possess fewer of the hard-to-measure interpersonal skills of leadership, problem solving, and creativity. Given that most factory jobs are destined to be filled by robots and computerized automation, and that some of the most intriguing vocations of today didn't even exist ten years ago, it is essential to rethink our education system and move away from the drills and rote learning of facts that can be better retrieved by computers than human beings. To really give our kids the best chance to flourish, we have to teach them how to think, lead, innovate, and contribute. Beyond the prospect of good jobs, we owe kids these better lessons so that they may forge good lives—equipped to be engaged, stimulated, complete human beings.

All of this was on my mind when I saw Vicki Abeles's film, *Race to Nowhere*, with hundreds of parents and teachers at a community screening in Santa Barbara, California, a few years ago. I witnessed the vibrant discussion afterward, as the audience shared their own similar stories, hopes, fears, and dreams for their students and children. Vicki's film stirred strong emotion in me too, as I have worn the shoes of a student, parent, teacher, and employer. In all of these roles, I've personally experienced the downside of high-stakes testing and standardized learning. My early school experiences were strikingly similar to many of those featured in *Race to Nowhere*. And the innovative high school that changed the trajectory of my life was strikingly similar to many of the inspiring schools that are written about in this book.

In both of her documentaries and now this book, Abeles has tuned in to one of the most important problems of our time. She is a brave champion for the widespread movement to change education from a one-size-fits-all factory model to a dynamic and personal approach that promotes our innate creativity and natural thirst for lifelong growth and learning.

I believe, along with Vicki and the other experts she cites in her book, that it is critical to place primary value on human creativity and wellness in order to create a viable economy for future generations and a balanced life for our children. Our current education system is not only outdated and ineffective, but it is dangerous to our children; the health effects of too much stress and pressure are resulting in physical and mental problems of epidemic proportions.

In our school system's zest to measure, grade, rank, promote, and punish, we have lost touch with what matters most—creating healthy, happy children who love to learn, want to contribute to the world, and can tackle the enormous problems of our times with innovative ideas and solutions. Because the truth is that success is not defined by grades, degrees, or money. It is reflected in the quality of life you lead and how you carry your values and purpose into making a positive impact.

Vicki's book tells the stories of students, parents, and teachers who are breaking free of the past and forging new systems of learning. She has devoted her life's work to telling the stories of the disenfranchised and disconnected, and presents solutions and research for how to change the system to foster thinking, creativity, wellness, and optimism.

Her words and research will shed new light on new information and actions that will reverse the tide of our broken education system. Change is not going to come from the top down, it is going to come from those affected by our broken systems. The time is now, and you can be part of this change. Join us, read and share this book, and be brave. It is time to stop perpetuating what isn't working and move toward a brighter and healthier future for all.

The stakes have never been higher for us to get it right.

"Numbered Identity"

Tira Okamoto, 17, Lowell High School, San Francisco

I am 2040, 31, and 3.67.
I am 500 words on the Common App.
I am the stacks of Scantron tests that lie on my bedroom floor.
I am the SAT, ACT, and AP test-prep books.
I am one of the millions of bubbles I will have filled out by the
*   time I graduate from high school.*
I am a student being taught by teach-to-the-test teachers.
I am instructional minutes and A-G graduation requirements.
I am the eight hours of high school.
I am the five hours of homework.
I am the less than five hours of sleep.
I am a test crammer who hardly remembers the information
*   after the test.*
I am the AP machine, the bubble robot.
I am the repeat.
I am a product of the system.
I am standardized.
What more do you want?
Why can't I be known as
A dancer with crazy curly hair
A bike rider who loves to read books.
An avid baseball fan whose passion is global communication
*   and relations.*
Why am I just a
Numbered Identity?

Introduction

IN HOMES AND classrooms across America, a silent epidemic is raging. It afflicts the eight-year-old lying awake, pulling his hair with worry over tomorrow's test. The seventeen-year-old straining to keep up in AP chemistry on top of the three other AP classes and two sports and four clubs that she thought she needed on her résumé. And the thirteen-year-old still studying past one a.m., wondering in the back of her bleary mind if *this*— this never-ending contest for credentials, this exhaustion, this feeling of meaninglessness—is all life is.

The scourge affects teachers, too, who feel pressured to push children through impossible piles of information instead of pursuing fewer, richer experiences that might teach them more. And it ravages families, who see their hard-studying teen little more than ten minutes a day and can't understand how such a curious, playful child became a spiritless workaholic.

This illness is the Race to Nowhere. Its source is an education culture gone crazy with competition, and a society so obsessed with one narrow vision of success that it's making our children sick. Once contained to ambitious adult professionals, the sickness now afflicts children, who absorb the message that sprinting for the "top" is the only way to succeed. Still fragile and impressionable, they feel they must outshine their peers with perfect performances in every realm: school, test scores, sports, arts, and activities. If they fall short, they believe they have failed.

As a result, some children have ended up in pediatricians' and psychologists' offices with stress-induced illnesses that could last a lifetime. Others will avoid medical trouble but will nonetheless miss the chance to enjoy their childhoods, explore genuine interests, and discover who they really are.

A grassroots movement is growing to cure this disease. In my travels across the country since the release of my first film, *Race to Nowhere*, and in researching my new film, *Beyond Measure*, I have found a veritable army of fellow change makers. There are hundreds of thousands of parents and students, teachers and school administrators, who all share the conviction that our kids deserve something better. We want to see our children for more than a hurried few minutes at dinner. We want schools to be a place where kids go to feel stimulated and supported, not ranked and sorted, and where the great poet, peacemaker, or political debater is valued as highly as the adept test taker. Like all caring adults, we want our children to grow into happy, healthy, financially independent citizens. But we see that the mad dash to outachieve one another is actually worsening their chances. The participants in this movement refuse to accept the false notion that the highest grades and the fattest childhood résumés represent the only path to a worthy life. Instead, we envision a world in which a child with a healthy body, a creative mind, and a contented heart—not simply an Ivy League diploma—is considered a success.

Brave trailblazers I've met across the country are fighting to create that world. In these pages, you'll meet them: a pediatrician-mother who spearheaded the awakening about student stress at her daughters' high school; a principal who insisted that her kindergarteners would fare better by reading stories after school instead of filling out worksheets; a teacher whose students' work improved when he stopped grading it; a superintendent striving to offer his community something deeper than test prep; a college admissions director who's personalizing the application process despite the risk of lowering his college's ranking; and a father who gently guided his kids toward genuine curiosity and away from the Ivy League.

This book tells their stories and many others. The actions they've taken (and the mistakes they've made along the way) provide a kind of playbook for other parents, students, and educators who crave change. More than that, their successes prove what is often so hard to believe in the midst of the madness: that change is possible. Their stories will empower you to start rewriting yours.

Prologue

Out of Nowhere

M Y OWN AWAKENING to the toxicity of the achievement race came the way it does to many parents: via years of trying to keep up with it.

I sensed the problem in my home before I could name it. My daughters, Shelby and Jamey, were in middle school, and Zakary was in third grade. They were still children, in the essential sense of the word. They still played hide-and-seek, treasured their American Girl dolls, and relied on me to make their meals. But their lives had mutated into an adultlike state of busyness that gave our home the air of a corporate command center.

Twelve-year-old Jamey, for instance—who still wore braces and fit into children's clothing sizes—would wake up before seven, cram in some extra studying over breakfast, and rush off to her school day, which lasted the usual seven hours. She'd go straight from there to a violin lesson or soccer practice, return home at six, and commence a daily homework marathon that took her well into the night. I'd see her hunched at her desk past eleven p.m., washed in the yellow lamplight, her long brown hair spilling over her books. The next day, she'd get up and do it again.

Now multiply that madness by three.

In earlier years, my husband, Doug, and the kids and I had spent weekends together, relaxing in the park, exploring museums, and playing games. We whiled away long hours reading books. I watched Shelby become a budding writer, Jamey fall in love with animals, and Zak develop into a garrulous drummer and athlete who could chat amiably with strangers. On weeknights we almost always ate dinner together as a family.

Slowly, though, I began to notice that our lives were less and less our own. During the week, the children would appear for dinner and then disappear into hours of assignments. Sometimes after a night's worth of homework, our dining table would be piled so high with books and papers that it looked like the conference table at a law firm. On weekends, if the children weren't practicing piano scales or traveling to soccer matches, they were often studying. They rarely simply went out to play with kids in the neighborhood; everyone else was enslaved to a schedule, too. I could scarcely remember the last time I'd seen my kids play, tinker, daydream, relax, invent a game, write or read for pleasure, or do *anything* that wasn't assigned to them by someone. They were so busy being little professionals that they had almost no time just to be children. Likewise, Doug and I were left with no time just to be the parents we wanted to be. We were too busy being chauffeurs, homework wardens, and musical taskmasters.

Worse, I began to see the constant demands taking a toll on my children's health. Jamey started complaining about headaches, stomachaches, and sleepiness, which she attributed to the pressures of school. Though she was just twelve, Jamey sometimes went to bed later than I did. Zak, only eight years old, also started getting headaches, from worry about all the work he had to do.

Believe me, I wanted my children to shine. I wanted them to earn good grades, cultivate their interests, and build the skills to succeed in high school, college, and life beyond. But as my once-curious girls withdrew from our family life and became worker bees, producing formulaic essays and correct answers and formidable extracurricular résumés, and as my once-buoyant boy cried in frustration over his hundredth set of math problems, I started to wonder whether the relentless pressure to perform was doing more harm than good.

————

So many parents have told me that the madness snuck up on them the same way. You want your children to learn deeply, so you push them to study. You want to give them opportunities to develop their interests—perhaps better opportunities than you had as a child—so you enroll them in whatever sports and art lessons you can afford. You think you're doing the right thing. And then, before you realize it, your life feels like it's spun out of control.

The rat race for our family began in kindergarten. The four of us (Zak wasn't born yet) bundled into the car one morning and set off to Shelby's kindergarten talent show, for which she had nervously decided to recite a poem. Puzzlingly, the expectations around the show seemed high. Were five-year-olds these days supposed to have finely honed specialties? Apparently so: the revue included impressive gymnastics routines and piano recitals, plus one particularly dazzling violin number, all executed deftly by tiny performers. Jamey, age three, immediately asked Doug and me if she could take violin lessons. Wonderful, we thought: music is educational! We said yes.

And we kept saying yes for many years thereafter. Both girls signed up for music lessons and soccer. When Shelby was in fourth grade and struggling with math, I learned that most of her classmates were taking after-school tutorials at the private Kumon learning center, so popular that it serves students in nearly fifty countries. Instead of wondering why a fourth grade math class was too hard for fourth graders, I enrolled her at Kumon, hoping to boost her confidence. Her siblings followed.

The kids' rigorous schedules also extended into our home as their homework loads grew heavier (and their enthusiasm for learning weaker) year by year. But the work seemed important. I understood it to be my duty as a mom to oversee my children's assignments and monitor their grades. I expected straight As, even made flash cards and marked up school papers with red ink. When I felt I couldn't help, I enlisted the support of teachers and tutors. I wanted to instill in my children perseverance and a drive for excellence because I believed those skills would carry them through life's challenges. I hoped they'd have better opportunities than the modest ones I had as a child. This, it seemed, was what devoted parents do.

"Children and families do not exist in a vacuum," Arizona State University psychologist Suniya Luthar would later tell me. "We exist in communities. Children exist in schools. There is a school culture, a community culture, in which there is this reverberating message: More is always better. Do more. Accomplish more. Achieve more. The schools and communities in turn exist in American culture, which again espouses the same message, the American dream. The more you can do, the better off you are. In fact, if you don't do more, you're going to be left behind."

I should have recognized the signs of overwork sooner, given my own history. My mother raised my two younger sisters, my younger brother, and me by herself, after our parents' divorce, in a small apartment on the outskirts of Miami. Seeing our mom's financial struggles made me determined to achieve independence. So I waited tables to fund my education at the University of Miami, and went from there to law school and then to Manhattan. Aiming for professional success and financial security, I joined a law firm on Wall Street and started working harder than I ever had before. Sometimes I wouldn't leave the office for days. Finally, a job move for Doug saved me. I transitioned to consulting, which allowed flexible hours, and we settled in Lafayette, a leafy San Francisco suburb where I imagined a healthier life for my family than the one we'd left behind. Never did I imagine that the frenzy of Wall Street would follow us there.

The upshot was that by the time my daughters entered middle school, our family had become enslaved to achievement. Jamey's violin studies had ballooned into a four-day-a-week gauntlet of lessons, group practices, and recitals. Her soccer team, which began as a cute exercise for second graders just striving to kick the ball straight, had morphed into a five-day-a-week commitment to practices and treks to tournaments hours from home. Even eight-year-old Zak had started soccer, piano, and Little League. We often ate meals in the car as we zoomed from one practice or recital to another. And always awaiting my kids when we returned was more homework. It seemed that anything a child did—every hobby, every interest, every lesson—had to be done at a near-professional level of commitment. Coaches and instructors expected no less. There was no room to dabble or just explore.

More and more, as I walked up the stairs to check on my children and saw Jamey through the crack in her bedroom door, she looked like my former self—hunched over her desk, joyless.

For my part, I woke up early and stayed up late to get my own work done, finding my days consumed with coordinating children's activities and studies. The expectations for parents seemed just as impossible as those for kids. How could we possibly manage all this and still have time to mind our own well-being?

"We're just really busy" was the answer I gave, reflexively, to grocery-aisle inquiries about how we were doing. Were everyone else's children handling it better? No one ever said otherwise. So we went about our busyness.

The saddest part for me is that we scarcely had to tell our children what "success" should look like. The prescription was plainly written: great grades and test scores, athletic and artistic awards, admission to a prestigious university, and, ultimately, a well-paid job in one of a handful of respected fields. Though I came to see that my husband and I had inadvertently pushed our kids too hard, they also pushed themselves. The extravagant expectations were all around them: In the impressive examples set by their friends. In the standards set by the schools, which increasingly expect all students to read fluently in kindergarten and perform feats of algebra by age thirteen. In the anxious questions overheard from other parents wondering how many AP classes their child should take for college applications. And in the shiny images of affluent lives on TV: the executives and stars in swanky New York apartments and Los Angeles mansions who appear to have reached the pinnacle of achievement.

This was the air we were breathing. And our young children, still searching for their identities, were breathing it, too.

In the spring of 2007, our family went away for Memorial Day weekend on the California coast. Shelby, whose seventh grade final exams were imminent, stayed inside studying the entire weekend. I'd never worked this hard—not in law school, not as an overburdened young associate in my first law job. Neither had Doug, who had survived the rigors of medical school. I thought: *This is nuts.*

———

Every parent who arrives at this realization immediately runs into a new set of vexing questions. Do we quit the sports and arts that our children seem to enjoy? Allow them to skip their homework? Abandon the tutoring that seems, at least in part, supportive of their confidence and progress? Pull them out of school? Each of these possibilities seems at first extreme. On top of the practical dilemmas, we confront deeper questions about the culture we are a part of. How in the world did we reach a place where school and enrichment activities, of all things, could literally be making our children sick? And how many other kids are struggling, too?

Searching for answers, I read books and attended lectures by experts in education, pediatrics, and child psychology. I started asking more people about their own experiences. What I found was staggering. The achievement-centered childhood that my kids were living was not a product of our particular family or town. It characterizes the lives of millions of children in diverse communities across the country. Nearly every parent and student I met understood the issue immediately and intimately. Everyone had a story—at least in private. Few parents wanted to publicly say that their children were being pushed beyond their limits. The kids didn't want to admit it either, having internalized the expectations of easy perfection.

Over the last couple of decades, I discovered, childhood has transformed into a performance. Not limited to the classroom or the ball field or the talent show stage, and knowing no socioeconomic or geographic boundaries, our collective focus on scores and numbers, awards and trophies, is robbing our kids of their childhoods, their health, and their happiness. This early experience with life-as-competition is shaping their nascent identities. Paradoxically, it's also swindling them out of their inborn enthusiasm for learning, challenge, and growth, thus dimming the brightness of their futures.

The deeper I dug, the more I became convinced: The pressure to perform—and its shadow, the fear of failure—represented a silent epidemic. Our competitive, high-stakes culture was the culprit. Our children were the victims.

At first I assumed that this pressure cooker was a perverse product of privilege, confined to upper-middle-class communities like mine in which success is often narrowly defined by high-status careers and elite college admissions. In some such neighborhoods there were epidemics of stealth tutoring, where every child had a tutor but no one admitted it. Yet I quickly found that students in working-class and impoverished communities suffer, too. In neighborhoods across the socioeconomic spectrum, I discovered that all students suffer in the impersonal contest that education has become, whether it be a race to ace an AP exam or to cover a year's worth of bloated content.

"I want to get into the best colleges I can," Isaiah, a high school senior in a low-income neighborhood in Oakland, told me. He was struggling in an AP government class that he took to fatten his transcript, staying up until midnight with the work. What for? He said, "Being an African American and taking AP classes is what people are looking for."

In many communities, even the nonoverachievers—the majority of kids—are afflicted. Children like my Jamey, a hardworking B student, feel marginalized by their school's limiting view of success. Meanwhile, *all* children in a system that mainly values bookwork miss chances to learn and express themselves in multidimensional ways. From the time they are toddlers, it thrills kids to count, sing their ABCs, observe bugs and birds, and build block towers. They have a natural drive to gain skills and achieve mastery, including and perhaps especially in areas where they are not yet proficient. But in too many cases, our impossible expectations for them after toddlerhood—expectations out of sync with their natural development—have made it too fraught or too frightening to continue. As our children get older, our cultural obsession with only one measurable version of intelligence—good grades, awesome test scores—discounts the value of diverse smarts and experimentation, leaving budding young poets, carpenters, and designers who don't test well to neglect their talents and doubt their self-worth.

Think of what we are losing.

And for what purpose, all this pressure? The presumed holy grail of a K-12 education in the United States is hardly a love for learning or an authentically engaged citizen. It is, against all odds, a "yes" message from one of a handful of expensive, brand-name universities that only a fraction of each year's three million high school graduates will be invited to attend. (And, it should be said, even that treasured invitation itself comes with no guarantee of lifelong happiness.) Whipped into a panic by hypercompetitive admissions practices and by hype, kids, parents, and educators pursuing that holy grail sacrifice terribly important things: time, money, health, happiness, and childhood itself. Without our even realizing it, our driving goal has become all about preparing for the college *application*, not preparing for the college *experience* or life beyond. Performing, not learning. Amassing credentials, not growing. Not even really living.

So, while it's true that resilient children need to cope with risk and failure as a part of life, we've set up their childhoods as a destructive march to likely defeat. "Success" equates to attending the most prestigious college and then netting the big house and the high-paying job. Winning the education race, we're told, is the way to get there. Rather than building their resilience, such a high-stakes education drives our children to chronic insecurity. Fear. Anxiety. Disconnection. Loneliness. Record rates of depression. And, as they get older, binge drinking, eating disorders, cutting, and even suicide. The clear message they hear from their environments is to produce, produce, produce at all costs, even if it means cheating, taking drugs, or working through the night to keep up.

The most painful irony is how badly out of step our frenzied educational practices are with science. Psychology and neuroscience journals abound with studies about how children learn and thrive, and how their brains grow, and none of it bears a remote resemblance to the spirit-crushing contest we're putting our kids through.

There's a "Goldilocks and the Three Bears" aspect to fruitful learning, explains Laurence Steinberg, Temple University neuroscientist and author of the book *Age of Opportunity: Lessons from the New Science of Adolescence.* In order to develop optimally, the brain needs just the right amount of challenge: enough to stimulate neuronal growth, but not so much as to overwhelm it. Our educational system today tends to "miss the sweet spot," he says, because "it confuses the quantity of work with the quality of the challenge."

The result? "Children are born curious, and it's pretty easy to facilitate that, to groom it," says Vassar College neuropsychologist Abigail Baird. "We're doing the opposite. We're squishing their desire to learn new things. And I think that's a crisis."

––––––––

Two incidents, one small and one large, pushed me over the edge into making my first film. The subtler event was a parent forum I attended at our school on the subject of student stress. As the guidance counselor ticked off symptoms, the parents and teachers in the audience nodded their heads; it all sounded too familiar. They asked what they could do. The unhelpful answer was that overwrought parents had to stop pressuring their kids. Besides, nothing more could be done until Congress and college admissions officers changed their policies. In other words, this was the fault of misguided individuals and policies beyond our control, not a cultural sickness or a responsibility shared by all. At the end of the evening, we left feeling as helpless as ever. No one, neither parents nor educators, had taken—or even envisioned—a step to actually *do* anything about it.

I came home feeling frustrated, even desperate, went upstairs, and found my daughter still doing homework at ten thirty p.m. Something flipped in me. Here before us was another inconvenient truth: a problem too many children and families were suffering from but no one was doing much to stop. This story needed to be told.

Soon after that night came the second, more potent catalyst: a friend called to tell me that a thirteen-year-old girl in our community, Devon Marvin, had killed herself. No one had ever guessed that this star student and budding musician felt so unhappy. Nobody, not even teachers or friends, had spotted warning signs; in fact, she'd been one of the success stories, one of the kids who had seemed to have it all. When I met her mom, Jane, she told me she had torn through her memories and Devon's emails and text messages, searching desperately for a sign as to why her daughter would end her life. The only clues she found pointed to a recent algebra exam, which Devon, previously a math ace, had flunked. "She was torn up about this math," Jane told me. "Here's a child who had always been so successful on so many fronts—and a stupid math grade."

I decided then that I'd do everything I could to make a difference, to tell this story so that people didn't feel alone. I read up on filmmaking, raised money, hired cinematographers, and in early 2008 started traveling the country, capturing stories. Our filmmaking team set out to give a voice to the young people on the front lines of this battle. Many of the students and parents I met had kept silent about their struggles until then, feeling pressure to make their exhausting achievements appear effortless. Once they were asked, though, many were surprisingly open.

"Kids are told that they need to be 'special,' that they need to stand out of the crowd," explained Samantha, a fifteen-year-old from San Diego. "Without that trophy, you are just another kid who plays soccer, or plays an instrument, or gets average grades, bound for community college."

Jeanine M., a mother in Newport Beach, California, wrote to me that as her kids grew older and became stressed and unkind to one another, she "felt my family slipping away."

Eighteen-year-old Emily wasn't afraid to recount how she slipped into a deep depression her junior year, and even considered suicide, as other swimmers surpassed her in water polo and it became harder and harder to maintain her once-perfect grades. She recalled, unflinchingly:

> *Junior year is supposedly the most important in high school and my effort just wasn't going to cut it, not if I wanted to go to a decent college, and without a degree from a top university I was not going to be successful. . . . I had failed. All those years of late nights studying for AP classes followed by 5 a.m. water polo or swim practices, what would they come to? Nothing, just like me. In a world where we must excel in not one but many areas, I had not done so in any. I would rather be dead than face the years to come, sure to be filled with constant reminders of my failure. In my mind, there was only one way out.*

Teachers, for their part, reported that they felt helpless, hemmed in by the curricular directives of their school districts, the pressures of preparing students for standardized tests over which they had no pedagogical control. "I wanted to really . . . change these kid's lives, and get them to see learning as a lifetime skill," said Emma Batten-Bowman, who taught English in a low-income community in Oakland. "But it's gotten harder and harder to feel like I could teach the things I believe in. . . . Things that actually get our students to think, and work together and care, are pushed aside."

In the end, the film's very title came from a teenager who pointed out on camera that his life had become a kind of treadmill: an endless competition with only vague and spurious rewards promised at the end. A Race to Nowhere. He was right.

———

Race to Nowhere premiered at the Mill Valley Film Festival in October 2009. Little did I know that afternoon that it would be the beginning of a whole new journey—a quest for solutions—that would ultimately lead me to this book.

I watched the film anxiously, unsure how it would be received. The moment the lights went up, I knew I'd struck a nerve. No one moved. The entire crowd remained in their seats, rapt, hungry for discussion. Hands flew up for the Q&A session. In the emotional conversation that ensued, concerns that parents had previously kept secret tumbled out. It was as if I'd stood up and shouted, "The emperor has no clothes!" Now the illness their families had been silently living with had a name. Now they knew that they were not alone.

Since then more than a million people have seen the film at seven-thousand-plus screenings in all fifty states and more than forty countries. Audiences in all kinds of communities, from leafy suburbs to remote towns to gritty cities, have responded much like that first crowd did. I have attended hundreds of these screenings and heard thousands of students and parents describe sadness, frustration, and something like grief about what the Race to Nowhere has stolen.

A father at a screening in Hinsdale, Illinois, stood up and said he felt like a failure as a parent for not giving his teenage son and daughter a different sense of accountability—an after-school job instead of a couple of those advanced classes, time together as a family instead of time glued to homework on the computer. "They need to have a broader experience of life, which is: it isn't all about studying," he exclaimed. "Getting an A in a class does not equal success in life. It just doesn't."

A high school student from Buffalo Grove, Illinois, wrote to me that she no longer had time to paint or walk her dog because of all her schoolwork. "I cry almost every day due to stress and anxiety," she said. "Please help end this race to nowhere so kids like me can get our lives back."

Everywhere I went, teachers, parents, and students of all stripes echoed the same wish: we all craved change. Yet inevitably, near the end of each discussion, we came to a question like the one I received from Cara Natterson, a Los Angeles pediatrician, author, and mom of two children in elementary school. She watched the film with friends and wrote to me, "The overwhelming response at the end was: Now what?! We who have children in grammar school can see what they are facing down the road. So how do parents step off the crazy treadmill and buck society?"

Natterson was right: It isn't enough just to identify the problem. We have to act to fix it. And we can't do it alone.

Yes, we as individuals can work to ease the pressures on students in our own homes and classrooms, to show them a broader vision of genuine success. That is crucial. But ultimately it won't be enough. We and our children still must answer to the pressures beyond our own four walls: the hypercompetitive college applications, the mountains of state-mandated curricula, the high-stakes standardized tests and rigid AP exams, the schedules set by club leaders and coaches, the constant well-meaning questions ("Where are you thinking of going to college?"). The crisis our children face calls for a whole movement—a radically altered vision for childhood and education and a groundswell of cultural change. Unless we build that, we'll just be erecting little storm shelters in a hurricane.

But here and there among the worried faces in the audience, I found daring people ready to make change—students, parents, and teachers presenting a fresh set of values and pressing their communities to uphold them. Some of these everyday revolutionaries live in wealthy, urban enclaves. Others live in middle-income suburbs, and still others on farms or in densely packed urban apartments. Their neighborhoods are dispersed from California to Kentucky, Montana to Manhattan. They send their children to, or teach in, public, private, charter, and parochial schools. Some of their victories are small; others are more extraordinary.

Every one of these revolutionaries has had the courage to stand up— sometimes against a tide of skepticism—and say out loud what our best intuition already tells us: that education is not a race. That busyness does not equal betterment. That a perfect transcript is not worth the cost of a lost childhood. And that no battery of tests can assess what most matters in life: Integrity. Determination. Empathy. Resourcefulness. Connectedness. A thirst for knowledge. Passion. Creativity. Adaptability. The aptitude to read not just books but also faces. Confidence and kindness. Respect. These are the qualities that adults who are truly prepared and engaged possess. They are beyond measure. And they are what we must actively cultivate in our children.

The Race to Nowhere movement that grew from those screenings proved to have a unique power. That is because it brings *whole communities* together in a new conversation about what those closest to our children—parents, educators, physicians, clergy members, coaches, and students themselves— actually want for them. Once the veil of silence is lifted, diverse stakeholders can become unified teams. And it is in the collective wisdom of each community that the solutions lie. This movement is not about promoting a standardized prescription; it is about healing from within.

Yet so many film viewers at first felt stuck on how to move beyond tiny fixes to big transformations. They couldn't imagine how education would look if it looked different. So I made my second film, *Beyond Measure*, to highlight innovative schools that are already showing how much healthier, more inventive, and more effective education can be. This book traces the stories of such change makers, including some who appear in the film as well as many others who appear only in these pages and who richly deserve recognition. In the chapters that follow, I chart their journeys—their determination, missteps, and victories—and I urge you to take heart in their triumphs and take up their charge. Each community's story is linked to one of the key ingredients in the Race to Nowhere, such as homework or testing, college admissions or overbooked time, though the truth is that everyone is working on multiple fronts, as we must do. In these pages I also spell out the scientific research that underpins our efforts. Years of psychology and brain studies clearly show that children learn best when they're supported, not constantly stressed, and when they're given the chance to grapple with deep questions that have no fixed answers. Something that, as parents and educators, in our guts we already know.

Let's make this clear: This movement is not about lowering standards. It's not about protecting our children from the inevitable stress and challenge of an engaged life. It's not about coddling or helicoptering or making excuses. Rather, it's about elevating the essentials. It's about questioning our spoon-fed definition of success and remembering what we truly want for our children: wellness, independence, purpose, and the spark of excitement in their eyes. It's about recognizing that it doesn't matter what college an unhealthy, insecure teen gets into—not if she's too stressed to learn or too anxious to grow. And it's about reclaiming for children and families the precious time that's rightfully theirs.

We can't wait for state or national policies to shift, or for the College

Board (maker of the SAT) to relinquish the keys to the college gates. That could take an eternity; our children need our help now. We must start immediately, joining together to launch change in our homes, schools, and our communities. This problem requires no technology or money to fix, only will. The will of each person to implement small changes as well as sweeping ones. We all create this culture—the current one and, starting now, the new one—by taking actions from right where we are. Call it the barn raising of a new American educational culture. Many layers of change will add up to an overall cultural shift that could quite literally save our children's lives.

In this shared effort, we will establish new markers of educational success and reprioritize what matters most to us, as parents and as Americans, for our kids and our future. We will insist upon raising a generation that can create, think, and thrive—not just produce. In our new vision, the reward sought for our kids will not be the trinkets of international test supremacy or name-brand college sweatpants. Rather, it will be the best gift we can give our children: the support and preparation necessary to enter the world ready to make it better.

Whenever I feel frustrated by the inertia we face and my energy flags (which it does), I think about my hopes for my own children, and for children like Samantha, the fifteen-year-old from San Diego. She wrote to me that kids' lives now are so scheduled that "it isn't until we have a shred of free time that we realize we don't even know who we really are." Though her peers tend to hide their problems, she wrote, "If you look closely, you can see how stress and the pressure to perform affect children and teenagers, even on a physical level: stomachaches, headaches, breakouts, delayed menstrual cycles, anxiety attacks, weight gain, weight loss, depression, even suicide."

Samantha concluded: "Something is very, very wrong, and it is up to us to fix it."

She is right. And we can. Courageous individuals and communities around the country are showing us how. Let's begin.

CHAPTER 1

Sicker, Not Smarter

I N LATE 2010 I received an email from Saint Louis University School of Medicine professor and pediatrician Stuart Slavin, who was concerned about the health effects of excessive performance pressure on children. One passage in it sticks with me to this day:

> My personal feeling is that we are conducting an enormous and un-precedented social experiment on an entire generation of American children, and the evidence of a negative impact on adolescent mental health is overwhelming. This is particularly disturbing given the fact that having mental health problems in the teen years predisposes to mental health problems in adulthood. It is even more profoundly disturbing when one considers that there is absolutely no evidence that this educational approach actually leads to better educational outcomes.

The science shows that Slavin is right: Our children are paying a high price for our cultural misdirection. Thousands of students are suffering from withering anxiety, depression, eating disorders, insecurity, dangerous sleep deprivation, and even thoughts of suicide. And it's not just our children's mental health that's in jeopardy (which would be worrisome enough by itself); it's their physical health, too. The result of the Race to Nowhere is a public health crisis on a scale that we have yet to fully recognize.

Before we turn to solutions, which are the heart of this book, it's important to take a chapter to demonstrate that students' stories are backed up by hard data—to take stock of the science of just what we're fighting for. In fact, the price of the achieve-at-all-costs approach includes more than sickness. It produces a drill-like mode of education that deadens lessons and narrows students' chances to explore broadly or think creatively. We see even young students disengaging from school experiences that feel impersonal and irrelevant, high school grads arriving at college in need of remediation, and rampant cheating among students of all ages. Ironically, the constant pressure also physiologically impairs children's capacity for learning. In other words, it backfires, undermining the very achievement that it's meant to promote.

All told, the outcome is a school environment that deprives children of both sound health and vibrant learning. These grave consequences are at the heart of what makes our work to transform childhood so urgent. What's at stake is no less than raising healthy, thriving kids and—as they become adults—a healthy, thriving society.

Fremont, California: A Crisis Visible

Irvington High School is a sprawling, single-story beige building wrapped around a central courtyard with picnic tables and a few redwood trees. The city of Fremont spreads out around it, pancake flat and pasted with strip malls and small ranch houses, the bare brown hills of California rising in the background.

Over the past five years, Assistant Principal Jay Jackson has watched this school community transform. He taught world history and sports psychology here for eight years before becoming an administrator. With close-cropped hair and the compact build of a lightweight wrestler, Jackson is the kind of compassionate teacher whom students instinctively trust. He has an Elvis Presley shrine in his office—replete with Elvis figurines, Elvis clocks, Elvis PEZ dispensers, and even a life-size Elvis cardboard cutout—made up of gifts from past students, who kept giving him the knickknacks as a kind of joke, even though he insists he's not *that* big of a fan. During his teaching years in the 2000s, Jackson recalls, the student population here was mixed:

primarily because they didn't have enough time to study or finish the assignment. Perhaps saddest of all, when asked, "What is your main purpose for being in high school?" more students checked "To get into a good college" than "To learn."

Stress levels were high when I visited Irvington in the fall of 2014. Sitting with a classroom full of juniors, I casually asked, "How stressed are you, on a scale of one to ten?" The teens replied with a chorus of groans: "Ten!" One said eleven.

I went on: "Who gets seven hours of sleep a night? Raise your hand." A couple of hands went up. "Six hours?" A few more. "Five?" And there the bulk of the class raised their hands. Growing ever more incredulous, I asked: "Four?" Up went the last couple of hands. Even as the discussion continued, many students were scribbling in their notebooks, not sparing a moment that could be spent on schoolwork. Finally, I put the critical question to them: "Is it worth it?" They mumbled yes. "Why?" One boy with a blondish mop of hair answered for his peers: "To better your future."

Afterward, Jackson strode down the hall away from the classroom, his frustration showing in his gait. "It pains me to go into those classes because they're really stressed, and my assumption is we're doing this to them," he said. "They're all messed up."

A student had died by suicide the previous spring. And just the day before my visit, Jackson said, he'd checked a student into the home-and-hospital program. That's an alternative education program for students who are too sick to come to school. What was this girl's ailment? The doctor couldn't diagnose the precise cause of her bodily pains and ulcers, but mysteriously, they went away during the summer and returned two weeks before the start of school. "It's driving me crazy," said Jackson, "because what's going on is flawed, but we're not brave enough to change it."

The fact is that he and his colleagues at Irvington actually *are* taking courageous steps to change the school's high-stakes culture and rebuild student health—most notably by restraining students from overloading on AP classes and working with Dr. Slavin to research what kind of support they most need, as we'll learn more about later. The progress is just slower than Jackson would like.

The questions I didn't ask in that classroom at Irvington were these: What about half of them were academically oriented and intent on college, the other half not. When, in 2010, the auto plant that had employed many of the students' parents shut down, taking nearly five thousand mostly blue-collar jobs away with it, the demographics of the school district began to shift. Around the same time, the district redrew neighborhood boundaries, delivering to Irvington a flood of students from a more affluent part of town. Many of these new students' parents were immigrants, drawn to the technology industry in nearby San Jose with high hopes for their children's futures in this land of opportunity.

The school's standardized test scores shot up—as did its rates of student anxiety, sleep deprivation, and stress-induced illnesses. When Jackson became assistant principal in 2012, the change was already under way.

"Two or three weeks into the school year, you start seeing students coming into the office with these issues, with stress, breaking down crying," even cutting themselves, he remembers. The problem hadn't been as obvious from the vantage point of his classroom, where students put their best face on and their late nights spent laboring over piles of do-or-die assignments weren't so visible. But you go to work in the school office, the crossroads of students' difficulties, and, he says, "You see enough."

Enough, that is, to deeply alarm Jackson, who's also a father of two boys in elementary school. It convinced him that Irvington has a serious health crisis on its hands. Jackson organized an online survey of students in fall 2013, to see if his instincts matched the teens' own experiences. The measure wasn't perfect—only about one in six students completed the survey. But this much was clear: if even a small percentage of Irvington students overall felt the same way as those who answered the questionnaire did, the situation was dire.

More than four in five of the teens who responded said they felt moderate or high stress about school. They reported doing hours of homework a night and sleeping too little. A majority were taking multiple AP and honors classes, and the most common reason they gave for enrolling in those classes (cited by 61 percent of students) was that it would help them get into a better college; trailing far behind, the next reason (cited by just 42 percent) was that they were actually interested in the subject matter. Nearly half of the teens admitted to cheating on tests or homework in the past year, primarily because they didn't have enough time to study or finish the assignment. Perhaps saddest of all, when asked, "What is your main purpose for being in high school?" more students checked "To get into a good college" than "To learn."

Stress levels were high when I visited Irvington in the fall of 2014. Sitting with a classroom full of juniors, I casually asked, "How stressed are you, on a scale of one to ten?" The teens replied with a chorus of groans: "Ten!" One said eleven.

I went on: "Who gets seven hours of sleep a night? Raise your hand." A couple of hands went up. "Six hours?" A few more. "Five?" And there the bulk of the class raised their hands. Growing ever more incredulous, I asked: "Four?" Up went the last couple of hands. Even as the discussion continued, many students were scribbling in their notebooks, not sparing a moment that could be spent on schoolwork. Finally, I put the critical question to them: "Is it worth it?" They mumbled yes. "Why?" One boy with a blondish mop of hair answered for his peers: "To better your future."

Afterward, Jackson strode down the hall away from the classroom, his frustration showing in his gait. "It pains me to go into those classes because they're really stressed, and my assumption is we're doing this to them," he said. "They're all messed up."

A student had died by suicide the previous spring. And just the day before my visit, Jackson said, he'd checked a student into the home-and-hospital program. That's an alternative education program for students who are too sick to come to school. What was this girl's ailment? The doctor couldn't diagnose the precise cause of her bodily pains and ulcers, but mysteriously, they went away during the summer and returned two weeks before the start of school. "It's driving me crazy," said Jackson, "because what's going on is flawed, but we're not brave enough to change it."

The fact is that he and his colleagues at Irvington actually *are* taking courageous steps to change the school's high-stakes culture and rebuild student health—most notably by restraining students from overloading on AP classes and working with Dr. Slavin to research what kind of support they most need, as we'll learn more about later. The progress is just slower than Jackson would like.

The questions I didn't ask in that classroom at Irvington were these: What about half of them were academically oriented and intent on college, the other half not. When, in 2010, the auto plant that had employed many of the students' parents shut down, taking nearly five thousand mostly blue-collar jobs away with it, the demographics of the school district began to shift. Around the same time, the district redrew neighborhood boundaries, delivering to Irvington a flood of students from a more affluent part of town. Many of these new students' parents were immigrants, drawn to the technology industry in nearby San Jose with high hopes for their children's futures in this land of opportunity.

The school's standardized test scores shot up—as did its rates of student anxiety, sleep deprivation, and stress-induced illnesses. When Jackson became assistant principal in 2012, the change was already under way.

"Two or three weeks into the school year, you start seeing students coming into the office with these issues, with stress, breaking down crying," even cutting themselves, he remembers. The problem hadn't been as obvious from the vantage point of his classroom, where students put their best face on and their late nights spent laboring over piles of do-or-die assignments weren't so visible. But you go to work in the school office, the crossroads of students' difficulties, and, he says, "You see enough."

Enough, that is, to deeply alarm Jackson, who's also a father of two boys in elementary school. It convinced him that Irvington has a serious health crisis on its hands. Jackson organized an online survey of students in fall 2013, to see if his instincts matched the teens' own experiences. The measure wasn't perfect—only about one in six students completed the survey. But this much was clear: if even a small percentage of Irvington students overall felt the same way as those who answered the questionnaire did, the situation was dire.

More than four in five of the teens who responded said they felt moderate or high stress about school. They reported doing hours of homework a night and sleeping too little. A majority were taking multiple AP and honors classes, and the most common reason they gave for enrolling in those classes (cited by 61 percent of students) was that it would help them get into a better college; trailing far behind, the next reason (cited by just 42 percent) was that they were actually interested in the subject matter. Nearly half of the teens admitted to cheating on tests or homework in the past year, makes you *so sure* it's worth it? Is this sprint to achieve a certain version of "success" (reaching the top of the class, the top college, the top job, and the top life) really helping? Or is it actually making you sicker, not smarter—the kind of sick that will likely last through your adulthood—and causing you to miss opportunities to build the real-life skills that really matter?

———

Let's examine the facts about what is happening to children's health. The implications are long-lasting, as there is an avalanche of evidence that an unhealthy youth sets the stage for an unhealthy life. I'll begin with the effects that we can see right now: the current frayed state of our children's and teens' health.

Unhealthy Hearts and Minds

Students these days are incredibly stressed. On the American Psychological Association's Stress in America survey, teens rate their stress levels during the school year higher than adults rate their own. Nearly one in three teens says the stress drives them to sadness or depression. And what are the top sources of their stress? Eighty-three percent of the thousand teens surveyed named school, and 69 percent named getting into a good college or deciding what to do after high school. Meanwhile, 30 percent of high schoolers said on a government survey that they had felt sad or hopeless almost every day for two weeks or more within the past year.

Young Americans' mental health has deteriorated dramatically since the postwar days of the 1950s. Jean Twenge, a psychology professor at San Diego State University and author of the book *Generation Me*, has scoured and crunched decades' worth of data to illuminate these trends. By her calculations, five to eight times more college students today report serious mental health problems than did students at midcentury. This doesn't bode well for their future health, as depression raises a person's risk of heart disease, diabetes, and other illnesses, and having depression early in life significantly increases the risk of having it again as an adult.

Federal data also show that suicide rates more than doubled among youth age fifteen to twenty-four between 1950 and 2010 and more than tripled (though the rate is still much lower) among younger children. What's less well known but equally worrisome is how many kids *consider* taking their own lives. In a Centers for Disease Control and Prevention (CDC) survey of high school students—children as young as fourteen—nearly one in six said they had seriously thought about suicide. Half that many had made an attempt within the past year.

It makes me wonder: How much torment happens below the surface, beneath the game faces that adults can see? And how much is hidden behind the airbrushed lives today's teens present on Twitter and Instagram, where one kid's seemingly effortless achievements only make the next kid feel she must do more?

Behind these numbers are stories like that of an alarmed mother in Orange County, California, whose seventeen-year-old son had once ranked first in his high school out of a class of 764, taking six AP classes (out of seven total) in his junior year and sleeping only five hours a night. His worried mother wrote:

> *I discouraged him from taking on this load, but he insisted and continued this into his senior year by taking the International Baccalaureate, and now the chronic stress and lack of sleep has taken its toll. . . .*
>
> *Prior to high school my son was a secure, outgoing well-liked person with many friends. He likes to surf and would design and paint patterns on his boards. He organized camping trips, booking at state parks and organizing his friends without any help from me. He would not be able to do this today. . . . He is now in his senior year and was diagnosed last month with major depression. He has a terror of going to school and has only attended school for about six days in the past two months. . . . We are working with a doctor, a counselor (who brought your film to our community) and the school to try and salvage what we can for him to graduate in June.*

What happened to this young man is sadly not uncommon. And unfortunately, our kids' poor health outcomes are anything but temporary. The unhealthy, unhappy patterns laid down in the grade school years stay with teens as they enter the nation's universities, where officials are battling binge-drinking episodes and reporting a rising mental health crisis, as well.

"They work their tails off to get here, and then reach the finish line and are accepted and get here, and then realize that there is no finish line," says Kevin Wehmhoefer, a Harvard University clinician and coordinator of outreach, counseling, and mental health services. "I got here and I was blown away by the level of acuity that kids were presenting with." Wehmhoefer observed extreme anxiety or depression in many students who came to his clinic—and counselors from the University of California to Appalachian State University in North Carolina report the same trend. Surprisingly, though, after final exams ended, Wehmhoefer saw the symptoms for some students resolve within days. That's not typical of clinical depression. The problem, he says, reflects "kids who have been measuring themselves by a lone metric for a long time," who have no tolerance for failure. And who, crucially, have never learned the emotional skills to manage the acute stress that results.

The scale of the problem is huge. In the latest National Survey of College Counseling Centers, 94 percent of counseling directors said they were seeing rising numbers of students with severe psychological problems. Indeed, more than half of college students in a recent survey reported that they'd felt overwhelmed by anxiety within the past year. One in three said they'd felt so depressed it was hard to function. Tulane University, particularly hard hit in fall 2014, lost three students to suicide by Thanksgiving.

"The increased need for mental health services on our campuses is outstripping our ability to provide those services," John Stobo, an executive vice president for the University of California system, told the *California Report* radio program that same fall. The number of students seeking help at UC counseling centers had jumped by more than a third in the previous six years. Reduced stigma around seeking mental health counseling could account for some of that rise. But the increased incidence of emotional distress among college students is dramatic nonetheless: UCLA has surveyed entering freshmen at four-year colleges and universities around the country about their own mental health since 1985. In 2014, these students' ratings hit a record low.

Unhealthy Bodies

Beyond the kinds of mental and emotional pains the college psychologists describe, the health consequences of the childhood rat race are also frequently physical. Many of the pediatricians I've met around the country have told me, with grave concern, that they're seeing physiological impacts of this stress among their patients. And not just among high schoolers: many report symptoms in children as early as elementary school, just like I saw in Zak in third grade.

Lawrence Rosen, a pediatrician in northern New Jersey, told me that over the past fifteen years he's seen more and more children diagnosed with depression, anxiety, and physical symptoms of stress such as motor tics and panic attacks. "Kids are coming here with migraine headaches, ulcers. I'm talking about five-, six-, seven-year-olds who are coming in with these conditions. We never used to see that," Rosen said. "I do a lot of work nationally with other pediatric groups and pediatricians and I'm hearing this from my colleagues everywhere."

From Highland Park, Illinois, pediatrician Susan Sirota emailed me the following: "Every day I see children with some condition that is a direct result of the stress they experience related to school. Interestingly, when I started practice we used to figure this out by asking about what happened to the pain on the weekend—it would go away; now there is no difference since so many children are continuing to 'do extra school' or just not able to relax on the weekends."

This is how extreme the physical symptoms of childhood stress can get. Edin Randall is a psychologist at a pediatric pain rehabilitation center at Boston Children's Hospital. Her clinic specializes in a poorly understood and severe illness called complex regional pain syndrome—which she describes as commonly associated with high-pressure educational and extracurricular settings. This rare disease was described as early as the American Civil War and affects youth and adults in various countries, but its rates are rising, probably due to increased awareness and diagnosis. Randall says a typical case starts with an injury, such as an ankle sprain in a dance recital. The acute pain persists beyond the normal tissue healing process and then becomes chronic. Then, for reasons doctors don't yet understand, the child's nerves become irritated such that "a light touch will feel like stabbing pain," Randall explains. Normal treatments don't work for some patients. The pain is so severe that the child stops using that limb, which becomes waxy and stiff from disuse. Many sufferers stop going to school or participating in other activities.

There's been no research done yet to identify a causal link between high-stakes education and such pain disorders, but Randall sees a connection. Many of the children she treats tell her they come from stereotypically high-achieving communities with intense competition and pressure to perform. "It's a common denominator for a lot of our patients," she told me. Randall is careful to point out that, though stress seems to make the syndrome worse, it's not the cause. Rather, the physical and emotional distress work in tandem: the pain heightens a patient's anxiety, and the anxiety, in turn, makes it harder to cope with the pain. "Pain turns out to be a good communicator," Randall explains. Many of her patients put great effort into appearing fine even when they're incredibly stressed. So, Randall says, "Oftentimes pain is an indicator that there's something else going on." That *something else* may include the extreme expectations of an achievement culture gone crazy.

The Young and the Sleepless

At every screening I've attended, without fail, a bewildered, exasperated parent takes the mic and says his teen is staying up until the wee hours, night after night, then pounding coffee or going through her days in a sleepy haze, and no matter how this parent tries, he just can't convince his kid to close the books and go to bed. I couldn't sympathize more. When my girls were in middle and high school, I lost count of the number of times I'd tell them to go to bed, only to find them hours later awake at their desks, afraid to show up at school with work incomplete. Finally, I started insisting: interceding when they reached for lattes to power through piles of homework and emphasizing that life would go on if they didn't get an A.

Studies demonstrate that chronic lack of sleep is practically an epidemic among American teens. This is one of the causes of greatest concern for parents and pediatricians alike. Not only can sleep loss make our children surly at the breakfast table, it also can spell serious consequences for their health—and for their learning itself.

Researchers from the CDC have reported that the vast majority of American teens get at least two hours less sleep each night than what's recommended for their age. In a national survey published in 2010, the researchers found that fully one-third of high school students sleep only five or six hours on an average school night. Contrast that with the National Sleep Foundation's determination that, for teens, nine hours is optimal, eight is borderline, and anything less is insufficient. And it gets worse in eleventh and twelfth grades, as college application pressures mount. The rise of sleeplessness has even spawned a whole new category of pricey specialists that some parents hire: sleep coaches, who provide individualized step-by-step plans for sufficient slumber. As Cornell University sleep expert James Maas has put it, "Every single high school student I have ever measured in terms of their alertness is a walking zombie."

Skeptics will be quick to blame video games, text messaging, and the like for the teen sleep crisis, and there's no doubt technology is among the many culprits. But don't mistake it for the main one. In a National Sleep Foundation poll, more than one in three parents said that *scheduled activities* make it harder for their child to get a good night's sleep. More than one in four said *homework* had been a sleep thief within just the past week. And among the surveyed students at Irvington High School, far and away the most common reason for getting fewer than seven hours' sleep (cited by 77 percent) was homework and studying. Social networking was cited by just 28 percent. A 2014 report on teen sleep by the American Academy of Pediatrics named all of these factors—homework, extracurriculars, and social networking—as significant contributors to the crisis.

Homework's impact on sleep is sadly ironic, given the clear evidence that sleep deprivation harms the very process schoolwork is supposed to foster. Sleep plays a key role in attention and consolidation of new information in the brain, reports Harvard Medical School, and thus "the quantity and quality of sleep have a profound effect on learning and memory."

Just how foggy does a lack of sleep make children? As reported in *New*

York magazine, Tel Aviv University's Avi Sadeh tested this by instructing fourth and sixth graders to go to bed earlier or stay up later for three nights. The later-to-bed group ended up getting about an hour less sleep per night, compared to the others. When, after the third night, a researcher went to school to test the children's neurobiological functioning, the difference was stark. "The performance gap caused by an hour's difference in sleep was bigger than the normal gap between a fourth-grader and a sixth-grader," the magazine recounted. "Which is another way of saying that a slightly sleepy sixth-grader will perform in class like a mere fourth-grader."

Clearly, chronic late-night study sessions are not a pathway to mental growth; on the contrary, they are a symptom of a system that broadly encourages children to complete tasks and fulfill expectations without considering the consequences. Insufficient sleep is known to lead to ill health effects such as depressed mood, headaches, and drowsy driving. And it nearly killed Hayley Eaton, now a graduate student at the University of Oklahoma, who shared her story of how dangerously far sleep deprivation can go:

> *My world finally came to a screeching halt when I fell asleep at the wheel of my vehicle and crashed into a tree in the fall of my senior year of high school. Until that October day, I had assumed that I could keep pushing myself without consequence. I was taking all the available AP and Honors courses at my school, leading various school clubs, participating in an internship, volunteering, earning awards, and really anything that would make a nice addition to my college applications. I was allowing myself an average of 5-6 hours of shut-eye a night before waking up and repeating the cycle of school, then after-school activities, then oodles of homework. Spending quality time with family was a rare occurrence and hanging out with friends even more rare. Time to exercise or even just relax was simply unheard of. . . . I joked that I would "sleep when I'm dead" without realizing just how close I would come to fulfilling that prophecy at an incredibly young age.*
>
> *The day of my crash was like any other: school, club meetings after school, run an errand or two, head home. I was driving care-*

fully, under the speed limit, wearing my seat belt. Like any other day, I was exhausted—this was simply a part of my reality. . . . Five and a half hours of sleep the night before—and the previous night, and the night before that—just wasn't sustaining me, like the ice on a frozen lake that finally starts to crack under pressure.

People say that their eyelids feel heavy when they are tired, but I was way past that: my entire body felt heavy, as if gravity was working extra hard on me, willing me to lie down and rest. I turned up the volume on my CD player a bit more, in the hope that it could keep me awake for about twenty more minutes of driving. . . . I was getting further and further away from the present moment until I finally fell asleep only a few miles from my house. I have a very brief memory of the ground under my vehicle changing from smooth pavement to shaky gravel and grass. I opened my eyes slightly and saw for a split second the tree in front of me, but my mind didn't even have time to register what I was seeing before the collision. I didn't have time to brake or scream out or shield my face or react whatsoever before the truck went from forty miles an hour directly to zero, and everything went black.

Hayley walked away, miraculously, with minor cuts and bruises and the determination to change her life. "Today I pay much more attention to my health and get plenty of sleep," she wrote. "The demanding course load and high academic expectations for myself are a significant part of my life, but nothing will come before my personal needs: healthy foods; sleep; exercise; and time to reflect, to relax, and to spend with family and friends are all vital to my well-being. Too few students have this perspective, however, and it is easy to see why."

Self-Medicated for "Success"

It's also easy to see why more and more young students these days are turning to prescription drugs for energy and focus. With the expectations that have been placed on them far exceeding what their minds and bodies can naturally sustain, they're using unnatural means to keep up. *New York Times* reporter Alan Schwarz has researched the problem extensively. For his 2012 story "Risky Rise of the Good-Grade Pill," Schwarz interviewed students and doctors in more than fifteen academically intense high school communities across the country and concluded that pressure for top grades and college admissions is encouraging students to abuse prescription stimulants such as Adderall. Schwarz wrote:

> *Pills that have been a staple in some college and graduate school circles are going from rare to routine in many academically competitive high schools, where teenagers say they get them from friends, buy them from student dealers or fake symptoms to their parents and doctors to get prescriptions.*

The availability of prescription ADHD medications is skyrocketing, with the number of stimulants such as Ritalin and Adderall dispensed having shot up more than eightfold since the early 1990s. Prescription rates for teens alone more than doubled in just over a decade. The medications do help bring calm and ease symptoms for people who have a genuine disorder, Schwarz points out—yet for those who don't, a pill can provide laser-like focus and the energy to jam through late-night study sessions and final exams. In many communities, the drugs are practically de rigueur for students taking the SAT and ACT—perceived to be as essential a supply as a No. 2 pencil.

A young woman named Taylor, by then a student at Northern Arizona University, confessed to me that she first took Adderall as a high school junior. "I knew a lot of people who took it and I would ask them for it every once in a while," she said. "It's hard to be the vice president of your class, play on the soccer team, and do homework. It made me feel focused and almost better because, 'Look, I can keep up with everyone now. I come to school and my homework's done.'" Her story underscores the irony that kids are taking the drugs to compete with other kids, who are in turn taking the drugs to compete with *them.* Taylor started using the pills more frequently her senior year, until they backfired, ultimately sending her to the emergency room. "All of a sudden, I couldn't breathe as well," she recalled. "It was scary. I'd be sitting there trying to catch my breath. I couldn't fall asleep at night."

There aren't solid numbers on just how many teens such as Taylor are taking stimulants as a study aid, not out of medical need. As one might guess, studies that rely on teens' self-reporting don't provide a full picture of the problem. In the national 2013 Monitoring the Future survey, 15 percent of high school seniors said they'd taken a prescription drug for nonmedical reasons in the past year, and about half of those named Adderall. Yet the teens and doctors Schwarz interviewed would call those rates low: they estimated the real number as anywhere from 15 to 40 percent.

The short-term boost young students are after comes at a cost. What kids may think of as a harmless "study drug" is actually a DEA Schedule II controlled substance, so designated because of its potential for abuse. The misuse of stimulants can result in loss of appetite, insomnia, anxiety, heightened blood pressure, and, at high doses, an irregular heartbeat. If a child or young adult becomes addicted, the problems can get still worse. Most students who misuse the drugs don't suffer serious harm—Schwarz's research indicates that about 10 percent of those who use these stimulants will develop an addiction—but it's hardly a risk we want our children to take for the sake of their studies. The mere fact that our kids feel they need to self-medicate just to meet expectations, like pro athletes propped up by steroids, is a sign that something's wrong.

Alas, this sign of distress, too, continues into college, where substances can serve not only as study aids but also as a form of stress release. Jarreau, who runs alcohol education programs at Stanford, sums up the general mental health status of students at the university in a word: "Anxious." (He emphasizes that he speaks mainly from his own experience as a Stanford undergrad, not as a university representative.) He observes that many of them have spent their young lives so focused on academics that they haven't fully developed their social skills. They turn to hard alcohol as a social lubricant and a stress reliever, but they don't have the experience to handle it. The results—getting sick, getting injured, damaging property, injuring others—are dangerous. It's not that students today actually drink *more* than students past, he says; they just drink *differently*. "It's about something different. I don't think it was as much about the social anxiety and about using alcohol as a coping mechanism in the past."

In the radio report on the surging demand for mental health services on UC campuses, Elizabeth Gong-Guy, director of Counseling and Psychological Services at UCLA, described the situation thus: "Increasingly, we find that many of the students who make their way to our counseling centers are seasoned perfectionists who've driven themselves to unsustainable positions in which their lives lack any semblance of balance or self-compassion. These are students with eating disorders, crippling obsessive-compulsive disorders, cutting histories, addictions, and illicit stimulant abuse."

That is not how I, or any parent I know, would define success for my child.

The Tidal Wave of Illness to Come

These are the immediate health effects of the chronic, extreme expectations we have placed on our students. And if these were the only consequences of our pressure-cooker educational culture, that alone would be enough for us to act. But it's likely there are consequences we can't yet see—domino effects that could undermine our children's physical and mental health well into the future.

The science on this is just emerging, and there is little awareness of it outside the scientific community. Research over the past decade or so has clearly shown that childhood trauma affects a person's health throughout adulthood. This work, originating with the landmark Adverse Childhood Experiences Study in San Diego in the late 1990s, demonstrates unequivocally that unchecked stress in the early years is linked not only with adult mental health troubles but also with disruptions of brain development, higher rates of illness, and even altered gene expression. The more trauma a person experiences in childhood, the more likely he or she is to suffer later from depression and alcohol abuse. More surprisingly, survivors of early trauma are also more likely to suffer *physical* ailments including heart, lung, liver, and autoimmune diseases.

To be clear, most studies have focused on childhood problems that go far beyond academic anxiety, such as parental drug addiction, abuse, and neglect. It should go without saying that one cannot compare such a trauma

with excessive academic pressure. What's new, though, and what researchers are just starting to flesh out, is the realization that the constant presence
of less severe stressors could take a similar toll. No study I know of—yet—
has *directly* examined whether the excessive pressure to perform in and out
of school could be the kind of chronic stress that becomes toxic. But every
scientist I've spoken to expects that that is what we'll find as research continues. That's because stress exerts the same effects on the body no matter what
the cause. In children, any kind of stress "can really impact how the structure
and architecture of the brain forms," says Andrew Garner, a pediatrician at
University Hospitals Medical Practices in Ohio and associate professor at
Case Western Reserve University. Garner cowrote the American Academy
of Pediatrics' 2012 paper on the lifelong effects of childhood adversity, and
he adds, "It doesn't really matter what the stressor is, whether it's poverty or
chronic abuse or the bully on the bus."

Stress begins its spread throughout the body in a part of the brain called
the amygdala, which triggers a cascading release of hormones that reach our
every cell. This hormonal jolt is calibrated to help us spring into action to
avoid an immediate threat such as a forest fire (or, in modern student life, to
avoid flubbing the SAT). But it is ill suited to see us through chronic, long-
term worries. In fact, when the stress response does drag on, unrelenting, it
creates a physiological strain that scientists call allostatic load. That burden
feeds inflammation in the body, suppresses the immune system, and even
enlarges the amygdala itself, making it more volatile and reactive to future
stress. In other words, by subjecting young students to excessive and constant stress in their formative years, we may be making them more vulnerable to stress for the rest of their lives. "The brain is like a muscle," Garner
says. "The parts you use get stronger."

It's critical to understand the difference between good stress and bad, lest
we mistakenly try to protect our kids from every little thing. A little bit of
the right kind of stress can actually be essential. Donna Jackson Nakazawa,
journalist and author of the book *Childhood Disrupted: How Your Biography
Becomes Your Biology, and How You Can Heal*, explains it like this: "Of course
we don't want a childhood in which nothing bad happens, because we have
to learn adversity and learn grit and resilience and determination, and those
things take a little bit of failure and hard knocks." The critical difference, she

says, is between the bumps in the road that we might expect in life—you miss the bus, you're unprepared for an exam, or your grandmother dies—and "chronic stress that keeps coming, doesn't let up, is unpredictable, and a child isn't getting the support they need from adults." These two kinds of stress hit our brains and affect our immune systems very differently, Nakazawa says, "and we sometimes confuse the two."

With temporary, predictable stress, we have a chance to recuperate and grow new neural connections in response to the problems we've encountered, learning to arrive at the bus stop early, study better, and cope with normal loss. It's chronic, unpredictable stress from sources beyond our control that gets toxic. And that is a pretty good description of what today's most pressured, overscheduled, underslept kids go through in the name of education. There's a perception that constant high demands will make kids stronger, says Nakazawa, "but biologically that is not the case; it's actually breaking down the brain rather than creating resilience."

In fact, a survey of the existing science in the 2013 *Annual Review of Public Health* concluded that "repeated exposure to less severe, but often chronic stressors is likely to play as large, if not larger, of a role in forecasting children's future mental and physical health," compared to extreme adversity.

What this means, in sum, is that we as a nation are not only making our kids miserable in the moment; we may actually be building a ticking time bomb of illness that will someday turn this generation of overstressed children into a generation of unhealthy adults. Research is under way that may show that bringing them up on a diet of unchecked stress is setting them up not for a happy, flourishing adulthood but for later waves of depression, anxiety, and even heart disease and cancer. And UC Berkeley health economist Richard Scheffler expects this ill health will come with both a human and a financial cost to society. "Many of the health effects are apparent now but many more will echo through the lives of our children," Scheffler says. "We will all pay the cost of treating them and suffer the loss of their productive contributions. Seeing these hidden costs now gives us a chance to avoid them."

Distribution of Health

By now you may be thinking, and not without good reason, that the pressure-fueled health problems described here only afflict children in upper-middle-class communities. Let me address that common perception head-on. Communities like mine, filled as they are with highly educated, financially comfortable parents who expect their children will attain the same, are undoubtedly hubs of the educational stress epidemic. And no one has made the case that children in upwardly mobile communities are suffering more vividly than has Suniya Luthar.

A psychology professor at Arizona State University and a native of India, Luthar has demonstrated over and over, in urban and rural communities and public and private schools from coast to coast, that the children of white-collar, well-educated parents in upper-middle-class communities are more likely than the average American youth to show "serious disturbance," manifested in mental health and behavior problems and substance abuse. These kids have higher rates of anxiety and depressive symptoms—sometimes at twice the national rate. Luthar's studies show that they are also significantly more likely to use cigarettes, alcohol, marijuana, and other drugs than are those from low-income settings (especially, it turns out, the girls). These youth don't appear particularly troubled as young children, Luthar reports, but—in a disturbing echo of what I saw in my own home—problems begin to emerge around seventh grade.

"Our sons and daughters are sort of living with this runaway train of who they're supposed to be," Luthar explains. Their aspirations for themselves mirror the status and accomplishments they see around them, in parents and community members and *especially* their peers, and thus they feel compelled to do everything at a peak level of performance. "The adage by which these children live is 'I can, therefore I must,'" she says. "You've got this mad rush to achieve, and that's sort of interspersed with this mad rush to relax, with whatever substances, and back to a mad rush to achieve." When a child defines herself and her self-worth by her accomplishments, Luthar adds, "That's a very tenuous way to live."

It's possible to take a cursory look at Luthar's work and the realities of inequity in America and dismiss academic stress as a rich kid's problem, an issue confined to kids with ample resources and one therefore not worthy of our alarm—or at least less worrisome than other social ills. Yet the causes for concern are manyfold. As Luthar herself notes, any population of children who are at risk, whether or not they fit our common perceptions of need, deserve to be protected. The pain these young people are experiencing is too excruciating—and the implications for our society's future are too real—to be ignored.

Besides, the knee-jerk assumption that academic stress is confined to privileged kids itself isn't true. The pressure to perform, while it pools within privileged neighborhoods, doesn't stay contained there. The troubling trends we've seen in depression and anxiety affect children from all kinds of schools and communities: affluent, middle class, impoverished, urban, suburban. School counselors widely report that the emotional distress they see in young people crosses socioeconomic lines and impacts children across the spectrum of academic ability. And they say it's worsening at a pace with which national surveys of adolescent mental health can't keep up.

Roy Wade Jr., a pediatrician at the Children's Hospital of Philadelphia, has seen the evidence. In interviews with Philadelphia youth from diverse socioeconomic strata, he has found that, though their external circumstances differ, they all describe feeling unsupported—an experience which is itself a stressor. In one study, Wade assessed stress levels in clients of five youth organizations, ranging from a homeless shelter to a running club that serves many kids from the affluent suburbs. "What we found is that if you took away the names of the organizations from the top of the report, you couldn't tell whose kids were whose," he said. "They all endorsed the same levels of stress."

No matter where we grow up, we are all inundated from birth with media messages about what makes success. Hint: it's not a modest job with a small house and a happy life; it's something at once much glossier and more limited. Perhaps it's the spacious suburban home with a smiling child eating Cheerios at the granite kitchen counter and a power-suited dad pulling his Lexus into the driveway. Or perhaps it's the übermodern city condo outfitted with slick Apple products and designer lighting. Our culture no longer celebrates the everyday travails of the blue-collar men who inhabited the bar on *Cheers*. Instead we idolize the urbanites of *Mad Men* and *Scandal*, their personal dysfunctions as grand as their lifestyles. Everywhere we look, someone is telling us to go bigger, to strive for more. Even a recently introduced line of Dreyer's frozen fruit bars (they're just Popsicles!) is named with a command: "Outshine!" All together, the glittering images that surround us fuel a status anxiety that's hard to shake.

Plus, the fierce competition for college admission among upper-middle-class students only raises the bar to entry for all students who hope to get in. For example, Mayra Valle, the daughter of Mexican immigrants in Houston, missed her last chance to see her dying grandmother because of school obligations. Her devotion to school came from years of watching her parents push their bodies to the limit. She'd seen her dad come home with white sweat stains on his green shirt from twelve hours working in the sun, and noticed her mom's calloused hands and chronic headaches from full days of childcare and cleaning. Mayra admired their strength but worried about their health, and wanted a solid education and career so she could relieve them from that labor. So, while not surrounded day to day by the trappings and expectations of affluence, she was nonetheless racing to compete academically. Mayra, vivacious and diligent, ultimately ended up at bucolic Connecticut College, in classes among peers who, by and large, faced far fewer challenges in getting there.

McKenzie Charlene Morrow, a student from a small town in western North Carolina, offers another example. As a high school junior, McKenzie wrote:

> I have lived my whole life stressing, worrying, focused on school. . . .
> I come from a family where neither my father nor mother graduated
> from high school. My parents always told me I needed to graduate
> and I needed to make something of myself. . . .

In eighth grade, McKenzie was thrilled to be accepted at a local early college high school, where students could take college and high school classes and graduate with both a high school diploma and an associate's degree. She felt as if all her hard work in middle school was finally paying off. Because her parents couldn't afford to pay for college, she felt excelling in school was her only path to a scholarship to a good college. McKenzie was determined not to squander the opportunity:

> *My freshman year I focused solely on school, no other activities, I*
> *spent 4 to 5 hours after school on homework. . . . If I made a 95 on*
> *a test, it wasn't good enough for me. . . . I would study all night, and*
> *run on 3 or 4 hours of sleep daily.*

She spent the summer after her freshman year reviewing SAT test prep instead of hanging out with her friends. Eventually, all that stress caught up to her.

> *My sophomore year was when it all changed. I pushed myself so*
> *much, I was at the breaking point. I wasn't getting enough sleep, I*
> *was worrying too much, I was stressing over school so much that it*
> *affected me physically. I became sick more easily, my hands would*
> *break out in eczema flares. It got so bad my doctor was going to*
> *put me on medication. He thought maybe I was OCD. That was*
> *when my dad told me to just stop stressing. It was going to be okay,*
> *I needed to just relax.*
>
> *So when spring break arrived, I spent it with some old friends*
> *from middle school. They were all so happy and so carefree. I wanted*
> *that. I made up my mind I wanted to transfer to the regular high*
> *school. . . . I wanted to go to pep rallies, to prom, to be able to relax*
> *and enjoy things. . . . I am now enjoying every day, and yes I still*
> *stress a little about my classes even though there is no need. . . . I have*
> *enjoyed knowing I can achieve, but now I am learning something*
> *I never knew how to do before and that is just to relax and let go!*

McKenzie ultimately graduated from the local high school with honors. Now she's studying at community college while working full time as a day-care teacher—a job she calls "the best thing ever"—and aiming to become an early childhood education director.

Edin Randall also sees evidence of suffering across the socioeconomic spectrum at the Boston Children's Hospital pain clinic, where many of the patients are affluent but a handful are also from lower-income families. "Interestingly, a lot of them are in the same situation," she says. "This is the good child. This is the child who's going to break out because they're such a good student."

That's just what I've heard from teachers, students, and researchers nationwide: kids in upper-middle-class communities may get a particular, potent dose of performance pressure, but children from many settings feel it. It's the precise genesis of kids' stress—whether from needing to keep up with inflated expectations or needing to escape poverty—that varies with a child's individual situation.

Impaired Learning

The excessive stress isn't doing much for children's intellectual strength, either. There's plenty of evidence that stress hurts cognition. As Garner points out, "That just makes sense intuitively. When you're panicked, you're not taking in a lot of information. You're certainly not making good decisions." Research has linked chronic stress with the loss of neurons and neural connections in the hippocampus, a brain area that's crucial to memory. Loss also occurs in parts of the prefrontal cortex, which is essentially the brain's conductor, a key player in so-called executive functions such as planning, problem solving, and self-control. The prefrontal cortex is still growing in adolescence, which means it's still being intricately shaped by the effects of experience (and which also explains a lot about teens).

In fact, the brain is particularly plastic in the teen years. We think of the years from zero to three as *the* critical period for brain development, but Temple University neuroscientist Laurence Steinberg underscores that adolescence is another one. "[T]he brain's malleability makes adolescence a period of tremendous opportunity—and great risk," writes Steinberg. "If we expose our young people to positive, supportive environments, they will flourish. But if the environments are toxic, they will suffer in powerful and enduring ways."

These sensitivities could have a serious impact on our children in school. Steinberg—who says schools chronically miss the sweet spot by overloading kids with assignments—explains that the key to learning is new experiences. These help to generate new synapses, or connections between neurons, which in turn create new links between different parts of the brain. A little bit of repetition can help strengthen those connections, but beyond that, repeated drilling produces no growth. "Novelty," he says, "is required to stimulate the growth of new synapses." So, by emphasizing quantity over quality, and content over mastery of complex skills, our traditional educational model is missing crucial opportunities to enhance brain maturation at a critical time. Plus, heightened levels of the stress hormone cortisol can injure the myelin, the protective white matter that surrounds brain circuits and allows them to function efficiently, Steinberg points out. So, school communities that place intense performance pressure on students, to the point of causing chronic stress, may actually be jeopardizing healthy brain function.

The misalignment of education with kids' real needs may explain why many check out and exacerbates the problems that cause some to leave school altogether. America's high school and college completion rates, once the world's highest, now lag far behind those of other developed nations. And while the high school graduation rate is rising, one in three students entering college requires remediation. These students made it through the exhaustive high school checklist, but the learning didn't stick. This is one of the reasons why 41 percent of students who start at a four-year college do not finish within six years. Such sobering statistics remind us of the big picture: that despite the trials we put high school students through in the name of academic preparation, our education system is still operating at a major loss. The hoops our children are expected to jump through on the way to higher education are, for too many, not hoops at all, but barricades.

"There are some kids that do need . . . to be taught how to organize, structure, manage their time," says Garner. "But we also know there are kids at the other end of the curve, crashing and burning." He argues that we must do better at helping kids stay more in the middle, where they're engaging but not burning out. Through our educational efforts to push every child to the max, he says, "We've gone off the deep end, and now we're doing more harm than good."

Less Prepared for Success

A youth spent in the pressure cooker also fails our children in one final way: by eroding the nonacademic skills that they also need to succeed in life. You'd think that a straight-A student who can manage four AP classes, run varsity track, and dominate the debate team with seeming ease would be perfectly poised to surmount challenges. In fact, we're seeing the opposite. College professors increasingly report that freshmen arrive on their campuses with the creativity strained out of them. Trained to color inside the lines, these students are afraid to take intellectual risks; they just want to know what it takes to make the grade. Then, as this stressed generation leaves college and enters the workforce, their employers report similarly troubling trends. Give them a discrete task, and yes, they can execute it like nobody's business. But more and more, surveys show, managers find young workers lacking in leadership, self-direction, critical thought, and collaboration skills—those essential, if immeasurable, qualities that truly determine success in today's world.

"Businesses often lament the lack of work readiness by recent college graduates" yet don't do enough to encourage change, says Bil Corry, a senior solutions engineer in information security at PayPal. "How can one expect innovative, creative thinkers that work well with others if the system they exclusively hire from does not value nor endorse those traits?"

We have, without really meaning to, transmitted to young people the idea that academic achievement is the most important way to measure their value as people, and that success in school exclusively assures success in life. Yet the Nobel Prize–winning economist James Heckman has decisively put that notion to rest. Analyzing thirty-five years of data that chronicled children's lives from preschool into adulthood, Heckman and colleagues demonstrated that character makes more difference than IQ for economic and social success. Improved character even boosted kids' standardized test scores, if that's what you care to measure.

The achievement-driven life appears even to be subverting our children's values. A 2011 analysis at the University of Michigan, which combined the results of dozens of personality studies of American college students over the course of thirty years, found that today's college kids rated about 40 percent lower on empathy than students in the late 1970s. Current students were comparatively less likely to agree with statements such as "I sometimes try to understand my friends better by imagining how things look from their perspective." Why? Researcher Edward O'Brien named "the hypercompetitive atmosphere and inflated expectations of success," and surmised that it all adds up to "a social environment that works against slowing down and listening to someone who needs a bit of sympathy."

A Harvard Graduate School of Education survey of ten thousand middle and high school students from diverse communities around the country found a similar distortion. When the researchers asked students to rank what was most important to them—achieving at a high level, happiness (feeling good most of the time), or caring for others—almost 50 percent picked high achievement as their top choice. Thirty percent chose happiness, and about 20 percent chose caring for others. When lead researcher Richard Weissbourd and colleagues compared the rankings head-to-head, they found that 60 percent of youth put achievement above caring. These values aren't mutually exclusive, Weissbourd explains. "We think you can be very happy and very caring and achieve at high levels. The concern we were raising is how out of balance they appear to be."

Evidence from the Josephson Institute of Ethics also reveals a disconnect. As you'd hope, 95 percent of the high school students the institute surveyed nationwide said trust and honesty are essential in the workplace. Yet, revealingly, more than half agreed with this statement: "In the real world, successful people do what they have to do to win, even if others consider it cheating." Similar to the students in Jay Jackson's survey at Irvington High School, more than 50 percent said they'd cheated during a test in school.

Even the so-called winners in the race may not ultimately gain. Daniel Kahneman and his colleagues have demonstrated that rich people don't actually feel any happier day to day than those with lower incomes. To be sure, it helps to have enough money to escape the pain of deprivation. But above an annual income of about $75,000, Kahneman and colleagues report, the link between wealth and happiness disappears.

"The irony here is all this focus on kids achieving may result in them achieving less, not more, because they're not developing certain skills that are going to be essential for their success" once they get out of the academic environment, says Weissbourd. Not to mention the skills essential for being good friends, romantic partners, and mentors, he adds, "and those relationships are probably the most important and durable sources of happiness that we have."

Cause for Action

Call upon all of this evidence when skeptics suggest that a healthy, sane education that's mostly free of anxiety is a soft one. I've encountered such resistance countless times. I've even encountered outright denial.

One screening of *Race to Nowhere* that I attended in Millburn, New Jersey, is seared into my mind. This came soon after the film's release, before it had been widely viewed and frank discussions about students' stress disrupted our national complacence. The moderator made audience members write their questions on notecards rather than speak them out loud, thereby silencing parents and students who had so much to say. Meanwhile, the evening's panelists (teachers and counselors from the local middle and high schools) said essentially that the schools weren't demanding too much of students, and that if there were problems with stress it was because of parental pressure and student procrastination. Afterward, in the lobby of the school auditorium, parents and students mobbed me to tell me just how acutely they disagreed with the panel. As one boy named Max put it to me, "I really feel that this movie is my life, and that the system truly needs change."

Change is hard. Even those who face the problem honestly still struggle to act—as I have myself, at times. Suggest to a coach that she take Wednesday nights off, and she'll say she can't because then her team will be less competitive. Ask a teacher to assign less homework, and he'll say his class might not then complete all the required content. Tell a student to ease up on her honors classes, and she'll say she might not get into Princeton. Everyone is afraid to be the first—or the only one—to change.

But those fears are unfounded. Change is already happening. And as the facts make plain, we must build on it; our children's health and preparation for the future are on the line. Even the gatekeepers at Harvard University say so. The dean and director of admissions coauthored an open letter imploring incoming freshmen to slow down their "fast-lane childhoods" and take a gap year before arriving, burned out and sapped of their souls, upon the vaunted campus. "The fact remains that there is something very different about growing up today," they wrote. "Some students and families are suffering from the frenetic pace, while others are coping but enjoying their lives less than they would like. Even those who are doing extraordinarily well, the 'happy warriors' of today's ultra-competitive landscape, are in danger of emerging a bit less human as they try to keep up with what may be increasingly unrealistic expectations." In other words, the price of maintaining the status quo is simply too high.

So "to better your future," to borrow the Irvington High School student's phrase, is actually to *stop* the automatic, unquestioned race we're all running and to redefine goals all our own. This is what the families and schools in this book have begun to do. They are not blaming each other, because they understand that the race is not the exclusive fault of any single group. It is the culture. Which is to say: it is everyone. We collectively create the culture, and it's up to us to change it.

That's what is so inspiring about the attitude of Irvington's Jay Jackson. He knows that change begins on the ground, in each community, with teams of people who believe in it. He knows this work will be hard, yet he insists upon pursuing it anyway, unflinching. "Let's try some things out," Jackson said the day of my visit after sitting with the roomful of exhausted teens. He knew his initiatives to ease students' stress and limit their overscheduling wouldn't work overnight, he said, ready for the challenges that inevitably come with change, "but let's see if we can tweak them and *make* them work."

When we look into our children's eyes and ask ourselves whether their "better future" should be the unhealthy one they're now marching toward, every parent and educator will offer the same answer: no. Instead we wish for them health, happiness, and the contentment that comes from being a good citizen of the world. We need to act *now* to preserve that better future for our children, and to protect them from the false ideals that threaten to take it away.

CHAPTER 2

It's About Time

THE WAY to reclaim a childhood stuck in overdrive has a lot to do with time.

I recognized this when the film crew and I went to interview Kelly, a close friend of Devon, the girl in my community who'd committed suicide. We found her saddened yet thoughtful, open to talking honestly about the pressures that beset her and her peers. Kelly, an eighth grader, had just one surprising request: we had to schedule the interview at eleven p.m. on a weeknight, after all her assignments, sports practice, and piano lessons were done.

The episode illustrated a key insight into the causes of the health crisis our children are suffering and the competitiveness that's diminishing their educations. At the root of all these ills, there is a universal pattern: our collective misuse of time. The problem is visible in the child falling asleep on her books or the parent spending all afternoon driving kids around, and visceral in the sense that our children's school years are speeding by. Time is at the heart of every single problem we will address in this book: poor health, runaway homework, excessive testing, narrow learning, and unchecked college competition. But it is also at the heart of every solution. Revolutionize the way we think about and use our time—and our children's—and we transform the way they grow and learn.

In our culture's manic mindset, often bent on one version of "success," we're constantly encouraged to "use our time well." And time used well is understood to mean one thing only: time used productively. Minutes spent at rest or at leisure, playing with friends or dreaming up stories, are considered frittered away. And so we stack our days with productive obligations, pursuing the achievement we understand to be primary, and then wonder why no time remains to do the simple things that make us whole. Schools, similarly misguided, grab huge chunks of children's time *outside of school*, commanding so many hours that our kids' school-to-life balance grows horribly lopsided. Meanwhile, the misuse of time *during the school day* keeps educators locked in old and unproductive modes of teaching.

Our children's treadmill schedules—which leave little room for deep learning, daydreaming, quietude, healthy habits, or human connections—are a symptom of this. And our collective misuse of time amounts to a societal disease.

"This disease of being 'busy' (and let's call it what it is, the dis-ease of being busy, when we are never at ease) is spiritually destructive to our health and wellbeing," writes Omid Safi, the director of Duke University's Islamic Studies Center. "It saps our ability to be fully present with those we love the most in our families, and keeps us from forming the kind of community that we all so desperately crave." It also steals the fleeting time we have to grow confident, considerate, creative kids with inquisitive, inventive minds.

The problems of the Race to Nowhere call for a total time redesign. It can be tough to imagine alternate ways to use our time—the task requires us to scrutinize not only the external structures and policies that frame our lives but also our own everyday choices. Yet some smart schools and families are already doing it, and the rest of us must follow their lead. Because time is not only a prime victim of our culture's distorted priorities, it can also serve as the most tangible and immediate tool with which to start setting those priorities right. If we examine which activities actually occupy a child's hours, then compare that accounting to the list of priorities we most value, we'll quickly see where values and realities misalign.

It is by reclaiming time that we begin to rebalance our children's lives and learning—and, as adults, our own lives, too. It's how we wipe clean the slate of *how things have always been done* and liberate ourselves to imagine how they can be done now.

In this chapter we examine some of the most conspicuous thieves of children's time, and we describe a variety of solutions that schools and families have created. These examples are not exhaustive; in your own schools and lives, you could surely find many more. What they all illustrate, though, is that *time* itself it is the most powerful lens through which to view our Race to Nowhere—and through which to see our way clear to something better.

Time and Values

Let's start by turning the lens on the daily life of one student: Tira Okamoto, the author of this book's opening poem.

We see her, a junior at San Francisco's Lowell High School, dragging herself sleepily out of bed at 6:10 a.m. She carpools in and arrives at school by the bell, barely, at 7:35, and then proceeds to lurch through seven straight classes. Precalculus: turn in homework, then zone out, wondering if this material will be on the SAT. AP English: beautiful books to discuss, though they were chosen by state policy makers, not this brilliant teacher. College and career seminar: daydream again, as the content is review for Tira. At 10:35, it's lunchtime—the only time slot where she could fit lunch given the courses she needed. Not yet hungry, Tira nips over to Starbucks, already reliant on caffeine to get through her long days and nights at age seventeen.

Next: Spanish (memorizing verb tenses), AP US history, and physics. Each forty-five-minute period contains perhaps enough time to check homework and attendance, introduce one new topic, and answer a couple of questions about it. Then—ring!—Tira moves on to the next class and does it again. A few classes a day are fifteen minutes longer, which in history today means the students have time to discuss current events. Otherwise, there's little time to consider what this math formula means in real life, or to delve beyond vocabulary into the cultural richness of Spain or Mexico. The content of one class is completely isolated from the next, and the amount of time devoted to each lesson is determined not by its complexity or potential to engage and inspire a student but rather by a soulless and inflexible warden: the clock.

Tira cares about physics, where the teacher is passionate and dynamic, but by that point, her sixth class of the day, with the coffee wearing off, she struggles to stay alert. Finally, her last class, advanced dance, awakens her.

She gets to finish the day doing something she loves, before the final bell rings at three thirty p.m.

Few adults in schools experience this churn themselves. But one veteran teacher and instructional coach from the Northeast, Alexis Wiggins, decided to try it firsthand. Before starting a new job, she followed a tenth grader around for a day, and then a twelfth grader for another day. Wiggins was shocked by what a passive, silent learner the regimen made her, and how exhausted she felt by all that sitting and listening by the afternoon. The experience startled her so much that she wished she could go back and change ten things about every class she had ever taught.

"By the end of the day, I could not stop yawning and I was desperate to move or stretch," Wiggins wrote in a blog post about the experience. "I was drained, and not in a good, long, productive-day kind of way. No, it was that icky, lethargic tired feeling. . . . It was not just the sitting that was draining but that so much of the day was spent absorbing information but not often grappling with it." She had planned to do more work that afternoon, but she was tired. She went home and watched TV, and went to bed at eight thirty.

So if the way we spend our time is a clear expression of what we value, what does a student's daily schedule tell us about what we value in school? A few words spring to mind: *Speed. Uniformity. Quantity.*

Certain other words—*depth, individuality, quality*—do not.

"If you were running a business with a thousand employees, and every forty minutes everybody had to stop what they were doing, go to a different room entirely, and do something else for forty minutes that they weren't so interested in, and then rinse and repeat six times a day, you'd be out of business in a week," Ken Robinson, the international education expert and author of *The Element: How Finding Your Passion Changes Everything,* said to me. "You would get nothing done, and people would become disaffected."

But the school day itself isn't even the whole picture for most students. Factor in the way schoolwork, sports, band, theater, and other school-sponsored activities extend ever deeper into afternoons, evenings, and weekends, and you see that, as imbalanced as adults' work-to-life ratio has become, children's school-to-life ratio is often worse.

Let's return to Tira's schedule in the hours after the final bell has rung.

She dashes to her locker, still in her dance clothes, to grab books and snack. Rehearsal for the school dance company lasts until six. Lugging her heavy backpack, Tira takes an hour-long bus trip home, showers, eats, and starts her homework at eight. She nods off sometimes while reading her textbooks. At midnight, bleary-eyed, she rushes through her last precalculus problems and goes to bed, setting her alarm early to get up and do it all again.

And this is a student participating in an unusually modest number of extracurricular activities: one.

So, what does a child's daily schedule tell us about what matters beyond school? Answer: productivity and performance. Clearly not reflection, connection, or rest. Certainly not family. Nor passion. Nor joy. When I think about children today, I often picture a dozen adults gripping each of them by their limbs, pulling them in all directions with demands on their time, pulling them to pieces.

Downtime Is Up Time

The result is that our children's balance—between rest and attention, compliance and exploration, self and work—is wildly out of whack. Time and again, I have shaken my head at how little resemblance my children's youth bears to mine. As a kid, I got all my homework done and still had time to read books, play with neighborhood friends, and even work an after-school job. Young people these days barely have time to blink. Even activities that appear recreational, such as softball practice, are scheduled, orchestrated, and directed by adults. Seduced by society into thinking that children must be filled with educational enrichment lest they lie idle and amount to nothing, we feel compelled toward what sociologists call "concerted cultivation." In other words, *Washington Post* reporter Brigid Schulte says, "You're trying to grow this hothouse flower," instead of a child with the natural inclination to find her own pursuits. Then, as our kids grow older, they absorb this idea from society and start overscheduling themselves, even when we parents sense it's gone too far.

"As parents, we want what's best for our kids but we've abdicated our parental rights and duties to the new societal norm," writes Ron Turker, a pediatric orthopedic surgeon in Portland, Oregon, who sees more and more overpracticed young athletes with repetitive-stress injuries that used to be rare. "We give in to the herd mentality along with our confounded friends so that our kids won't be seen as outliers."

What we parents, educators, and coaches may forget amid all the racing around is that this modern childhood time suck comes with a huge opportunity cost. All the hours our children spend dutifully taking direction are hours they don't spend imagining, experimenting, inventing, connecting, or creating and solving problems all their own. They're missing a critical window to develop the skills that come with organic exploration and spontaneous play. While we all know intellectually that each day, every day, only has twenty-four hours in it, we often fail to note that our children's schedules are a zero-sum game. Gain an hour of piano lessons and you'll lose an hour of outdoor play. Lose an hour of homework, and you get that playtime back. It's that simple, and yet it's that hard.

Research confirms that children's downtime is dwindling. A team at the University of Michigan found that over just the two-plus decades between 1981 and 2003, American children ages six to seventeen came to spend significantly more time in school and studying. Probably not coincidentally, over the same period, children's time outdoors dropped precipitously— nearly in half. University of Washington researchers found in 2015 that even kids in preschool are given only forty-eight minutes a day for free and active play.

Boston College psychologist Peter Gray has found evidence showing a continuous decline in children's outdoor play since the 1950s. The realization really hit him on a trip about a dozen years ago to the Dominican Republic, where he saw lots of kids freely playing outdoors: "I realized: this is how I used to play. And wait a minute, I don't see that anymore back home. When I see kids outdoors they're in uniforms. They're on manicured soccer fields doing what the coaches are telling them to do. They're not playing. They're doing something that's adult directed. They may be enjoying it, but it's not play." Our lives are so scheduled, Gray laments, that "even those kids whose parents let them go out to play, there aren't other kids to play with."

We forget in the push for productivity that much of what is lost is what happens below the surface of free time. Building a fort, daydreaming, or inventing a game might seem like dreamy luxuries—but these idylls of child-hood are far from idle. It's in these unstructured moments that children develop essential capacities for reflective thought, creativity, social skills, and self-control. And these opportunities, which now grow ever more rare, are irreplaceable.

"Downtime actually isn't down time," said the Harvard Innovation Lab's Tony Wagner when we met. "Downtime is up time. The research is very clear that the brain needs time off to synthesize, to integrate. Why is it that so often many of us get some of our best ideas when we are shaving or in the shower, or taking a walk or doing yoga?"

An explanation of what makes downtime—true downtime, not staged recreation—so important comes from University of Southern California neuroscientist Mary Helen Immordino-Yang and colleagues in the journal *Perspectives on Psychological Science*. Reviving an old John Lubbock quote that "rest is not idleness," they cite evidence that "wakeful rest" (daydream-ing, reflection, what researchers call the brain's "default mode," with no task at hand) is essential for healthy psychological functioning. In that state, you develop stronger memory, cognitive skills, divergent thinking, and social-emotional skills such as weighing the moral and emotional effects of your actions. The researchers argue that our ceaseless demands for kids' exter-nally focused attention, in and out of school, may be harming their growth. They write, "Safely indulging mind wandering may be critical for healthy development and learning in the longer term."

The author Tim Kreider, deploring our constant hurry, puts it this way:

> *Idleness is not just a vacation, an indulgence or a vice; it is as in-dispensable to the brain as vitamin D is to the body, and deprived of it we suffer a mental affliction as disfiguring as rickets. The space and quiet that idleness provides is a necessary condition for standing back from life and seeing it whole, for making unex-pected connections and waiting for the wild summer lightning strikes of inspiration—it is, paradoxically, necessary to getting any work done. . . . Archimedes' "Eureka" in the bath, Newton's apple, Jekyll & Hyde and the benzene ring: history is full of stories of inspi-rations that come in idle moments and dreams.*

It follows, then, that some researchers also blame the dearth of down-time for our nation's growing creativity crisis. Kyung-Hee Kim, a professor of creativity and innovation at the College of William & Mary, published a bombshell study on this in 2011. She examined the scores of more than 250,000 children and adults on a widely respected creativity test, the Torrance Tests of Creative Thinking, from 1966 to 2009. Children's scores on this test are powerfully linked to their later life accomplishments, far more so than IQ. The data showed that indicators of creativity had flatlined or declined during that time. Looking just at the years since 1990, the picture was worse: even as Americans' IQ scores generally rose, creativity scores significantly dropped, especially in kindergarten through third grade. Breaking the creativity measure down into its component parts, Kim wrote that over the last twenty years:

> *Children have become less emotionally expressive, less energetic, less talkative and verbally expressive, less humorous, less imaginative, less unconventional, less lively and passionate, less perceptive, less apt to connect seemingly irrelevant things, less synthesizing, and less likely to see things from a different angle.*

That's not exactly what I wish for my children. Nor does it bode well for American ingenuity. And it may help explain why high-tech universities are doing more educational gymnastics to get incoming students to think outside the box. One MIT undergraduate dean told science journalist Annie Murphy Paul, "We scour the country looking for young builders and inventors. They're getting harder and harder to find." So MIT now offers classes and activities "devoted to taking things apart and putting them together," Paul writes, "an effort to teach students the skills their fathers and grandfathers learned curbside on weekend afternoons."

Alongside creativity, there's still another endangered species in our children's minds: a critical capacity called executive function. This is your child's basic tool kit for functioning in life, and it includes the ability to set goals, make plans, manage one's time, and control one's impulses and emotions. "When you're playing with other kids and working on your own projects, it calls for a lot of self-regulation and executive functioning," explains Paul,

who's also the author of *Brilliant: The New Science of Smart*. "When you're being ferried from one activity to another, and always told what to do, that capacity for executive function doesn't have the opportunity to develop."

Indeed, a 2014 study from researchers at the University of Colorado at Boulder found that children who spent more time engaged in less structured activities were far better at setting and accomplishing goals than peers who participated in more formal, structured pursuits. The bottom line: in constantly pushing our children to do more, we may be setting them up to pursue and achieve less. "It's strangely, ironically, unproductive to over-schedule kids," says Paul. "For parents who think they're giving their kids a leg up by having every moment of their day structured, it's having the opposite effect."

Productivity does not necessarily equal good growth for older kids or teens, either. Abigail Baird, the Vassar College neuropsychologist, explains that chatting and hanging out is some of the essential work of adolescence. Just like the most critical—and easiest—window for learning a language is eighteen to twenty-four months, she told me, "The adolescent years are the prime time for social experience, to learn everything you need to about yourself and how you relate to your community. That's the perfect time." So you may do okay learning your social skills later in life, she said, "but in the same way that learning a language late in life leaves you with an accent, you'll never sound exactly like a native."

The Youth Sports Vortex

Take, as a time-thief example, the great maw of recreational sports. These seem like an unlikely bad guy. They provide opportunities for physical exercise, perseverance, discipline, and teamwork—all good things for our kids' growth. But over the past few decades, youth sports have gone off the deep end, requiring way too much time, exertion, and specialization at an ever-younger age. Practices and games engulf fifteen or twenty hours a week, while travel teams for nine-year-olds drag families across the state, gobbling up their budgets and weekends. (My extended family hasn't gathered for Thanksgiving in years because my nephews always have obligations to

hockey.) It's not unusual to drive past a soccer field at eight p.m. and see eight-year-olds at practice. In my childhood, we were in bed by then.

Because everyone else is doing it, parents feel they have to do it to keep up. *Start training hard at age five, or your kid will never be a ready enough competitor to play high school sports* is the implicit or even explicit message we get from well-meaning fellow parents and coaches. Or: *Top performance in sports is your ticket into an elite college.* ("Fear-based sports marketing" is what one sports mom I know calls it.) Children themselves notice that their peers are attending summer soccer camps or slotting in extra private lessons in between team practices. So we accept these excessive schedules rather than organize for change. The consequences, besides lost time and opportunities, include high rates of repetitive-use injuries (as Dr. Turker has seen) and many kids who utterly burn out on sports and quit by the time they reach high school.

"Many parents have come to believe that more (more teams, more practices, more intense and competitive games) and earlier (travel teams at age seven!) is somehow better," reports the youth sports website MomsTeam. But "the majority of studies suggest that early specialization can have 'significant negative consequences on the development of an athlete over time.'" Many parents, including me, simply want our kids to have the chance to play sports but find the only opportunities are all-or-nothing rec teams that demand Total Commitment. Whatever happened to a bunch of kids playing informal baseball in someone's front yard with an old sweatshirt used as second base?

Even unsuspecting recreational players get swept up in the sports machine. Stacked against their overtrained peers, they often don't feel "good enough" and quit because they sense there's little value placed on having fun. Or they try so hard to catch up that they end up with the same overuse injuries or overscheduled days as their more competitive friends. This kind of overdrive is part of what drove Zak out of adult-organized sports. After a few years of soccer and Little League, he decided he preferred skateboarding, snowboarding, and surfing, where he could stretch his own limits without having to answer to coaches' and parents' ambitions.

Emily Cohen, a Berkeley mom of two and host of the youth sports podcast

TeamSnap, recalls when her daughter had finally had enough. She'd played A-level club soccer through seventh grade, but when practices were set to increase to four times a week, leaving her no time to play tennis, she declined and joined rec soccer instead. "What do you mean, she's not all in on soccer?" fellow parents asked her mom. "Your daughter's not going to get a college scholarship," said the coach, echoing a sports-can-get-you-scholarships perception (sometimes oversold) that also drives many hopeful families to pursue athletics to extreme degrees. Cohen replied, "I don't care, this is about her, what she wants." And she considers it one of the best decisions her daughter has made.

School-Life Balance

Yet the imbalance in kids' lives is hardly all due to overzealous soccer leagues. Nor can it mainly be chalked up to parents' and kids' overeager scheduling. In fact, by the time students reach middle school, if not earlier, the demands dictated *by schools themselves* account for by far the most sizable part of the problem.

Start with the thirty-five hours a week a typical student spends in school and commuting there. Add in a very conservative ten hours for one sport or school-sponsored activity, and you've already exceeded the demands of a full-time job. Beyond that, assignments, additional activities, required community service, and recommended tutoring encroach ever further beyond the last bell and even into the evening, appropriating the personal and family time that schools do not own and cannot see. Outside of abandoning academic responsibilities and quitting activities that they care about, kids and families feel like they have little say. Homework is, of course, among the most egregious means of these time grabs, so much so that I devote the entire next chapter to its origins and solutions. Here, I'll focus on the numerous other ways schools reach across the school-home line—through sports and activities that are inherently valuable but have been taken too far.

Emily Cohen remembers how high school sports teams, for instance, simply picked up the baton of extreme scheduling from the youth leagues. One day her daughter got a list of expectations from her high school soccer coach. It said: *You are a student first.* Then it said: *All doctor's appoint-*

ments and family commitments should be scheduled outside of practice and games. "I nearly threw up," Cohen recalls. "Family commitments should be scheduled around the games? What world are we living in? When it's my mother's ninety-second birthday, no, we're not going to the game." Even when coaches say schoolwork comes first, she's observed, the kid who skips practice to study for two finals the next day may get benched, "so there's a punishment for it."

The expectations have grown so out-of-control that in 2014 the California Interscholastic Federation capped high school sports practices at eighteen hours a week or four hours a day. As if even those limits were reasonable. In my own home, I found that when my older daughter decided to play high school softball, she had to head to practice the moment the last bell rang, five days a week, and then didn't get home until after seven, delaying our family dinner.

Plus, sports are only part of the broader problem of extracurriculars going overboard. School debate teams, yearbook staffs, dance troupes, and other activities can command at least as many hours as athletics. These are wonderful experiences that contribute greatly to kids' growth, but they've become professionalized to such a degree that participating in even one of them now allows a child little chance to try anything else.

Science has a lesson for us here. Psychologist Edin Randall, whom we met in the last chapter for her work with pediatric pain patients, also specializes in research on extracurricular activities. One study of hers revealed that students at a diverse, urban high school who participated in more than about ten hours of activities per week saw diminishing returns. They enjoyed benefits from moderate participation, including social confidence and connectedness. But those benefits leveled off around five to seven hours per week and started dropping around ten. Randall's subsequent research reveals an important wrinkle: it matters not only *how much time* you spend in activities, but also *why* you do them—whether for enjoyment or a sense of obligation. Children who spend oodles of hours in activities they adore, purely for the fun of it, tend to be happy and well adjusted. Those who participate because they sense pressure to do it may fare worse. The essential question for the kids, Randall concludes, is: "Why are you doing this? Because you're enjoying it, or because you feel like you have to?"

TeamSnap's Cohen has tried some rebellious tactics to spare her own children from being caught amid competing demands from authority figures they respect and trust. "Adults like to use the word *mandatory* to make the kids feel like they have to do something," Cohen says. Once she got back-to-back emails about two of her daughter's activities, both claiming to be mandatory, at times that conflicted. Since then, she says, "I have a ban on the word *mandatory* in my house."

Even spiritual leaders are joining the ranks of those concerned about overscheduling. Pastors and rabbis frequently tell me they're finding kids and families losing touch with their faith and community because they simply don't have time, just as I saw happen with my children. "Youth ministry has become extremely difficult," says pastor Doug Burford, who leads a small church in Overland Park, a Kansas City suburb high on the performance-pressure scale. Youth group meetings, Bible study, service projects—it all takes a back pew to other obligations, he says. "It's almost impossible to schedule anything."

Burford once saw a kid at church in a soccer uniform at ten on a Sunday morning. He asked if the boy had a game later, and the boy said no, he'd had one at six thirty a.m. because that's when the field was available. "In the morning?!" the shocked pastor asked him. "If I as a pastor asked for that kind of meeting time, people would look at me incredulous that I had the audacity to request that."

Without the time for cultivation of the soul, Burford senses a void in kids—a hunger that they can't quite name. "An idol can be anything that takes first place over God," he says. "And to me, frankly, sports has become that."

Too Early to Rise

It's worth noting one more important way in which school schedules are poorly aligned with our children's needs: the indecent and science-defying hours at which they roust our teens out of bed. Alarm clocks across the country go off at six a.m. or earlier to get kids up in time to stumble blearily into class as early as 7:20 a.m., poorly rested and unready for learning. School start times are determined by a host of factors—competing bus schedules, interscholastic sports, tradition. But too often missing from that list is an essential one: medical evidence.

"We're starting to see schools change their schedules to accommodate the fact, and it is a fact, that circadian rhythms change in adolescence, and making them get up at six is really dumb," says Abigail Baird. "Adolescents can only physically grow when they sleep, so disrupting their sleep cycles is really not smart."

The reason is that adolescents' natural sleep-wake cycles, governed by the timed release of hormones throughout the day, begin to shift by up to two hours as puberty begins. Teens are naturally driven to stay up later and sleep later, and our traditional school schedules directly contradict their bodies' needs. The American Academy of Pediatrics cites strong evidence that early school start times are a critical contributor to chronic sleep deprivation among American teens. Its official recommendation is that middle and high schools start at eight thirty or later—but an AAP report in fall 2014 noted that 85 percent of American high schools do not.

We saw in the last chapter that teen sleep deprivation is linked to anxiety, depression, and other ill health effects, as well as a marked drop in mental functioning. So it stands to reason that studies have found schools with later start times see fewer tardies and absences, improved student attention, and higher grades and standardized test scores. One alarming study in Virginia even found a connection between teen sleep and car accidents. The neighboring cities of Virginia Beach and Chesapeake are demographically similar, researchers reported in 2008 in the *Journal of Clinical Sleep Medicine*. The major difference for students is that the cities' high school start times are seventy-five to eighty minutes apart. Perhaps as a result, the research team found that earlier-to-rise Virginia Beach saw significantly higher rates of weekday car crashes among teen drivers than Chesapeake did.

So what our school start times tell us about our values is that, until now, logistics and traditions have trumped health and learning. Thankfully, that is starting to change. Two high schools in Boulder, Colorado, for example, pushed their first bells back from seven thirty to eight or later. Fairfax County, Virginia, high schools and the Minneapolis school district have delayed their starts. The Emery/Weiner School in Houston reset its start time by forty-five minutes after a *Race to Nowhere* screening. Rock Bridge High

School in Columbia, Missouri, pressed by a sophomore and A student who told the *New York Times* she had to set three alarms to get to class at 7:50, changed its start time to the adult-work hour of nine a.m. Other schools across the country are following this lead.

Enslaved by the Bell

And what happens when students, sleepy or not, arrive on campus? As the glimpse at Tira's schedule showed us, the hurried pace of learning during the school day only quickens the spin cycle. Overcrowded schedules fragment our kids' learning time, thus crowding out opportunities for deep consideration. The inefficient use of the school day is also part of what pushes school obligations, such as assignments and tutoring, past the last bell.

Teachers are not to blame for the mind-numbing march that school days often become. Even the most inventive among them must work within the inflexible constraints of a system created in the Industrial Age, when factory schedules framed the zeitgeist and influenced the design of public schools. The stubbornness of that system came home to me in a head-spinning story told to me by Larry Rosenstock, cofounder and CEO of San Diego's High Tech High, one of the most vibrant and innovative schools I've seen. He considers the traditional school schedule, regimented into fixed chunks of time, the single greatest impediment to educational innovation. While explaining what drove him to exit the public school system and start a charter school, Rosenstock recalled a moment working in Cambridge, Massachusetts:

> We had a schedule that really was designed for adult convenience, not for students' convenience. It made no sense to a lot of us. So, I met with sixteen teachers. I said, "We need to change the schedule," and they all sat there very somberly, and one of them said, "Well, we can't change the schedule. The schedule won't let us," as if it were sitting at the table. And it took me six years to realize that that person was right. The schedule wouldn't let us.

In other words, Rosenstock said, the schedule had been rigidly fixed for so long that people assumed it could not be disrupted—yet those very assumptions prevented them from exploring avenues for change. It was a self-fulfilling prophecy. On top of such tunnel vision, schools trying to reshape their schedules run up against practical obstacles: bus schedules, sports schedules, objections from teachers unions, and the organization of high-stakes tests and teachers' credentials around narrow subjects. Many states still have antiquated "seat time" requirements for public schools, based literally on how many hours students have spent sitting in class, regardless of how much they've learned. The resulting rigidity reflects another misalignment of our actual use of time and our values.

A number of schools across the country have successfully upturned tradition, redesigning school time around a new set of priorities—depth, personalization, creativity, connection, meaning—and restoring some of the after-school time that rightfully belongs to students and families.

Walter Payton College Preparatory High School, for example, has used several smart tactics to shake the schedule monkey off its back. The downtown Chicago magnet school draws academically high-achieving students from all socioeconomic strata from across the city. The foundation on which Payton's layered strategies are built is the block schedule, where students spread their classes out over two days, attending only four classes a day instead of sprinting quickly through all eight. The classes come in big ninety-minute blocks, which allow teachers and students to settle down and dig in—tackling more complex lessons and deeper questions. Plus, with students only having to prepare for half their classes each night, Principal Tim Devine explains, "That allows focus."

Block schedules are not uncommon in American high schools and represent a good, if basic, starting point. Research confirms their benefits. In 2001, Michael Rettig and Robert Lynn Canady, then professors at James Madison University and the University of Virginia, respectively, took stock of a decade's worth of science and found evidence that block schedules can bring a host of improvements: better student and teacher attendance, fewer discipline referrals, and higher grades.

Payton puts some unique twists on its block schedule. First, it devotes the last forty-nine minutes of each day to a period called Enrichment. This is, essentially, flex time: Payton students' all-in-one tool for addressing whatever they need on the day when they need it. Those who need one-on-one tutoring with a teacher can go to that teacher's classroom and get it. Athletes can start practice or set off for away games without missing class. Others might work together on group projects, hold meetings of academic clubs, exercise, or just get a jump start on homework. (Personally, I could use an Enrichment period every day.)

Second, Payton devotes every other Wednesday to ungraded seminars: deep dives into decidedly nonacademic subjects that expand students' minds and worlds. Teachers, who get to invent seminars based on their own interests, enjoy them, too. The subjects range from the gritty to the goofy— recent seminars include the basics of stocks and trading with researchers from Morningstar, improv comedy with performers from the sketch comedy company Second City, belly dancing, beginning guitar, and elementary astronomy.

Making these time-shifts at Payton involved clearing some common hurdles—especially skepticism about changing the status quo. In spring 2012, when the whole city of Chicago was poised to lengthen its school day, Principal Devine seized the chance to explore how to use all school time better. Payton hosted dozens of conversations with students, faculty, and parents, closely examining the benefits of potential approaches. A majority of people in all those groups ultimately embraced block scheduling, enrichment periods, and seminars—and that broad-based support helped Devine convince reluctant district officials to let Payton break the mold.

For recent Payton grad Lucian, the net effect was to create a more relaxed learning environment and deeper lessons. He says the seminar days, in particular, "allowed me to explore how to understand a new concept, idea, solution, or entire world without the stresses of a regular academic course" and "kept us excited about our other classes since there isn't the constant drain of being in the same class every day." Rising senior Daniela finds the enrichment periods especially important, "because when a chunk of school time is devoted to extracurriculars, there is more time after school to finish homework, spend time with family, and, of course, sleep."

Devine, meanwhile, is watching closely to see how Payton's reforms affect all students. So far, so good: three years after implementation, the school's impressive student outcomes remain strong. About four in ten Payton students live in poverty (and counting those who are just "a snowball's throw away from poverty," says Devine, it's closer to six in ten). Yet 98.5 percent of them go on to college. And more than 95 percent of Payton students attend school daily, on regular class days and seminar days alike, a sign that they find it worthwhile to be there.

Far west from Chicago, Saint Mary's College High School, in Berkeley, took a different approach to allowing more time for deep study and restoring balance to students' lives. As the Catholic school began looking several years ago at how to shift its focus from breadth to depth, Principal Peter Imperial realized: "The schedule sets the RPM of the school. . . . You can't go into depth if you have seven classes at night to go home and study for." He and his staff discussed it and determined that there had to be a better way. The solution they settled on: trimesters. By switching from semesters to trimesters, Saint Mary's reduced the number of courses students take at one time from seven to five—only four of which are typically academic. "It also reduced the number of classes teachers teach," noted Imperial, "because they, too, are on this wheel."

And at High Tech High, a charter school free from some of the standard constraints, Rosenstock and colleagues abolished schedules entirely. Instead of segregating lessons by subject, they give each group of about fifty freshmen just two core teachers: one for science, one for humanities. Each pair of teachers decides together on the best way to use each school day, working with students as a whole or in smaller groups, expanding or contracting different parts of the day depending on their purpose.

Radical schedule changes are possible at the elementary school level, too. After screening *Race to Nowhere*, the community of Potomac, Montana, a sleepy hamlet outside Missoula, created a task force and ultimately decided on a change that was nothing short of extraordinary. The K-8 Potomac School shifted to a four-day week, holding class from eight a.m. to four thirty p.m. Mondays through Thursdays. The extra ninety minutes a day became time for children to study what they most needed, get extra help from their teachers, and complete what would otherwise have been homework—not unlike Payton's Enrichment time. With this time built into the school day, Potomac eliminated homework for the elementary grades, thus evening out some inequities, enabling students to get just-in-time help from the experts (their teachers), and honoring children's time at home.

The four-day week was a true break from America's educational convention. But what it enabled Potomac to do on Fridays was even more uncommon. Every Friday, families may choose to send their children to school or not. Those who come are treated to the Potomac Explorers program, aptly described by the local newspaper as a kind of math, science, and art camp for experiential learning. The 2014–2015 calendar included rock climbing and snowshoeing trips, a robotics lesson, a visit from a mechanical engineer, geocaching, a pinewood derby, kids creating their own stop-motion movies, designing and building sets for the school's holiday show, and a "spooky science" day on Halloween. Alicia Vanderhyden, a mom of one son, said the schedule change was scary at first. But ultimately she saw it as a chance for kids to escape the everyday churn, to experience "the process of joyful learning . . . so that they carry that with them through the rest of their life, so that they don't give up."

As at Payton, Potomac's dramatic transformation came through a careful process of research and discussion involving all kinds of constituents—and it started because several people in the school community dared to question our educational habits and to put students' real needs at the heart of the answer. Taking the time to bring a majority of the community on board, and to make structural changes rather than just slapping on extra programs, really matters. "Because this was built into the culture of the school," says then-superintendent Tim Johnson, "these ideas last."

At the end of Potomac's first year under its new schedule, the school surveyed families on their opinions. More than 90 percent said the four-day week and the Friday field-learning program should go on.

Just One Night

Hundreds of schools have tried a simple experiment to counteract the over-commitment of kids' *after-school* time: a night off. This strategy has parallels in the business world, where even the elite Boston Consulting Group has made efforts to ease the 24/7 demands that were leading burned-out employees to leave the firm. Working with a Harvard Business School professor, BCG moved to make sure each employee had at least one night off per week, while fellow team members covered for that person. Relieved employees, who could at last plan a family dinner or outing that wasn't at risk of last-minute cancellation, embraced the reform.

Nights off for schools are a starting point for change. There's no way a single night could really ease our kids' overstretched lives, but it can provide a snapshot of the many other valuable things children might do with their time, a glimpse of what we're missing. These evenings fit into a broader national movement to encourage communities to schedule regular times to reset their health, such as Meatless Mondays and Wind-Down Wednesdays (the latter being a Race to Nowhere call for schools to pilot a midweek night off). And if a work-crazy consulting firm can try it, so can a school community.

Irvington High School's first-ever Community Night Off took place on a Monday in fall 2014. Assistant Principal Jay Jackson sent the whole school community a letter explaining the night's purpose—to spend quality time with family and friends—and urging everyone to follow three guidelines: no homework, no extracurricular activities, and no electronics. He encouraged teachers to take the night off from grading, too.

You would think that a single free night would be an easy sell, but Jackson had to fight for it at a faculty meeting. In the end, 80 percent of the faculty voted to approve it. "That's the 80/20 rule," Jackson told me: anytime you try to make a healthy change, 80 percent of people will support it and 20 percent will object. "But I find that 20 percent is very vocal."

The results were positive. Not every teacher honored the no-homework rule (was one night really too much to ask?), and not every student truly took the night off. But those who did embrace the evening described it as "great" and "wonderful." Some families played cards or went out to dinner. The girls' volleyball team replaced practice with a parent-student scrimmage, followed by a potluck. Aneesha, a sunny-tempered sophomore who leads the school's Edjoycation Task Force, assisting Jackson with health promotion, went to a movie with her mom.

By spring, Jackson and the Edjoycation students were collaborating to plan another, improved night off and expecting even stronger participation the second time. Dozens of other schools have made their nights off monthly, and Aneesha planned to take it upon herself to contact the elementary and middle school principals in town and ask them to participate, too, so that whole families could truly enjoy a night together.

Retaking the Reins

Nowhere does the lens of time reveal a more topsy-turvy picture than when we turn it to the realm of family. And looking at that picture can be hard. Because whenever I write about the pace at which my children live—their ceaseless sprint from obligation to obligation, distraction to distraction—I start to get the uncomfortable feeling that they remind me of someone: myself. I realize, with chagrin, that I model the marathon for them. And our respective rat races have a multiplier effect. It is not simply that the kids are busy and I am busy. *We* are busy. Our family together forms an interconnected system of busyness, a constellation of ever-spinning whirligigs, helping to propel one another.

In families, "You have a whole system that is formed and predicated on the notion that we are busy, that busyness is good," says the *Washington Post*'s Brigid Schulte, who wrote the book *Overwhelmed: Work, Love, and Play When No One Has the Time*. "It's how we show our status, it's how we derive value, it is what we do as a family. You get so busy that you never have time to stop and think about *why* you're so busy, what is all the busyness for."

If you, too, cringe as you recognize your children's mad dash as your own, take comfort in the fact that it's not entirely our fault as individuals. Overscheduling has deep societal roots. American workers clock on average 10 percent more hours per week now than we did in 1979. Schulte notes that extreme hours also afflict people at the lower end of the socioeconomic spectrum, who take on multiple jobs because it's no longer possible to support a family with just one. And stubborn gender norms take an especially high time-toll on mothers, who, on average, still do twice the housework and child care as fathers.

As a result, many of the physicians and psychologists I've met in researching my films speak about their concern for parents' health as well as that of students. We are an overworked, underslept, overscheduled bunch constantly expecting ourselves to excel at everything (work, parenting, fitness, marriage). We harbor profound anxieties about our own success and our children's futures, and those anxieties seep out of us and into our children without our even realizing it. Our kids see and absorb it all.

"A lot of times parents will bring their kids to me because I'm a pediatrician," says Lawrence Rosen, who practices in northern New Jersey. "But what we realize when we ask questions about family life is that the same issues we're seeing in the kids, the physical symptoms of stress, the depression, the anxiety, we're seeing in parents, too. . . . Nobody's taking the time to take care of themselves."

It's painfully clear that we adults need a remedy for our "dis-ease of being busy," too. I know this as well as anyone. I removed from my car the school supplies that my kids had used for on-the-go studies—but when they're not there I still make my work calls from behind the wheel. My colleagues often comment, with a shake of their heads, that they've received one email from me at midnight and the next one at five a.m. It's hard to shake the compulsion to busyness once it's in you—which is why we must work to wean our children and our families off of it as early as possible.

Breaking the habit can be hard. Zak started ninth grade with no commitments outside of school, which I supported. But as I watched his classmates practicing with their sports and debate teams, while Zak skateboarded and played with our dogs, I worried that I was failing him as a parent, letting him miss important opportunities. What if he literally did nothing?

A couple of months into the year, though, Zak and a friend started tinkering with hand planes (wooden paddles for bodysurfing), invented their own, and explored turning this into a business. The next year, he spontaneously took up cooking; I came home one evening to find him sitting at the table with two friends for whom he'd made dinner. When I doubt my better instincts now, I remind myself that downtime is a catalyst for self-discovery and autonomy. To survive as an underscheduler in an always-busy world, you have to keep faith in the value of space and time, of allowing a child to explore the new interests to which an unplanned afternoon may lead.

What about children with the opposite tendency, who will voluntarily run themselves into the ground unless you restrain them? Ridgewood, New Jersey, pediatrician Anne Robinson says that's where we parents need to step in. "The parent's primary role is to be the balance keeper," she explains. "Just the way you prepare a meal with the idea of balancing out their nutritional requirements, and you think, 'I want to have a little bit of meat, a little vegetable, a little bit of starch,' you have to think about a child's day that way."

Or, if a day is too short a horizon, think about your child's balance over the course of a week. "Have they had some academic work, but also had time for their friends and family?" Robinson asks. "Have they had time for fresh air and exercise? Have they had time for adequate sleep, time for activities that they enjoy and that enrich their lives? If you think of that balance all the time, when you start to see the balance tipping, figure out how to get it back on track."

————

As we will see in the ensuing chapters, some of the remedies for restoring our misspent family time lie in actions we can take as individuals in our own homes. Yet many of the important steps for resetting the balance involve advocating for school change.

To do this well, it is critical that we come together to build support networks. If we are going to shake off society's norms and define ourselves by something other than our productivity, we need backup. Your wingmen and -women might be neighbors, friends, or an organized group like the McLean, Virginia, PTSA. Past PTSA president Wilma Bowers is campaigning, alongside local clergy and the high school's college counselor, to convince parents and school officials to place more value on "authentic success," which naturally entails a redesign on the use of time. So far they've succeeded at moving the high school start time back forty minutes, organizing an annual summit on teen stress, and persuading school administrators to discourage students from taking more than three AP classes at once.

I believe that each of us who undertakes this work has the same ultimate hope: that we'll look back on our lives someday with satisfaction, seeing that we have spent our time and energy on what most matters—and that our children will someday be able to do the same. What most matters, of course, is not the number of credentials we've earned or competitors bested or records broken. Not what columnist David Brooks calls "the résumé virtues."

But rather "the eulogy virtues," the kindness, honesty, courage, and love that grow from a life lived in concert with our values.

Each person will define his or her truest priorities a little differently. Whatever they are, there should be just a few of them. And these are the pursuits to which we should devote most of our time. Success, to me, means making just a little bit of progress each day in the movement to end the Race to Nowhere, keeping a strong connection with my family and friends, and maintaining a healthy mind and body.

Everything else is optional.

CHAPTER 3

Homework:
Take Back Our Nights

Now we come to the Big Three—the trio of forces that demand the most of kids' time and do the most to disrupt their health and learning: homework, testing, and college admissions. These are also the ripest areas for reinvention. I'll take the first one first.

———

Stephanie Brant started seeing the ills of homework in her students during her first year as principal of Maryland's Gaithersburg Elementary School. She spotted it on her morning rounds, in the look of gloom on children's faces. "I started noticing students that came into school very discouraged," she said. "So often our students would be confused or feel bad about what they didn't get done at home."

Brant, a chipper dynamo who started her career as a teacher and literacy specialist, raised the concern with her staff. The Gaithersburg faculty read the research on homework and examined its effects on the young children they served. Ultimately, their investigation led them to a stunning fact: there is no scientific evidence to support the value of most of the homework our children are assigned. This supposedly wholesome practice—which has spiraled to such extremes that it shreds family life, steals children's chances to explore and play, and deprives growing minds and bodies of essential rest—does not even help students learn. So the teachers sought a better way to enrich the kids' learning instead of squashing their enthusiasm for it. And in so doing, they upturned this toxic old educational tradition that has typically gone unquestioned.

Homework holds a special place in the American psyche. This insistent, uninvited guest possesses a mythology all its own. We have long considered homework a rite of passage, a necessary evil, part of the training required for success in college and life beyond. Idiomatically, someone who "does his homework" is a diligent, well-prepared person. And at one time, I myself was a believer, even directing my young children to spend weekend time studying instead of playing if their grades were down. Like most of my friends, I accepted my children's ceaseless nighttime slog as the hallmark of a strong education, a vehicle for learning the value of self-discipline and persistence. This idea of developing a fierce work ethic felt especially important to me, as someone who grew up amid financial insecurity and saw education as the way out.

Yet our devotion to the myth—and a myth it is—has reached the absurd. We have confused quantity with quality, busywork with challenge, conformity with discipline. We consistently ask our still fragile and growing children to put in second and third shifts, logging more hours in a day than many adults I know. As parents, we give up our authority over the after-school hours, allowing schools to claim as much of our family time as they desire. Combining their time in school with school-sponsored activities and homework, many children's work hours today remind me chillingly of the unhealthy way I worked while on Wall Street. Aren't seven hours of school, plus perhaps a sport or a music lesson, enough for a child?

The Intruder

As *Race to Nowhere* screened in communities across the country, parent after parent stood up and identified homework as one of the most malignant aspects of the race. They worried about how to get their teens to go to bed before one a.m., or grew heartsick watching the spark of curiosity fade from their kindergarteners' eyes. Instead of playing board games or reading books together with their children, parents were engaging in nightly battles with eight-year-olds who (understandably) didn't want to do a lifeless worksheet after a full day at school. It was clear that the truckloads of assignments being dumped on children today are nothing like the modest homework our generation had as kids, when we could finish our work, get to bed on time, and still hold an after-school job and ride bikes with friends. Homework has become an act of home invasion.

"Now that my daughter's in fifth grade, three hours of schoolwork comes in the door with her," said a mom and professional therapist at a screening on the Stanford University campus. "I'd rather she come to this movie, or go to my music group with me, or work on just making pasta the way she likes it or making a musical instrument out of rubber bands. That's what counts to us."

In working-class Castro Valley, California, a grandmother who had also trained as a psychologist worried about the anxiety she saw homework causing children in her hometown.

And a girl named Amanda, from Miami, who said she consistently misses her nine o'clock bedtime and goes to sleep at eleven thirty, wrote:

> Now, when I have just started the sixth grade, I have been piled up with homework to high heaven! . . . I only partake in one after-school activity, which is on a Friday so I can complete homework from that day over the weekend. I have literally no time to be a kid anymore. I am a writer in my very sparse free time, and I have barely written anything for myself this school year. To tell you I'm angry would be an understatement.

One father of three—a sitting school superintendent, no less—said to me bluntly: "Homework is destroying my family."

I saw the same problems in my own home. Every day, including weekends, was cast under homework's shadow; every errand, family outing, and gathering with friends had to be shoehorned into the few hours of space that remained. If I convinced my children to meet friends for lunch, they'd be studying in the car en route, asking for vocabulary help instead of chatting. Even over holidays the kids spent long weekends and winter breaks bent over their books, trying to keep up. And this was *after* Doug and I had made deliberate efforts to lighten their course loads and reduce their commitments! Jamey had quit violin and soccer, Shelby stopped ice skating and playing piano, and Zak left his soccer and Little League teams. Instead, Jamey took up cheerleading, Shelby studied for her Bat Mitzvah, and Zak zoomed around on his skateboard. Yet no amount of cutting back felt like enough. The race seemed inescapable, even for a family that no longer believed in it, and homework was a primary culprit.

This has got to stop—and it *can*. I know because I've seen it done, by pioneering schools and families across America.

In the wake of screening *Race to Nowhere* and reviewing the research showing that homework does not improve learning, the public K-8 Hillcrest School in Oakland courageously abolished homework entirely for the primary grades. The superintendent of schools in Swampscott, Massachusetts, declared a monthly homework-free night. Galloway, New Jersey, banned weekend homework for children in grades K-6. Mango Elementary School in Fontana, California, replaced homework with "goal work" tailored to individual children's needs and completed on a flexible schedule. At the Brooklyn School of Inquiry, a public "gifted and talented" program, homework is optional.

These changes might seem radical, yet the sky has not fallen. Indeed, it seems brighter than ever for the children in these districts.

Meanwhile, parents have secured similar reforms in hundreds of communities by banding together and insisting that teachers, schools, and districts provide relief. In their own homes, many individual parents now simply say no, opting their child out of homework when sleep, health, and other life lessons and experiences are more important.

Of all the aspects of the race that need changing, homework is actually the easiest place to start. Change can begin with individual parents, teachers, administrators, and students. From there, it grows, as families and schools work together to take back our nights.

A Short History of Homework

It is not your imagination. Children today actually *are* being asked to do vastly more than we did as kids. Here's a bit of history:

Homework has played a central role in American family life for centuries.

It was standard issue at the colonies' first public school, Boston Latin, where the Puritan notion that "practice makes perfect"—the precursor to "drill and kill"—reigned supreme. Complaints cropped up in the mid-1800s, when some citizens worried about the effect on pupils' health. By the turn of the twentieth century, organized objections to take-home assignments were taking hold. Assignments of that era tended toward rote memorization, including notoriously awful spelling drills of obscure words. In 1900, *Ladies' Home Journal* magazine campaigned with the support of the country's pediatricians to abolish homework in favor of fresh air and exercise. The campaign fueled the rise of a national antihomework movement, which convinced numerous cities to place limits on after-school assignments for young children.

But the resistance couldn't hold for long. In the competitive frenzy following the Russians' launch of Sputnik in 1957, the pediatricians' philosophy was eclipsed by a "more is better" maxim. Homework loads increased (though not yet to the levels seen today). Amid worries that other countries would outrace our economy, outbuild our bombs, and outeducate our students, homework became—and remains—a symptom of our fear that our children will be left behind.

The freer-thinking 1970s (when I grew up) offered a brief respite, when afternoons were reserved again for child's play—but then the modern age of homework madness began with the 1983 publication of *A Nation at Risk*, a report by the Reagan administration that once again amped up the fear of global competition. The report noted the substandard test scores of US students in relation to their peers internationally, and identified the preceding decrease in the amount of homework as one culprit. As a result, the commission recommended "students in high schools should be assigned far more homework than is now the case."

We all know where that has led. A University of Michigan study found that between 1981 and 1997 the amount of homework done by children aged six to eight more than doubled. A later Michigan study that looked at the average homework load across all ages from six to seventeen found it rose by 50 percent between the early 1980s and 2003. And that was largely *before* President Bush's No Child Left Behind Act and President Obama's Race to the Top fund—federal initiatives that applied carrots and sticks to students' standardized test scores—further upped the ante. Now teachers are under increased pressure to plow through an impossibly long list of state-required content. As a result, many of them send home what can't be covered in school. The mounting college arms race also fuels the misguided notion that children should do more, faster, sooner, so as to be prepared to do more, faster, later.

By 2005, parents surveyed by the Lucile Packard Foundation for Children's Health named homework as the greatest cause of their kids' stress, far more frequently even than divorce or family financial troubles. And the burden has only grown heavier in the decade since then. (Some news stories have proclaimed that homework levels are unchanged, but that's based on data from an exam called the National Assessment of Educational Progress, which asks test takers how much homework they did the night before—yet teachers typically lighten the load the night before a standardized exam.)

The problem is not that *every* assignment in this mounting pile is meaningless; amid the busywork, my kids have also written thoughtful essays and completed substantive science projects. The intentions behind these assignments are undoubtedly good. The trouble is that attending school alone is a full-time job for a child. Even meaningful assignments are overtime.

So deep is our ingrained faith in the virtues of homework, though, that we've developed a punitive attitude about kids who don't do it. It's not just about learning—it's about character. Children who don't complete their assignments receive a collective *cluck-cluck* from society; they must be slackers. There's little recognition of the countless other important needs and activities that command kids' time. Even when a child is sick, she's often required to do her homework or, impossibly, to make up days of backlogged work once she recovers. That's what happened when my daughter missed eight days of school in seventh grade. The school demanded that she complete all eight days of schoolwork and homework, while continuing to do new assignments, even when she still needed energy to fully heal. I said no.

A brush with such rigidity was also part of what convinced Etta Kralovec to become a homework researcher. The University of Arizona education professor and coauthor of *The End of Homework* had, earlier in her career, conducted a study for the Maine Department of Education in which she interviewed dozens of high school dropouts who had enrolled in alternative schools around the state, asking them, "When did you know you weren't going to make it through school?" These teens, most of them from poor, rural homes, contended with health, transportation, and family problems. But although it was far from the only factor, homework became a decisive one: the inability to keep up had helped to push all of them over the edge. "We were stunned," Kralovec says. "I'd never seen homework discussed as a contributing factor to dropping out of school."

The prevailing attitude is that there can be no exceptions. It's not about the learning; the fixation is on completion of the assignments themselves. Once, at a screening in New York's Westchester County, students admitted to the crowd they'd be up until two a.m. doing homework to make up for time lost to attend the event. I was shocked that their principal, in the audience, offered them no flexibility. To heck with sleep, health, and the value of participating in a discussion of important issues with their community—the Almighty Homework God had to be appeased.

No doubt some parents exacerbate the pressure on schools to assign homework by buying into the idea that homework equals learning—as I used to. Now we even have software programs like School Loop that allow parents to watch, hawklike, how their child fares on every single assignment every single day. Schools encourage this in the name of parental engagement. Yet this can transform a loving parent into yet another adult who's constantly measuring and micromanaging them. I avoid logging into these systems, finding that my children will share more with me about their school experience, and will gain a stronger sense of responsibility and autonomy, when they don't feel I'm looking over their shoulders. But many parents, with the best intentions, do just that.

Still, the vast majority of parents I've spoken to believe homework has gone way too far, and they are exasperated and baffled about what to do. Rick and Casey Sasner wrote a letter to the school superintendent after their son fell asleep at his desk at eleven thirty one night, then woke up two hours later and tried to keep studying. The letter was so candid that it still moves me. Rick and Casey agreed to let me share excerpts:

> *We are at a breaking point in terms of frustration with the over-load of junior year. It's surreal that our child is BEGGING US to*

entirely cancel our family's spring break—a four-day trip that was originally a six-day trip but was cut back because of his workload.

Over the past three weeks, our son has had nine math tests, three history tests and a string of other quizzes, tests, projects and papers. . . . He is trying to operate consistently on five hours of sleep a night and being forced to skip classes in order to prepare for other classes. His physical and mental health are in jeopardy and there's not a thing we can do about it except to say, "if you fail a test or a class or get a C, it will be okay!" We are saying that, but you can imagine how any high school student would receive that.

The Sasners described "feelings of sadness and hopelessness for our own child because we honestly believe he's being robbed of a life." For Kralovec's part, though her own children are now grown, she recalls, "I hated homework because it interfered with my family life. I didn't have a lot of time with my kids, and I didn't want to use it fighting with them over homework. . . . I don't want the state telling me how to spend my evening with my kids."

Kralovec and the Sasners, to their credit, had the clarity to realize that the system—not their child—is broken. Yet as I know from personal experience, many parents whose children strain under the weight of so many assignments are less certain; with no clear norms to guide them, they wonder if the teachers are assigning too much or if it's simply too much for their one kid. And schools often confirm those fears. For students who aren't advancing in lockstep with everyone else, I've found, the school typically suggests tutoring. The message is: the problem is you.

Why do we tolerate this? Homework is such an entrenched part of the modern idea of school that many families rarely question it. I have asked myself, as I look back and cringe at the thought of all the time lost with my children, how I let it go on so long. But that is because we as a culture consider it normal. Because homework is tradition. It is a child's educational pill to swallow. And objecting to it makes you, the parent, also seem lazy, indulgent, or unduly freewheeling. Simply put, homework is assumed to be virtuous: it is what we did (in smaller quantities) and what our parents took for granted was good for us, too. We do this because this is what is done.

Homework Doesn't Work

Luckily, this irrational, unquestioned acceptance of homework is starting to change—slowly—in schools and families across the country, as more research shows that excessive homework does more harm than good. Indeed, there is now a growing movement of schools, particularly in the elementary grades, putting the brakes on the runaway train.

Scientific research demonstrates that in many cases, homework does nothing to improve students' academic performance, as we have always assumed it does. In fact, those hours of assignments can hurt both health and learning.

On the homework-doesn't-work score, here's what the science tells us. In 2006, Duke University's Harris Cooper surveyed fifteen years' worth of homework studies conducted across the country. The conclusion: homework was found to have *little to no benefit* before high school and diminishing returns for high school students as the hours spent doing it increased. Another study in 2011 reinforced this finding. In that experiment, a pair of economists crunched numbers from 25,000 eighth graders and found that a little extra math homework (amounting to about fifteen minutes per weekday) did boost students' math scores slightly (just over 3 percent). But piling on an extra weekly hour of English, science, or history assignments, beyond average levels, made *no impact whatsoever* on scores in those subjects. So even if you believe that high test scores are the hallmark of a high-quality education—which I don't—after-school assignments aren't getting us there.

As for that bit of daily math practice that does help with mastery, students can do that best *in school*, Etta Kralovec explains. "The work of *good* homework, what we think is important"—that is, a little practice and making the learning one's own—"that needs to happen in the presence of a teacher who can help them with their learning. . . . Parents are not substitute teachers." Happily, once teachers aren't spending part of each class assigning and checking homework, they'll have time for that. Some schools are also capturing more time during the school day for independent work and assistance, through strategies such as Walter Payton High School's block schedules and Enrichment period. Others provide in-school study halls or use central assignment calendars to avoid overloading students with a deluge of tests and assignments from different teachers on the same day.

We get obsessed with debates over how much time kids of certain ages should spend on assignments each night, but that's the wrong question. The right question is: What is the best way for each child to grow and learn? The fact is that there are no proven standards for the "right" amount of homework time. Much is made of the oft-cited "ten-minute rule": ten minutes of homework per night per grade level—i.e., ten minutes a night in first grade, fifty minutes a night in fifth grade, and so on. It sounds sensible enough on the surface but is ultimately arbitrary. There is no research establishing the magic of those ten minutes; rather, the guideline is grounded in the questionable (but often unquestioned) premise that homework must be assigned each day, and therefore must be limited. Furthermore, the guideline fails to recognize that time spent on a given homework assignment can vary substantially from one child to the next. And it ceases to work entirely once students hit middle and high school and have six different classes per day, with each teacher assigning homework, unaware of what other teachers are also requiring. (Imagine if you had five to seven bosses, each sending you home with separate assignments every night and weekend, entirely beyond your control.)

There's an even more pernicious problem: homework exacerbates inequality between families. Some children go home to high-speed Internet connections and private bedrooms and parents with advanced degrees who can serve as at-home teachers. Others go home to cramped quarters and parents who lack the time, education, or English-language skills to help them. These children may also hold jobs or care for younger siblings to support their families. Still others spend their after-school hours on violent streets and in drug-infested apartments with scarcely a stable adult around. Our public education system strives toward equality—yet when it comes to homework, we expect all children to perform the same with vastly unequal resources. As Isaiah, the Oakland Tech High School student, said to me, "Academics has become a new way to test a person's character: whether they can handle the rigorous classes, the pressures of holding both a job and going to school on time, whether they can, you know, watch their little sister and write an essay at the same time." (These same inequalities prompted

French president François Hollande to propose banning elementary and middle school homework for his entire country in 2012.)

A classic counterargument to reducing homework, a favorite of politicians, is about global competition. It is the same argument that was effective in the Sputnik 1950s: Why are hours of at-home drill essential? Because children in the world's other advanced economies are doing it. *Just think of how hard the Chinese are studying while your little Johnny fritters away his time and gets left behind!* Aside from the deep flaws in our measures of "achievement" (which I'll lay out in the next chapter), there's an even more fundamental error in that statement: it's not universally true. Homework is not the key to success in these other countries. Indeed, its use varies widely. Many of the countries that score highest on international tests assign the *least* amount of homework. For instance, the PISA, the international exam that's given by the Organization for Economic Cooperation and Development, is more respected than most as a means of gauging good thinking skills. One of the consistent superstars on this test, Finland, logs the least homework time—an average of less than three hours a week for fifteen-year-olds (and Finnish students spend fewer days and hours each day in school than their American counterparts).

Precise numbers for the US are hard to pin down. OECD researchers put the US homework average at more than double that of Finland, and among the highest of the thirty-eight countries studied. Depending on whom you ask (teachers, students, or parents) and when and how you ask them, other estimates of the weekly hours an average American high school student spends on homework range from seven to nearly eighteen. In some communities, homework time can climb to five hours per *night*. More salient than the exact number is the matter of what all this desk time means for the quality of our kids' lives and learning. When OECD researchers looked at average homework loads for fifteen-year-olds in each country, they concluded that "after around four hours of homework per week, the additional time invested in homework has a negligible impact on performance." That is frustrating news when your kid is sitting inside studying chemistry equations on a lovely Saturday afternoon and you'd rather take her hiking.

What's more, our little night-and-weekend warriors rarely get assignments that are tailored to their individual strengths and needs, or that afford them the opportunity to direct their own learning. Often, all thirty kids in a class get the same to-do list, no matter who they are. The only time I saw homework stimulate my kids' appetite for learning was when they were guiding the work. In fourth grade, Jamey's class was given optional "go-getter" projects on subjects of the students' choosing, and she and her friends would spend hours together researching questions that excited them. Opportunities to engage with the world outside of school, such as interviewing a family member or a local historian, can also extend learning beyond the classroom. But alas, teachers are spread so thin that creative and personalized work is the rare exception. Too often, homework assignments are a reflex, not a rich learning experience.

The writer Karl Taro Greenfeld famously did all his daughter's homework for a week for a story in *The Atlantic* in 2013. Greenfeld struggled through consecutive late nights of algebra problems, readings from a deadly earth sciences textbook, Spanish verb conjugations, and assignments to read as much as seventy-nine pages of a novel per night. "Memorization, not rationalization," his thirteen-year-old instructed him. Barely able to sustain his energy or interest through Thursday, he asked: "Are these many hours of homework the only way to achieve this metamorphosis of child into virtuous citizen? . . . I have my doubts."

But wait—doesn't homework at least instill a sense of organization and discipline? Americans have long clung to that idea, too. Yet here there is even *less* evidence to support that assumption, as it has never been tested. Kralovec explains, in her characteristically spirited tone: "If there were one shred of evidence to prove that, I would be very compelled by those arguments, but there has never, ever been research done about any of that. That's a blind faith. That's akin to religion."

Her advice instead, issued with a note of irony: "If you want a kid to learn time management, get them four dogs and make them walk the dogs after school." Human beings learn perseverance well by taking on challenges that matter to them. Meanwhile, we have imbued homework with all kinds of powers it doesn't truly have.

One thing that we know actually *does* reinforce rich learning is—of all neglected things—rest. We've already seen how downtime supports creativity and psychological growth. It is also essential for our brains to process and remember what we've learned. So if a kid goes out skateboarding after school, that is not wasted time, according to pediatrician Anne Robinson: "He's processing the information of the day. He's using math and physics to navigate that board around. And he's using the skills that he'll need for the rest of his life to navigate the world. This is the piece that our students are missing out on, when they're spending so much time with a book."

In fact, the more challenging the work we expect our students to do, the more rest they need. In a seminal 1993 study, a trio of European psychologists examined how experts learn. Studying violinists at various skill levels, they determined that the most elite performers slept substantially more than the middling ones. They even took regular afternoon naps! All told, the experts engaged in intensive practice (what you might liken to studying) only around thirty hours a week, or a little over four hours a day. They typically spread that work out into short, manageable chunks of about ninety minutes each—not unlike a block schedule in school. Experts in other fields are frequently the same; the researchers cited evidence of similar work patterns among professional athletes, famous authors, and prominent scientists. Creativity and genius spring only from well-rested minds.

"If you look at adults, there's four or five hours in the day that you can actually do really serious, creative work," says UC Berkeley psychology professor Alison Gopnik. "You can do kind of make-work for the rest of the time, but there's only a limited period of actually being able to do really serious, intellectual work, and then you need downtime" to consolidate it.

All of which is to say: driving students to slave away over their books almost every spare minute of the day is not doing much for their education. For those who want to truly reinforce learning, the best practice is to prescribe as little as possible—only occasional, personalized assignments that involve experiences that can't happen at school—and to allow the student's brain ample time to explore fresh ideas and absorb and process what it has learned that day.

Opportunity Cost

What troubles me most as a parent is not just homework's lack of utility. It is the harm that excessive, unrelenting hours of assignments do to children's health—with all the lasting physical and emotional consequences we traced in the first chapter. And it is, less conspicuously but quite importantly, what homework takes away. All those hours *not* spent making up games, peering under rocks, talking with friends, tinkering with tools, looking up at the sky and puzzling out the constellations, or putting a nose in a book for long, lost hours—the many nonacademic pursuits that can shape a child's personality, aspirations, and dreams. Since when is *school* the only source through which children learn and grow? These lost experiences amount to numberless childhood hours that can never be recovered, even a loss of childhood itself.

Homework is responsible, first of all, for countless hours of stolen sleep, lost at a phase of life when children acutely need rest for healthy development. More than four in ten parents in a 2014 National Sleep Foundation poll said homework had made it hard for their child to get a good night's sleep within the past week. And researchers at Northwestern University who asked teens to keep a time diary discovered, unsurprisingly, that more hours spent doing homework predicted fewer hours of sleep. Exercise, too, is so often supplanted by homework that Sara Bennett and Nancy Kalish, authors of the book *The Case Against Homework*, coined the term *homework potato*. That effect is especially worrisome in light of the research linking too much everyday sitting with a higher risk of obesity, depression, heart disease, and cancer.

Yet homework steals many valuable things that are harder to recover than sleep and exercise. It's difficult to count them all. There is, first and foremost, family time. We parents have a very short period with our children, all things considered, to share daily meals and provide them with all the lessons and experiences that we consider important. Time outdoors also has dwindled to such a rarity for kids that we now talk about "nature-deficit disorder," an utterly modern ailment that journalist Richard Louv links to rising rates of obesity, attention disorders, and depression. Moreover, reading for pleasure drops off just as homework loads ramp up. A 2006 Scholastic study of five hundred children and their parents found that reading for pleasure decreased dramatically after age eight (after which only 29 percent of students read every day). Parents identified homework as the number one reason their children didn't read for fun.

Our communities suffer from our children's absence, too, as young students step back from unassigned community service in order to study. Participation in religious communities also goes by the wayside (both of my girls' attendance at Hebrew school waned and eventually ended when their homework loads got too heavy). Youth ministers across the country, from all kinds of denominations, have told me they can scarcely get young people to show up for anything after sixth grade.

Even after-school jobs—once the all-American training ground for traits like responsibility and financial prudence—are becoming nothing but a quaint historical notion for kids who don't have to work to support their families. I recall the jobs I had when I was a teen, working as a candy striper and a cashier in a grocery store, where I learned how to manage my time and be responsible to others who were relying on me, in addition to earning income to support my education. Now many teens get such first-job experiences only as college students, when the combined burden of class time and homework becomes, ironically, more manageable than it was in high school. "Contemporary children have very little experience with the kinds of tasks that they'll have to perform as grown-ups," even basic skills like cooking and caregiving, says Gopnik, the UC Berkeley psychologist. "We give them this very specialized, strange thing, which is: we teach them how to go to school."

Homework is obviously not the only reason for these growing gaps in modern childhood, but it is a substantial factor in all. It crowds out the kinds of experiences that help kids develop the very qualities we say they need, such as creativity, communication, and collaboration. And the cultural expectation that school assignments trump all other commitments gives homework cover. Instead, we parents should trust our instincts when homework starts to supplant other healthy experiences and insist that academics are not the only way to learn. We can be the whistle-blowers.

Extracurricular activities are a favorite scapegoat for homework apologists: *It's not his homework that's the problem; it's his frivolous softball practice and saxophone playing!* But extracurriculars should not be cut out of kids' lives to make way for more studying. As long as activities are done for genuine interest, not résumé padding, and their hours are kept moderate, a balance of exercise and fun is essential to healthy, happy growth. They're also a

chance to cultivate a whole world of interests and intelligences beyond strict academics. Kelly, a senior at Ridgewood High School in New Jersey, grew exasperated when teachers suggested she and her peers cut activities after they complained of too much homework. Kelly said: "I do my extracurriculars because it's a way to break free from the academic stress. I do them because I'm passionate about them and I love doing them, and the fact that they want us to cut down so that we have more time to do the homework is counterproductive in and of itself."

Research backs up Kelly's perspective. William Damon, education professor and director of the Stanford Center on Adolescence, has spent decades investigating the importance of one overlooked ingredient in young lives: purpose. "The biggest problem growing up today is not actually stress," Damon told his local Palo Alto newspaper as the town reeled from a cluster of teen suicides. "It's meaninglessness." Damon's research has demonstrated that a strong sense of purpose is critical for building resilience, vigor, self-esteem, and determination, whereas a lack of it can be linked with self-absorption, depression, addictions, low productivity, and unstable relationships. Alarmingly, Damon finds, the chance to develop purpose is too often missing from modern kids' lives. His studies show that nearly one in three adolescents falls into a pattern of "high activity, low purpose," and the implications aren't good.

Extracurriculars can be one key step in that direction. As Damon explains, the path to finding purpose requires that young people have the chance to explore various pursuits, to risk failure, to play, and to work hard at things *they choose themselves*—not to be consumed by tasks chosen for them by others. In that context, kids are more likely to persevere through setbacks and find in them opportunities to grow. Simply working hard on an external goal like getting into Stanford isn't enough to cultivate purpose; the work has to mean something to the person doing it and to the community at large. "We all need a purpose," Damon told the paper. "But at the formative period of life, when you don't even know who you are, you really need it."

Another significant casualty of too much homework (and another favorite scapegoat for students' scant free time) is socializing. Critics tend to cast it as a lazy frivolity, but that couldn't be further from the truth. For young

children, a huge raft of evidence shows how important play is for developing everything from self-control to creativity. The United Nations Convention on the Rights of the Child even names "time to rest and play" among the essential rights of all children. For teens, socializing is some of the primary work of adolescence, a crucial way they develop as social beings and define their identities. I can see clearly how Zak, for example, becomes invigorated, more content, and more productive after spending time with friends. Yet in 2014, UCLA's annual survey of incoming college freshmen revealed that they'd hit a record low in high school social time. In the 1980s, some 38 percent of freshmen said they'd spent at least sixteen hours a week with friends. By 2014, the percentage had plunged to just 18 percent.

Anne Robinson, the pediatrician, underscored to me how essential it is to restore kids' social time. In our youth, kids of Robinson's and my era chatted for hours with friends on the phone. This new generation does some of that socializing on Twitter and Snapchat. Whatever the medium, online or in-person, social time matters. "The fact is that's a requirement, too, just like drinking water or eating their vegetables," she explained. "They have a social requirement."

Finally, and perhaps saddest of all, I have seen over and over again that homework overload steals from young minds the desire to learn. Putting in a second shift after seven hours in school does not help a child become a confident, lifelong learner with an intrinsic sense of curiosity and joy in discovery. Excessive hours hunched over assignments—too many of which amount to pointless practice of what one student already knows, or what another student still doesn't understand—actually kill kids' natural motivation for and excitement about learning. No expert on child development is surprised by this.

Danielle Allphin, a mother and former Los Angeles elementary school principal with a doctorate in education, wrote this to me in late 2014 about her daughter:

> *Today, homework broke her spirit. . . . On this 54th day of kindergarten, homework sucked the inquisitive, eager-to-work-and-learn soul out of my child. On this 54th day of school, I find myself heartbroken. . . . I have a smart, funny, creative, sensitive child who*

went to bed in tears, with knots in her stomach over "three more boring pages" yet to be done in her kindergarten homework packet.

I found myself and my husband launching into the rite-of-passage lecture about the fact of life that is doing things we find boring— laundry, dishes, taking out the trash, reports for work, etc. . . . But why should a five-year-old who loves learning and has a solid grasp on all things one through ten have to spend her evenings re- petitively drawing and/or circling sets of various items in groups of 1 through 10?

Allphin's daughter had already demonstrated mastery of those skills on a kindergarten entrance assessment the previous spring. "Yet she has now completed 37 pages of review," Allphin wrote. "And there it is, folks, the mo- ment that learning stopped being fun. Day 54, page 37. Such a tragedy."

Students themselves can articulate the pain of the dying flame. Alexan- dra, a middle schooler in Redondo Beach, California, sent me this in a letter:

I used to be a very happy tomboy. I picked up water polo three years ago and I was always playing football with the boys at lunch. I loved to play and learn. As I always describe it, I had more questions than people had answers for. I dreamed of going to medical school. I spent hours just thinking of all the wonderful things I could do with that one piece of paper . . . be an army surgeon, a doctor on a cruise ship, or the team physician for the national water polo team. Now, I am an extremely stressed-out student, suffering from depression and anxiety. Even if I finish my homework in time for practice, I some- times don't have the energy for it. Medical school is still a dream, but it's also four more years of school I'll have to go through. I am a completely different person.

In my home, the difference between frenzied overwork and joyful learn- ing was obvious years ago, between the hair-pulling anxiety experienced by a second grader racing the clock to scratch out twenty timed addition prob- lems and in the way that same second grader's face lit up with joy when he could accurately add the number of dogs he'd seen on a neighborhood walk.

If, in our devotion to the busy-worker ideal, we are actually raising a generation of children who lack purpose and creativity, who have missed formative real-world experience, and who are sick, sleepless, joyless, and disengaged, then I have to ask: What kind of "success" is that?

Gaithersburg and Menlo Park: Free to Learn

Homework is the low-hanging fruit of Race to Nowhere reform. Even that may sound daunting—how could decades of this entrenched habit be overcome? But it's possible, and it's already being done by forward-thinking parents, teachers, and schools nationwide.

First, there are examples of educators who have done it themselves. Stephanie Brant, in Gaithersburg, started with a concern about homework's effect on equity. The vast majority of Brant's students come from immigrant families and live below the poverty line, often with multiple families squeezing into a single apartment. Their parents, many of whom clean houses or do construction in other suburban towns around Washington, DC, frequently work two or three jobs to get by. Many speak limited English. So when one of those young students takes home a history research project or a set of tough math problems, she's on her own. She might not get through the work, or, without guidance, she might spend hours doing it wrong.

Once they came to this realization, Brant and her staff "started looking at the quality of the work we were sending home, and it was really just rote worksheets," she told me. Sometimes the assignments involved useful practice, but mostly, the staff realized, they were just sending something home to send something home. "It's not worth it," staff-development teacher Laura McCutcheon explained. "The kids are not getting enough out of this to take away from what little time they do have with their parents between jobs. We wanted kids to enjoy their time at home and come back to school the next day feeling good about themselves and not feeling really badly because they didn't do a math worksheet that research tells us probably isn't doing much for them anyway."

Now, in place of traditional homework assignments, Gaithersburg Elementary asks students simply to read a book—any book they like—for thirty minutes a day. The focus has shifted from rote practice to an attempt to "*extend* what students know," Brant said. Through reading, "We can increase their vocabulary and their background knowledge." Plus, "it gives students the opportunity to get lost in a book and become that character for a while." In the summers, the indefatigable Brant personally drives a "bookmobile" (a.k.a. her own Acura RDX) around the community, giving away books to her students.

Three years later, the new program is still humming along smoothly. In addition to changing the rules on homework, Gaithersburg had simultaneously made a major change to *in-class* work, as well, shifting to an emphasis on creative problem solving and personalized lessons that it calls "Curriculum 2.0." So, in Patricia McCaffrey's fifth grade class the day I visited, there was no lockstep lesson with the teacher lecturing at the front of the room. Instead, McCaffrey was in a corner doing a reading assessment with one small group, while the other students sat at clusters of desks working on various tasks amid a soft murmur of voices. Each child's particular assignment depended on what he or she most needed to work on.

At one set of desks, a cheerful ten-year-old named Victoria explained that she lives alone with her mom since her dad stayed behind in his native El Salvador. She often goes to a friend's house after school while her mother works at McDonald's. "We normally play in the snow or play outside or ride bikes, or anything like that," Victoria said, giving me visions of childhoods in days gone by, before homework took over. "We always do our thirty minutes of reading before anything else." When Victoria's mom gets home, the day's work is done for both of them. "We usually cook dinner, we clean the dishes, sometimes we even do games," said Victoria. "It's really fun."

Sitting opposite her, Ezra, who sported intellectual-hip black glasses and a ready opinion on everything, said, "I have a lot of better things to do than homework." Like what? "Like, where do I start?" he exclaimed, with a slight note of exasperation. Ezra likes writing and not being told what to write. He finds homework too easy. On the merits of homework overall, though, he added, "I'm kind of in the middle. It depends on the homework and it depends on the kid. Some kids learn from homework, some kids learn from reading, some kids learn more from not having homework." To set one system for all kids, he concluded, would be "irresponsible."

Brant recalls that some parents were resistant to the change at first. Without daily assignments, they understandably feared they wouldn't know what their children were studying in class. Other educator-reformers have encountered similar obstacles. When Manhattan's P.S. 116, an elementary school, eliminated homework in early 2015, some parents were outraged, with the mother of one third grader complaining that besides watching more TV, her daughter was also spending more time in her room—gasp!—playing. Meanwhile, across the country, Principal David Ackerman said he, too, had to invest a lot of time in reassuring parents when he dramatically reduced homework at Menlo Park's Oak Knoll Elementary in 2006. In the affluent heart of Silicon Valley, Ackerman observed, "There's a solid set of parents who believe that homework and a rigorous program are the same thing."

So Ackerman penned a now-famous letter to parents explaining that research shows otherwise. He wrote that "large amounts of homework stifle motivation, diminish a child's love of learning, turn reading into a chore, negatively affect the quality of family time, diminish creativity, and turn learning to drudgery." To the oft-aired fear that children who don't practice homework in elementary school will be unprepared for homework in middle school, Ackerman retorts, "You don't prepare them for torture by torturing them early." Students who graduate fifth grade with strong skills and confidence, he reasons, will readily adapt.

Ackerman had to convince skeptical teachers, too, who feared students' test scores would drop if they trimmed homework. But as time went on, and teachers experimented with new methods, he said, "They found they were just as successful as they had been before." The school's standardized test scores continued to rise.

Brant assuages parents with a weekly newsletter that suggests what kinds of questions they might ask a child, by grade level, based on what they're studying that week. Gaithersburg also hosts community learning nights; I attended a math night where teachers led parents and kids through math games that they could play together, and each family took home a gift bag of dice, cards, and other playing pieces they might need. Teachers here also offer families optional projects that they can try at home, such as creating a tennis-ball catapult or building a tower out of household supplies—exercises based on some of the reading and science that students have done.

What ultimately won over parents in both schools were simply the results themselves. Over time, it became apparent that their kids were still doing just fine (as of spring 2015, the number of Gaithersburg students reading at or above grade level was up 8 percent over the year before). That, and having their family time back. Milagros Flores, a mother of three boys who has volunteered in Gaithersburg classrooms for six years, said she misses having little homework packets that showed her what was going on in class. But now the atmosphere at home "is calmer, there's less pressure," she said. She and her kids can go for walks without worrying about the time.

Flores has also found her boys developing more independence, now that they're given more control over how they use their study time in and out of class. That's one of Brant's key selling points for her reforms: showing parents how confident children can become as leaders of their own learning when schoolwork is personal and meaningful. "When parents see their children motivated to do more and to extend their own learning through a book or a blog or just getting information from the environment or the Internet," Brant said, "it's those sparks, it's those goose bump moments for parents that we want to create."

Ridgewood: Homework Change for Health

Often the instigators of homework reform are not educators but parents and students. This is especially true in high schools, where homework is a tougher nut to crack than in elementary grades. So it was fitting that the leader of the charge in Ridgewood, New Jersey, was both a parent and a pediatrician. Anne Robinson, energetic and approachable, could make her case not only as the mother of two daughters at Ridgewood High but also as a medical professional with a clear view of the physical and mental damage that excessive homework was wreaking on teens.

Ridgewood is a leafy New York City suburb and an academic pressure cooker. When Robinson's campaign began, her message about health was one that many in the community were already anxious to hear. A junior named Laura confessed that, after five or six hours of sleep, "I'm basically asleep the first three periods of school." Even Assistant Principal Jeff Nyhuis—himself a father of a third grader, able to see firsthand how intrusive homework is in a child's day—knew most of his students were staying up studying until one or two o'clock in the morning, a statistic that upset him.

Robinson organized a few other parents to meet with school administrators in an attempt to get them to address student stress. Finding an ally in Nyhuis, she joined forces with him to make presentations at PTA meetings and faculty meetings. The reformers had to contend with many common fallacies, and they had to be ready to answer the perennial skeptical questions from parents and teachers who did truly care: How is this going to affect student achievement? How can we get through an AP curriculum if students have only two hours of homework, total, per night? Are you sure it's not just that students have too many extracurricular activities? If we free them from homework, won't they just waste their time on social networks all night?

"Practices from the past just kept rearing their ugly heads," Robinson recalled when we met. "We are stuck in a system that is used to doing things a certain way." The biggest challenge, she said, was convincing people that achievement and wellness can coexist, that they're even complementary, "that well-rested, well-balanced students will perform better academically and in every aspect of their life."

(On the fear about social media, I have a special note to add, as I've heard that ill-conceived reason for keeping up homework so many times. "But they'll just spend all that time on Twitter!" someone inevitably says when I suggest at film screenings that schools curtail homework. Many parents think homework is what "protects" kids from technology's pull. Perversely, however, those students who become addicted to Twitter, TV, or video games are often, in fact, the product of an education system that has stifled a love of learning, a curiosity for new hobbies and ideas, and an impulse to play outdoors, volunteer in the community, or bond with friends and family. Reducing homework loads and restructuring assignments to those that promote such goals could arguably reduce the hours most students spend in escapist screen time by empowering students and parents to exercise more control over their afternoons and keeping them more engaged in their physical world. Parents do indeed face a tough challenge in trying to regulate their children's technology use, but piling on mind-numbing bookwork is not the answer.)

The Ridgewood organizers named their campaign the Smart Balance Initiative, underscoring that it's possible—and wise—to strike a balance. They continually emphasized the research on what is actually healthy for kids. And when they asked a number of students to use time diaries to record what they did in a twenty-four-hour day, the resulting diagrams proved to be a game changer. "What shall we eliminate to make time for more homework?" Robinson asked at a faculty meeting, displaying the data they'd gathered. "Do we want to X out the time they need for sleep? Do we want to X out the time they need for family and friends? Is it fresh air and exercise? Which thing are we willing to sacrifice in order to add more academic work?"

It took patience and persistence, but eventually the resistance started to crack. The first change the school made was to institute homework-free holiday breaks (which should be a given). "These breaks are specifically placed into the academic calendar for the purpose of providing relief to students and their families," Robinson explained. "Just like you rest the muscles to come back a stronger athlete, you're resting your brain to come back a stronger thinker. . . . Burned-out students are not good students." Although homework-free holidays are a relatively small reform, Robinson quickly found that they were a powerful conversation starter.

That change, which began at the high school, was eventually adopted by all the schools in town. Then hundreds of schools across the country followed suit as Ridgewood became the launching point for a 2011 Race to Nowhere campaign to ban holiday homework. The swiftness with which the change spread contains a lesson for anyone working to transform any aspect of school: you can try anything for a short period of time. Homework bans, flexible deadlines, qualitative grading—try it for a week and see what kind of perspective it opens up. Or, as in the case of Irvington High's midweek community night off, try it for a day. The limited time frame makes the experiment more palatable to skeptics, and whatever the outcome, the experience is guaranteed to open eyes.

Some secondary schools have taken their homework restrictions still further. In Potomac, Montana, for example, when the K-8 school there transformed its weekly schedule, it also stopped grading homework in the middle school grades (while ending assignments entirely for the primary grades). The educators effectively made homework optional: to be done only when it fits a family's priorities and helps a particular child learn. And Potomac students continue to fare well.

In tackling homework, Ridgewood instituted another inspiring and widely applicable reform. Administrators created the Principal's Advisory Group, a set of students who meet regularly with Nyhuis to discuss issues of student well-being. This reform starts to address the widespread problem of disenfranchising young people from decisions about their own education; students, who know best how well our educational practices are working and have the most at stake, are often the last to be consulted. Olivia, a junior and lacrosse player in the advisory group, felt empowered by the change: "We have such a greater voice than we had before. . . . We see differences being made after we've told Mr. Nyhuis problems or things that upset us." Students in the group also invite their teachers to meetings and describe best practices that they've seen in other classes. For example, they lauded one math teacher who experimented with giving an "exit question" at the end of class: if students could successfully complete that problem, then they didn't need additional practice at home.

Despite all this progress, everyone at Ridgewood acknowledges that they still have a long way to go. Students still have much too much homework. Assignments tend even to creep into the homework-free breaks, when kids continue to study for tests and work on long-term projects due a few days after the holiday. I've seen the same happen with Zak, who had to read and annotate *The Great Gatsby* during a supposedly no-homework weekend. This is a reflection of how hard it is to break our entrenched educational habits. For this reason, schools would be wise to appoint a homework ombudsman to field students' and parents' concerns and ensure that policies are truly followed.

Ridgewood students also told me they want to see more flexibility on homework—a bit of understanding from teachers that some days there is simply more to do than they can get done. Nonetheless, Ridgewood has taken that all-important first step, and now stands as a model of what can happen when parents, students, and educators work together to make kids' health the highest priority.

Drawing the Line

Ultimately, the homework equation comes down to this: Just as adults increasingly find their work following them home, the boundary between school and home has blurred, almost to the point of vanishing. Somewhere along the line, we parents began letting schools decide how our children will spend their out-of-school hours and how our families will use our precious time together. It is time to reclaim that authority.

According to both scientific and anecdotal research, it is clear that homework should be the exception, not the rule. Even the most inventive or meaningful assignments still infringe on the time that belongs to families. Making this change will not only improve our children's physical and mental health, level the playing field for rich and poor students, and make more time for exploration and enrichment beyond academics, it will also be a huge step forward in eliminating our cultural misperception that education is a race, and our children competitors.

To help guide families and educators who want to restore homework sanity, I've worked with Kralovec and other education experts to create Race to Nowhere's **Healthy Homework Guidelines**, inspired by the parents and faculty who ended homework at Hillcrest School in Oakland:

- *Homework should advance a spirit of learning.* Forget the old assumption that homework will be assigned each night in certain quantities. Educators should send home an assignment only when there's a compelling reason to do so, when it advances curiosity and inquiry, and when it provides a unique learning opportunity that cannot be had within the confines of the school setting. (This might include experiential activities like asking children to take an inventory of the bugs in one square meter of their neighborhood park and catalog the findings.) There should never be homework for homework's sake.

- *Homework should be student-directed.* Educators at all levels, but particularly in the elementary and middle grades, when children need ample room to explore, should limit homework assignments to projects chosen by students themselves. For example, send a child home to read a book of his or her choosing. End the practice of sending home standard-issue homework packets that require the same exercises of all children regardless of their individual strengths, needs, or interests. For equity's sake, all homework should also be reasonable for students to complete without a parent's or tutor's help.

- *Homework should honor a balanced schedule.* Educators at all levels should avoid assigning homework on weekends, holidays, school breaks, or on the days of major all-school events when at-home time is scarce for most children. Even on regular school nights, parents should be given the flexibility to opt their child out of assignments when they judge that to be best, such as when the child is sick or when take-home assignments conflict with family, religious, or community obligations.

If schools are too worried about their competitive status to try optional assignments, we parents can do it ourselves, making homework opt-in by simply opting out. Other parents may give their child homework if they like, but their preferences are not a reason to force homework on mine. If enough of us enact this bit of civil disobedience together, the system will be forced to change.

School communities are likely to resist reform at first, often by trying to pass the buck. "It's a situation where everybody believes they don't have any power," explains Ackerman, the veteran principal from Menlo Park. "Teachers believe the principal has all the power, and the principal believes the teachers have all the power. The superintendent believes the principals have all the power. And parents are the same way." Ackerman's advice is to keep at it: "Schools respond to pressure, they really do. School boards respond, superintendents respond. It goes slowly because, like any bureaucracy, the first thing they do is put up a wall and give you all the reasons why they're doing the right thing and can't change—but they are responding. They are talking about it, and if you keep the pressure up, institutions change."

Don't discount the impact you can make, even as just one person. In my neighboring community of Danville, a mother of two, Kerry Dickinson, made the local paper for taking action. After reading Alfie Kohn's book *The Homework Myth*, she got ten friends to read it. The writings and advice of homework activist and author Sara Bennett further informed her. Then, instead of just settling for the usual parent gripe session, Dickinson teamed up with another mom and lobbied the district to form a homework task force. The task force ultimately created a new policy that discourages weekend and holiday homework and spells out teachers' responsibilities to prevent homework overload and test stacking.

In spring 2015, some of the schools in Dickinson's community took her work a daring step further. They declared an entire week in May free of homework, for all grades (another example of testing out a reform for one nonthreatening week). The explanatory letter to parents, signed by the principals of all seven schools in the Dougherty Valley region, proposed that we "encourage our children to spend a significant portion of the free time outside . . . something that will allow the sun to warm their soul and rekindle a love for outdoor play." Kirby Hoy, the district's director of instruction, told me the week off was symbolic, a conversation starter about the best uses of families' time and a way to show that the world doesn't fall apart without homework. Delightfully, he said, the parent response has been entirely positive.

Educators themselves can make a big impact—even when they have to go it alone. Mike Miller, an English teacher at Thomas Jefferson High School for Science and Technology in Fairfax County, Virginia, entirely reversed his stance on homework in 2013 after nearly two decades of teaching. "As a younger teacher, I used to think, 'What will I assign for homework?'" he recalls. "I needed to concoct something for homework, because if I wasn't assigning homework then I wasn't doing my job."

Then Miller became a father of twins, and he started reading books on both sides of the homework debate. He was swayed. Miller found a forgotten regulation on the Fairfax County books that limits high school homework to two hours a night, total. (When he tells students about this, they think he's kidding.) On the academic integrity committee he serves on, he pointed out that homework overload encourages cheating (in fact, a Josephson Institute of Ethics survey of tens of thousands of US teens found that three in four had copied someone else's homework). The committee is now working to bring assignments to a reasonable level, but in an intensely performance-oriented community, it's slow going.

So Miller decided to do what he could in his own classroom. "I haven't waited for the school to do anything. I've seen the research," he says. It used to be that Miller would automatically assign half an hour of homework a night, not really doing the math that thirty minutes for each of six classes amounts to three hours. Teachers "tend to think in isolation," he says. Now he needs "a very compelling reason to assign outside homework." And when he does, he frames assignments in terms of time, not quantity. Instead of asking for a page of analysis, he asks students to write for about forty minutes over the course of two nights. This way, they can write at their own pace.

Around the same time, Miller made the bold move of eliminating letter grades on everyday assignments. Instead of grades, he gives narrative feedback, sometimes as much as six hundred words on a single student's essay. At the end of the quarter, each student assembles a portfolio and discusses her work one-on-one with Miller, and he converts that assessment into a letter grade. The net result of Miller's single-handed reforms is not that his students have become lazy Twitter-heads with nothing better to do in the evenings. What he's found is that his students, relieved of daily drudgery and the threat of constant judgment, are more engaged and willing to take creative risks. "I don't see a decrease in the quality of what they're producing," Miller observes. "If anything I see an increase. They're writing better. They're reading more deeply."

For him as a teacher, the transformation has breathed new life into his job. "It's been a shift from more of a learning factory to a place where we talk about books and write some interesting stuff," he says. "It's begun to blur the lines between play and work."

———

As parents, of course, the most immediate thing we can do is to support our children. In my home, I stopped asking my kids reflexively about homework the moment they walked in the door. Instead, I focused on taking the time for conversation and reflection. "How did your day go?" I would ask. "Who did you have lunch with? Did anything surprising happen today?" I eventually learned, by the time Zak was in elementary school, to say "Lights out" at bedtime, whether his homework was done or not. When he couldn't complete his assignments and also honor his needs for exercise, family dinner, and sleep, I wrote an explanatory note to his teachers. This is a small but important act of resistance, one that I'd encourage other parents to try. Many teachers, to their credit, were accommodating. Even when they disagreed, at least Zak was learning where my priorities lay.

Our children need our understanding. Sometimes they need us to help them talk with teachers and principals about overwork. They need to hear us say "Your grades are not you" and "It's okay to do less," and to emphasize as early as possible, before other ideas set in, that there's no shame in failing. Sometimes our kids simply need us to tell them that they're not crazy. A New York mom named Diane posted the following example on our Facebook page:

> When, after six months of struggling in her senior year to complete all the requirements of her IB program, my daughter finally said, "Enough!" we were able to listen, and advocated on her behalf with her school to scale back the requirements. Recognizing your limits is not the same as quitting—it's the mature response to an impossible situation. We are proud of our daughter for standing up for what she needed, and grateful we were able to hear her.

Millions of young students, entrenched in a system that tells them they must sacrifice sleep, health, hobbies, and joy in order to succeed, also need to be supported and heard. Start by requesting a meeting with your child's teacher or principal, or by encouraging your student, if she's old enough, to join you in taking up the cause. Start by talking honestly with other parents about your concerns, finding allies among them, and requesting an agenda item at the next PTA or school board meeting. Start by considering which everyday activities are most important to your family. Or start just by telling your children you care more about their health than their homework.

Whatever you do, start tonight.

CHAPTER 4

Testing:
Learning Beyond the Bubble

O N A cold, rainy morning in February 2011, I stood with three hundred students outside the brick facade of Briarcliff High School in the New York City suburbs. The young people around me held umbrellas and hand-lettered signs asking: Where is *learning* in our budget? The teens had arrived on campus at least an hour early that morning to protest a school board vote that condensed their schedules from nine periods to eight. The change was intended to provide the students more instructional time in core subjects—those in which they would be tested. But the shift came at a cost: the students would be squeezed out of study periods and electives they cared about.

As yellow school buses rolled by, a skinny sixteen-year-old organizer named Philip took to the megaphone. For too long the school system had thought of students "as merely numbers and statistics," he proclaimed. "Today's system doesn't think of any of us as the boy who loves music, but instead the boy who has a 1600 SAT score and a good amount of extracurriculars. Are we not the leaders of tomorrow?"

The outrage at Briarcliff was a symptom of a growing nationwide discontent. The cause: the blind quantification of our entire education system. We are suffering from a slavish devotion to numbers—tests, and the scores and rankings they produce—that's dehumanizing our schools, increasing homework loads, and enshrining the belief that canned questions asked on paper are the ultimate measure of educational "success."

Our young students spend weeks a year regurgitating information onto computer screens and Scantron forms instead of learning. There are the annual state tests, the pretests, the practice tests, the district tests to check readiness for the state tests, and the field-test tests. Combine those with the extra deluge that comes in high school—the AP exams, SAT, PSAT, and ACT—and children take as many as twenty standardized tests a year, averaging ten tests a year in the tender grades of three through eight. Even when they're not being tested, students are frequently being subjected to deadening test prep. All the while, our testing obsession earns billions of dollars a year for the private companies that write, administer, score, and tutor for these exams.

The testing machine is massive, but here again, there is much that we parents, students, and educators can do about it, and that many are already doing. The Briarcliff protest was an early glimpse of that. It did not stop the students from losing their beloved art classes to the tightening grip of testing, but it did earn Philip (a guitar player who does indeed love music) an appearance on the *Today* show. More important, that morning signaled the beginnings of something far bigger. The Briarcliff students were early voices in a chorus of protest that soon erupted from coast to coast.

At Castle Bridge elementary school in New York City's Washington Heights, so many parents refused to let their young children (kindergarteners and first and second graders!) take a multiple-choice test that authorities canceled the whole exam. The teachers at Seattle's Garfield High School outright refused to give their students the district-mandated Measures of Academic Progress test, which they contend is misaligned with the state curriculum they must teach and wastes precious instructional time. In doing so, they put their jobs on the line. In Providence, a crowd of students in zombie costumes, complete with green skin and blood-spattered clothes, staggered up to the doors of the Rhode Island Department of Education, protesting what they called the "zombifying effects" state testing was having on young people. (The Providence group later administered a set of sample problems from Rhode Island's high school graduation exam to fifty accomplished professionals, including lawyers, state senators, city council members, nonprofit directors, and college professors. Only 40 percent passed.)

The protests reached a fever pitch in spring 2015, when the parents of more than 175,000 New York State students had their children sit out state tests, more than double the number the year before. Opt-out groups cropped up in Florida, Iowa, Colorado, and more. The previous fall, nearly five thousand high school seniors in the Denver area refused to take state science and social studies tests, contending that the exams were out of sync with what they'd learned and wasted valuable educational time. According to the national organization FairTest, eight states have laws granting parents the right to keep their children out of standardized tests: Utah, Colorado, Wisconsin, Pennsylvania, Minnesota, Oregon, Washington, and California. Everywhere else, opting out is an act of civil disobedience.

Meanwhile, signatures on the National Resolution on High-Stakes Testing mounted into the tens of thousands, and the National Education Association, the nation's largest teachers union, launched a campaign against what it calls "toxic testing." The campaign aimed to "end the abuse and overuse of high-stakes standardized tests" and "put the focus of assessments and accountability back on student learning."

Such actions now constitute nothing short of a national movement, and the protesters have very good cause. Standardized testing may have originally been based on the sensible idea that we should make sure all schools are doing a comparable job of teaching kids what they need to know. But America's devotion to exams has spun out of control. The occasional fill-in-the-bubble tests of my youth—which were dull but low-stress for students and used only as a temperature check for schools—now sound like a dream. In their place we have a nightmare, a national testing obsession of monstrous proportions.

The outcome is *not*, as the tests intended, a good education for all. In fact, it is nearly the opposite. Standardized tests have driven American education into a vise grip of regimentation. Now there is one narrow set of things to learn and one way to learn them—all at one uniform pace. Stressed teachers race to get through reams of content, any of which might be tested, at the expense of depth and personalization. Students, for their part, are demoralized by the constant judgment and competition. Young people whose minds don't fit the one-size-fits-all mold disengage from school and doubt their own worth. Even those who do fit miss the chance to plumb their own ingenuity or to nurture a lifelong love of learning.

Policy makers made matters even worse when they attached powerful consequences to standardized test scores—teachers' job evaluations, schools' funding, and students' high school diplomas and college admissions—thereby plunging the entire American education system into a stultifying culture of fear. The product of an education system that judges success through narrow, fearsome exams is not a nation of geniuses; it is a nation schooled in narrow, fearful thinking. This is not the way for our country to cultivate the curious spirits and creative minds that will thrive in a dynamic global economy—or in life.

Zombie Nation

I don't believe that the authors of the No Child Left Behind law in 2001 understood the monster they were creating. They saw a society in which massive gaps in education and achievement persisted between rich and poor, and between whites and Asians on one side and other minority groups on the other. They wanted to insist that our education system attend to those inequities—an important and laudable goal. The lawmakers also (mistakenly) saw high-stakes testing as a key weapon in a contest among nations to produce the smartest, most successful workers.

So they mandated a national exam regime in which every child in the country would be tested on reading and math every year from grades three through eight, plus once in high school. The idea was to hold kids from both affluent and less privileged communities to the same high standards, to try to level the playing field. Scores would be public, and schools would be penalized for poor results. Then, in 2009, President Obama and Education Secretary Arne Duncan doubled down with their educational initiative Race to the Top, a $4 billion competition for states. In order to get a slice of the federal funding pie, states had to agree to evaluate teachers in part on their students' scores, to adopt "college and career-ready standards" that would become the hotly debated Common Core curriculum, and to test kids on those standards every year. Teachers and principals in schools that weren't performing would be fired. What began as an effort to raise standards became a punitive accounting strategy.

At the same time (as I'll address more in the next chapter), the pressure on students to take ever more Advanced Placement and SAT and ACT tests, and to score ever higher on each of them, was mounting.

The sum total of these developments is that today's kids are the most tested generation in history. This has not translated to greater success. Indeed, the negative consequences are so numerous it would be hard to list them all. Yet two are particularly important to address: the deadening effect of excessive high-stakes testing on the character of education and the sickening stress and self-doubt it causes in kids, who are misled by the twisted message it sends about what matters.

To the first point, test worship is squeezing the life out of our children's learning, both in *what* schools teach and *how* they teach it. Within the first few years of No Child Left Behind, schools scrambling to boost math and reading scores on the annual tests started cutting back on all kinds of other classes. The nonpartisan Center on Education Policy found that, by 2007, more than 40 percent of the nation's school districts had trimmed time from nontested subjects to make way for more reading and math in elementary schools. The cutbacks included such throwaway subjects (ahem) as science, social studies, art, music, and physical education. Many schools had even shortened recess and lunch. All told, the decreases amounted to an average of nearly thirty minutes a day lost from those other important subjects. And the trend has continued: more than half of the teachers in a 2011 national survey said that the extra focus on math and reading was resulting in "disappearing curriculum" in other areas, with the cutbacks at their worst in elementary school.

"When you look at the force of standardized testing, what they're testing pretty much is mathematics and reading comprehension," says Tim Devine, principal of Chicago's innovative Walter Payton College Prep High School. "So where does that leave science and social studies and arts and music programs? They become afterthoughts. They become the stepchildren of education, and that's not where they should be. Our kids are much more dynamic than that."

Ironically, the distorting of priorities plays especially heavily on children in schools in low-income communities with generally lower test scores—precisely those whom No Child Left Behind was intended to help. In the CEP study, these districts reported cutting elementary school recess alone by fifty minutes a week (not to mention other academic subjects). That's especially counterproductive when you consider the ample evidence that physical activity is essential for brain function.

Zoom the lens in closer on the *way* students are actually studying those subjects that remain, and you'll see that our sledgehammer approach to accountability is incentivizing what Harvard educator and author Tony Wagner calls "stunningly mediocre" teaching and learning. "And that's not the teachers' fault," Wagner says. "That's what they have to do to get kids to pass multiple-choice, factual-recall tests."

Sadly, it's true: most standardized tests really are shallow tests of basic skills. And that's partly by necessity, since the tests are annual and universal—it would be awfully hard to design and score a deep and personal assessment that elicits complex thought and individual talent for every single American child every single year. Researchers at the RAND Corporation looked at seventeen states whose tests are regarded as the most thoughtful and demanding. Even among these supposedly standout states, the researchers found the cognitive sophistication of their math and English tests was low. Using a range of criteria, they concluded that a mere 1 to 20 percent of state reading tests, and around 30 percent of state writing tests, tapped truly deep thinking. None of the math tests did.

Teachers know that they and their students will be judged mainly on their ability to regurgitate content or produce cookie-cutter written responses for these tests. So lectures, textbooks, and problem sets become the default vehicles for teaching, and in-class tests remain the main way to gauge learning along the way (recall that the Sasners' son suffered through more than a dozen teacher-given tests in just three weeks!). The testing obsession perpetuates an obsolete and unscientific vision of learning that's focused on facts. Moreover, the high stakes of failure scare schools away from trying new innovations. Glance into many modern classrooms and you'll still see students regimented into rows of desks, staring blankly and miserably as the teacher drones—looking, indeed, very much like zombies. In this staid system, the *product* of children's learning—an expected answer to a prescribed question—becomes more important than the *process*. And in the inexorable forward march to cover it all, there's little time left for kids to pursue original questions, take risks, or explore anything that's not on the exam.

"Go down the assembly line, get some math. Go down the assembly line, get some social studies," quips Walter Payton High's Devine. "And out comes a perfect Model T Ford."

Obviously certain schools and classrooms succumb to the drumbeat more than others—but the fixation on soulless metrics is alarmingly pervasive. And this drill-and-kill method tends to squash deep thought, creative collaboration, and sometimes the possibility of a trusting relationship between teachers and students, since it discourages students from asking questions and leaves less time to develop that essential rapport. The effect of this mindset extends even beyond standardized testing and the prep that precedes it, as it shapes everyday lessons and activities that remain stuck in stale old methods of evaluating student learning. Quizzes, worksheets, short-answer exams—even "fun" activities like spelling bees—all treat students' minds as merely inert receptacles for information.

Our everyday reliance on easily quantifiable tests and grades also flies in the face of everything we know about human motivation. Daniel Pink, author of *Drive*, explains that schools are mired in methods that tap a shallower, *extrinsic* kind of motivation rather than students' *intrinsic* drive to think and discover. They rely heavily on "if, then" rewards—if I memorize these Civil War facts, then I will get an A on the history test. "Those kinds of rewards are very effective for simple, straightforward routine . . . adding up columns of figures, turning the same screw the same way on an assembly line," says Pink. Yet fifty years of social science tells us they don't work well for motivating original thought. "If you want people to come up with the next iPad mini, a solution to the climate crisis, new medicines to fight diseases," Pink adds, "they do it better under conditions of autonomy. We can't 'if, then' people into creativity. It just doesn't work." The result in schools, he says, is that you find some students who are compliant and some who are defiant, but few who are truly engaged.

Nicole, a high school student in Oakland, knows the feeling. She told me her Spanish classes had never been presented as relevant to her real life, despite the obvious applicability of speaking Spanish in heavily Hispanic California. Instead, the lessons were just part of the foreign language admission requirement for the University of California system. "You think, 'Oh, all right, I'll take it. I'll get an A,'" Nicole said. "I took three years of Spanish and I can't put a sentence together. You memorize, you spit it out, and once you do you move on to the next chapter."

Research echoes Nicole's experience. In one study, Clark University psychologist Wendy Grolnick gave kids a passage to read about the history of medicine. She told some that they'd be tested on it and told others just to see if they found it interesting. Afterward, she asked all of them to repeat all the information they could remember from the passage, and to say what they thought the main point of it was. Those who expected a test could cough up just as much rote information as the others, "but they were worse in terms of their conceptual understanding," Grolnick told me. "They would focus on some detail and not on the main point." Two weeks later, she saw the students again and asked them to repeat all they could remember. Those who'd read the passage purely for interest had retained a lot more.

"So when we are focused on grades, focused on outcomes, whether in the learning environment or the home environment, it narrows kids' attention," Grolnick said. "It makes them focus on specific details, prevents them from getting the larger picture or other things that weren't specifically supposed to be learned."

Scared Sick

Tests are also a huge source of unhealthy stress on children. Kids as young as six or seven understand that their performance on a certain test on a certain day at a certain time can have big implications for their teachers, whom they don't want to let down. Children internalize the message that a test says something significant about who they are: smart or not, good or not, worthy or not. Our testing obsession fuels the notion that every individual can be weighed, measured, tallied, categorized, and ranked against others—and that each one should be.

Parents and students in nearly every state have told me how the specter of an upcoming test can turn even very young kids into anxious insomniacs, crying or yelling or even pulling their hair out with worry. California, in fact, has a protocol for what to do when a child vomits on a test—put the test paper in a sealed Ziploc bag and mail it in. The irony is that anxiety triggers a cascade of chemicals in the brain that interfere with clear thinking and memory. Eleven-year-old Becca, a fifth grader in Radnor, Pennsylvania, sent me this letter describing how testing affects her:

> *It's always test after test after test: math, social studies, spelling, spelling pretest, science, health, music. Then there are the standardized tests . . .*
>
> *I feel so tense when I take these [standardized] tests. The teachers tell us to get a good sleep and have a good breakfast. They don't say that on normal test days. That makes me worry more and sleep less. The "what ifs" start running in my mind at night and I can't sleep. "What if I get stuck?" "What if I don't finish on time?" "What if I don't know an answer?" "What if I don't do well?" "What if I don't get in the best class?" "What if I don't get enough sleep?" And then I don't get enough sleep. . . .*
>
> *I had a conversation with some of my friends a little while ago. They say that if you don't get into a good class, you won't do as well in school and you won't get into a good college.*
>
> *It's just worrying, worrying, worrying.*

In the case of math, for example, Stanford University professor Jo Boaler notes that we know from neuroscience "that speed is extremely detrimental to math. . . . Timed tests are the early onset of math anxiety for kids. Yet speed is emphasized in every math classroom. The one who gets the right answer first is the one who's valued. . . . What's interesting about that is mathematicians are some of the slowest thinkers of all."

The pressure of the exams also prompts schools to push advanced content into ever-lower grades. A University of Virginia study found that even in kindergarten, teachers in 2010 spent more time than those in 1998 on advanced literacy and math, and substantially less time on art, music, science, and activities chosen by children themselves. Schools now routinely press all kindergarteners to read, despite scant evidence on the educational advantages of that practice. (In fact, evidence suggests the opposite: children in less academic kindergartens perform *better* in school years later.) And algebra, once sensibly situated in ninth grade, now starts in seventh grade for any student who wants to appear "advanced." This is not the universal norm in countries with the strongest education systems; Finland, for example, doesn't even start compulsory school until age seven.

At a film screening in Castro Valley, California, a teacher of thirteen years stood up and called upon the entire audience to mobilize and ask Congress to quit its unrealistic expectations. "This was my son's latest third grade math problem," she told the crowd. A bar graph showed twenty lunches of various types. The question was: *What number times three, minus sixteen, equals the number of lunches on the graph?* In other words: an algebra problem assigned to eight- and nine-year-olds! "Now, you tell me what eight-year-old on their own is going to figure that out?" the teacher and mother exclaimed, incredulous. She said her son, a strong student, cried over the problem and said to his dad, "I'm afraid you're going to be mad at me because I didn't figure this out by myself." The woman went on: "What curriculum writer would do this? Piaget must be turning over in his grave." The audience applauded.

This march for more-sooner-faster may also be partly fueling the dizzying rise in ADHD diagnoses in recent years. To illuminate the link, professors Brent Fulton, Richard Scheffler, and Stephen Hinshaw at UC Berkeley looked in 2015 at ADHD rates among children from low-income families attending elementary and middle school in the years after NCLB began. They compared states that had already issued rewards and punishments for standardized test scores *before* NCLB was enacted with states that only started issuing consequences *after* the law was passed. Their striking finding was that while ADHD diagnoses rose everywhere, rates shot up far faster in states where the testing pressure was new. Writing in the journal *Psychiatric Services*, the researchers concluded that high-stakes tests "provide incentives for teachers to address and refer children having academic difficulties" for treatment.

For teens, the pressure only intensifies as AP and college admission tests—and, in some states, exams required for high school graduation—loom. The stakes of the tests are so high and the pace so relentless that many students are tempted to cheat. A case on Long Island in 2011 made headlines when the Nassau County district attorney actually criminally charged more than a dozen teens with paying other, high-performing students as much as $3,600 to take the SAT or ACT for them. At Middleton High School in Wisconsin in 2013, administrators made nearly 250 seniors retake a calculus test after finding that some had stolen copies of it and sold photos of questions. Beyond the punishment, the incident served as a wake-up call for school staff, prompting them to consider what kind of learning environment makes it seem okay to cheat—or so important to do well that stealing a test seems like a reasonable risk. To their credit, they decided to change their system by crediting students more for the skills they demonstrate throughout their learning process and less for a single examination at the end.

Besides cheating the old-fashioned way, a distressing number of teens now turn to chemical aids for an advantage. "I used Adderall before taking the SAT so that I would be able to stay focused for the whole time," one eighteen-year-old from the Northwest told me. "I actually don't regret taking it because I wouldn't have gotten as high of a score without it. . . . Most kids I know took Adderall or some type of performance drug for the SAT just because it's so long and rigorous."

How serious is the stress? Lawrence Rosen, the New Jersey pediatrician, said he sees more children come to his office in the spring testing season with headaches, stomachaches, and other stress-related symptoms than at any other time of year. "I have kids as young as first grade, second grade, who are being subjected to these tests, who are coming in with migraine headaches and ulcers, and not eating well," he said, "to the point where parents are really thinking about pulling their kids out of school for that week and just saying, 'Enough. I'm not going to engage in this.'"

So let me make this clear: protecting kids from excessive test pressure is not coddling. It's not the equivalent of insisting that every child needs to get a trophy. It is a critical mission to preserve our children's health and provide a kind of education that truly nurtures their minds. And it's a call to arms that's backed by research, which consistently tells us that testing does a very poor job of measuring or encouraging the learning that matters most.

The Blunt Instrument

Susan Engel, an education psychologist at Williams College, recently reviewed more than three hundred studies of K-12 academic tests and came to this startling conclusion: "Most tests used to evaluate students, teachers, and school districts predict almost nothing except the likelihood of achieving similar scores on subsequent tests. I have found virtually no research demonstrating a relationship between those tests and measures of thinking or life outcomes."

You would think that kind of decisive science would end the debate; research shows the tests are a red herring. What's tricky about standardized testing, though, is that the principle of it sounds so simple: teach kids some stuff, then ask them to repeat it, and that'll tell you what they learned. What could be wrong with that? Yet the reality is incredibly more complex, and so boiling it all down to a single measure can do tremendous harm. Psychometricians—the scientists who make and study tests—themselves will tell you so. Daniel Koretz, a Harvard psychometrician and author of *Measuring Up: What Educational Testing Really Tells Us*, explains that for tests to serve a useful purpose in education, they have to honor a fundamental principle: "Don't treat 'her score on the test' as a synonym for 'what she has learned.' A test score is just one indicator of what a student has learned—an exceptionally useful one in many ways, but nonetheless one that is unavoidably incomplete and somewhat error prone."

That's because, scientifically speaking, a test is merely a small snapshot of one particular kind of performance, gauged in one particular kind of way, taken from a vastly bigger picture of knowledge, behavior, and skill. It is a blunt instrument, not a surgical tool. So can a state achievement test tell you approximately how well a new curriculum is working across several cities? Sure. Can a set of AP exams indicate whether the classes are generally covering the material the College Board assigned? Most likely. But neither can really tell you whether *this* school or teacher did a good job, or whether *that* student is well prepared to thrive. Unfortunately, that's what we're using them for.

Even if the exams *could* show us everything a child understands about reading or math or AP biology or AP history, that still would be only a fraction of what counts. We all know that persistence, adaptability, creativity, and charm account for just as much of a person's success as his or her book smarts do. And experiments such as those by Nobel Prize–winning economist James Heckman have demonstrated that those noncognitive traits have just as much, if not more, to do with a person's accomplishments in work and life as the kinds of cognitive abilities covered by tests. Yet that's not what our education system communicates to kids.

"Formal education systems tend to confuse academic ability with intelligence," says British educator and author Ken Robinson. Plenty of people who aren't that comfortable with writing or numbers are actually brilliant with music, dance, craftwork, or gardening, or they're intuitively skilled at caring for people or animals, Robinson says. "These aren't mindless activities; they're different ways in which human intelligence expresses itself."

Erin, a high school junior, actress, and writer in California, knows just how confining schools' narrow definition of smarts can be. "Art is my release, my hallelujah, my break," she says. But in schools, "art is the first thing to go. . . . There's a specific thing the school wants you to shine in, and if you don't shine in it, then you don't [shine at all]. . . . I feel like they're trying to make us into one person."

Character and creativity also have a whole lot to do with the success of nations. "Innovation comes from innovative people," writes Yong Zhao, chair of educational methodology, policy, and leadership at the University of Oregon. The countries that will flourish in the modern age will be those whose people burst with original ideas and readily adapt to change. Yet those aren't the qualities our test culture is cultivating or rewarding.

In his book, *Catching Up or Leading the Way,* Zhao has chronicled one of the great paradoxes of American education: we are pushing ever more narrow-minded testing in an attempt to compete with the likes of high-scoring China, while at the same time the Chinese are trying to create a more flexible and creative kind of schooling that they see as more American.

The Chinese, coming from a long tradition of rigid examination, have learned from experience that test worship is the enemy of innovation. Zhao underscores his point with a cautionary tale. China's historical devotion to testing, he writes, has produced huge numbers of students "who score well on tests but have few skills that are usable in society." This is such a big concern for the Chinese that they even have a name for that sort of academically stunted person, *gaofen dineng*. The flourishing of Chinese labor and the floundering of its invention so worries authorities there that in 1997, the national education ministry issued a screed against what it called "test-oriented education." This "tendency to simply prepare for tests" and "blindly pursue admission rates while ignoring the real needs of the student," the ministry wrote, "emphasizes knowledge transmission but neglects moral, physical, aesthetic, and labor education" and "relies on rote memorization and mechanical drills as the primary approach." The upshot is trampled motivation and squelched creativity.

Sound familiar?

The Chinese authorities concluded that test-oriented education violated Chinese education law and must be replaced with "quality education"—a goal they're still pursuing, even as America moves in the opposite direction.

By contrast, Finnish children, whose performance on international exams is the perennial envy of other nations, undergo almost no standardized testing. The Finns' dominance instead seems to stem from educational practices far different from our own. In place of punitive, top-down mandates, Finland recruits and pays teachers well, grants them respect and autonomy in their classrooms, and both prepares and trusts them to design their own curricula. Teachers assess students' individual progress in the classroom, not en masse on external tests, and provide personalized lessons without tracking kids into separate groups by ability. Plus, young children are given minimal homework and more playtime, while high school students also have more opportunities to choose electives than peers in the United States.

There are obvious differences between tiny Finland and the massive melting pot of the United States. But this much is clear: even if stellar scores on international tests are your goal (they're not mine), you don't have to enslave children and their teachers to an endless run-up of standardized exams to get there.

America now faces a choice. We can break the chains of standardization and embrace a kind of education that nourishes the creative thinkers and compassionate leaders of tomorrow. Or we can keep insisting on the same outmoded protocol, trying to quantify all knowledge and churn out "educated youth" like uniform items on an assembly line. One California college professor told me about the day he assigned his students—a generation groomed on multiple-choice education—to examine the facts of a Supreme Court decision on church and state and reach their own conclusion. One asked: "What's the right answer?" The professor was aghast. "There is no right answer," he said. His highly educated students had been tested to the point where they were unable to think for themselves.

New York City: Learning Goes Deep

None of this is to say that we should not be evaluating students' skills and knowledge. Assessment is an essential part of education and, if used wisely, can actually help to drive deep and powerful learning. The proof is in the schools that are doing it well.

The Institute for Collaborative Education, a public school in the Gramercy neighborhood of lower Manhattan, occupies two floors of a stately, century-old school building with a columned cement facade. Just under five hundred students, in grades six through twelve, are enrolled here.

Mike Hills's sunlit classroom is on the fifth floor, at the top of the building. The classroom isn't fancy—wood floors, high ceilings, whiteboards, and twenty-some of those terrible plastic chairs with attached desks arranged in two concentric semicircles. But the educational activity going on there is impressive. When I visited, Hills was leading his eighth grade humanities students through a discussion on juvenile crime, to kick off their monthlong unit on the US justice system. A simple enough assignment, except for the caliber of the conversation.

A reserved-looking girl with dark hair hanging in her face (who turned out to be not reserved in her opinions at all) was countering a classmate's argument that juveniles are more vulnerable than adults to peer pressure. "I don't think peer pressure for adults is nonexistent. I just think for adults, they use a different word, and it's more about competitiveness," she said. She cited the example of a friend in another school where many of the kids live in elegant brownstones, making her friend's mom feel they need a brownstone, too. "Your parents are also bragging about your grades to their friends, so it's the exact same thing, they're just older and taller than you," the girl said. A couple of her classmates nodded vigorously.

Hills, with his long red beard and calm demeanor, listened attentively to his students' points and interjected now and then to steer the conversation toward challenging questions. "So when should a person legally become an adult?" he asked them. A skinny boy, who looked young for eighth grade, said confidently that it should depend on the crime, as kids at different ages have different understanding of the wrongness of certain offenses. Even an eleven-year-old knows killing is wrong, he said—but he or she may not understand the consequences.

Every time there was the hint of a lull, at least four hands shot up from students keen to talk. "Self-awareness really determines how you can judge or grade a person," argued another boy, who spoke eagerly and sported a Yankees shirt. "What makes somebody an adult is they're very aware of what they're doing and are intentionally trying to hurt a community."

These were eighth graders? When my kids were in eighth grade, I don't remember them having many assignments this profound. No one asked them to deeply challenge their opinions, to publicly defend their beliefs, or to listen intently to differing viewpoints from their peers. And they certainly never showed this kind of verve for their course material. Yet in fifteen minutes of constant discussion in Hills's class, not a single student spoke twice. When Hills cut off the conversation, five hands were still up high.

Meanwhile, down the hall, eighth graders in a science class were designing their own hydroponic systems to grow lettuce. They'd studied different types of systems and nutrient mixes, and they were working to see which group's design would produce the biggest yield. (Try to put that kind of collaboration and inventiveness on a test.)

What makes Hills and his fellow teachers at ICE feel free to invest time in deep inquiry is that the school is exempt from New York State's standardized Regents exams, the subject-area tests required to graduate from high school. (Technically, the middle schoolers there are still supposed to take state tests, but many of their parents opt them out, and the school makes clear when parents visit that test prep is not on the program.) ICE is a member of the New York Performance Standards Consortium, a group of more than two dozen public schools that possess a little piece of educational gold: a waiver. The only Regents exam their high schoolers take is in English. The consortium was founded in 1997, before high school seniors had to pass the

Regents as a graduation requirement, and it has fought to keep its test-free status. It has succeeded—so far—in part because of its impressive results. Students in the consortium come from comparable socioeconomic backgrounds as those in New York City's other public schools. Yet they graduate from high school and go on to college at substantially higher rates. Of those who enter a four-year college, more than 93 percent return the second year, far more than the national average of 75 percent.

Don't think, though, that just because consortium students skip the standardized tests they go unevaluated. Far from it. In place of multiple-choice and short-answer questions, the consortium schools use performance assessments: meaningful tasks that challenge students to think and demonstrate their skills *while they're doing them*, not by proxy on paper at the end. Students take on these kinds of learning tasks daily and weekly, in place of traditional tests. Rather than receiving a single, onetime grade on each assignment, they engage in a deep revision process with their teachers' help. Plus, students must complete four larger performance assessments—one in each core academic subject area—to graduate. And they are grueling. "They're really hard," said Erica, an ICE senior. "We're not talking about Googling your topic. We're talking about reading pages and pages and pages of journal articles."

The assessments range from conducting an original science experiment to writing a social studies research paper: a deep and lengthy work of scholarly quality on a subject of your choice. ICE senior Joya, for instance, wrote a whopping thirty-two pages on post–World War II economics and its effect on minorities. When students complete larger projects, they don't just hand in their work to a teacher to get a grade; they have to present and defend it to a panel of judges, including teachers, peers, and members of the broader community—similar to a graduate thesis defense. How can the school be sure students are getting the essential math and reading skills the state requires? The mastery shows in the students' work—along with equally important skills such as analysis, persistence, organization, communication, and original creative thought.

"Our school really teaches us how to think, instead of telling us, 'This is correct,' and, 'This is what you need to know,' and, 'This is what you need to know two months from now on the test,'" Erica said. Teachers still give

students quizzes to check for understanding, but the quizzes don't count toward their grades. Most consortium schools don't offer any Advanced Placement classes, either; they feel they can educate students better when they're not simply driving toward a factual exam. And the lack of APs doesn't hurt their graduates' college applications; colleges know the consortium's policy and simply consider what students did with the offerings they had.

The ICE students talked about one particular aspect of their education that means a lot to them: choice. This is a refrain I've heard from students across the country. As Ridgewood High School recognized by creating its student advisory group, education becomes a far more engaging experience when you have a voice in what and how you study. Yet student choice is utterly lacking in traditional, overstandardized schools, where teachers feel they have only enough time to stick with the program. At ICE, choice *is* part of the program.

Erica, Joya, and their friend Jordan told me about their recent study unit on new journalism—the long-form, literary nonfiction pioneered by writers like Tom Wolfe and Truman Capote. After reading and analyzing Capote's *In Cold Blood*, each student wrote his or her own true-to-life story. Erica, a stylish dresser who wants to go into fashion, wrote her story on attending New York's Fashion Week. Jordan described a day in the life of her family, which she said helped her notice small details she never had before. And Joya did a sociological exposé of Macy's at Christmastime, a setting she detests.

Joya said coming to ICE and being allowed to make choices and asked to think for herself changed her whole experience of school. "It's a shift in emphasis," she said. "It's learning for yourself instead of learning for someone else."

Experiments actually show Joya's experience to be broadly true—people of all ages thrive when they have some independence. Wendy Grolnick, the Clark University professor, explains, "What we know is that kids feel most engaged in school when they have a sense of autonomy, when they have some volition or some choice. That doesn't mean that we can't give kids tasks to do sometimes that aren't things they would spontaneously do. But to have that sense of autonomy is really important to sustaining motivation. We don't value that as much in schools as we could."

That same week in New York, farther uptown, I met a student at a consortium school called Urban Academy for whom deep inquiry and choice had made an especially big difference. Jameel came to Urban Academy as a sophomore after flunking and repeating ninth grade at another school. He'd earned straight As in middle school, "but that wasn't saying much, because they didn't really challenge us," he said. High school was a whole different ballgame. Jameel went to an elite college-prep high school reputed for its high standards, aiming to be the first in his family (he's the youngest of four siblings) to go to college. But he quickly found he could not keep up with the school's huge quantities of hard work—most of it geared toward textbook answers. His teachers cared but seemed unaware of what he was struggling with, and he didn't feel free to ask for assistance.

The Jameel I met that day at Urban Academy was worlds happier. Now an eighteen-year-old senior, he was rehearsing for the school musical and interning weekly with a small film director. He shook my hand firmly, spoke in a resonant voice, and frequently flashed a smile that pushed his cheeks up high. He told me he'd found that at Urban Academy, where the teachers weren't caught up in the march through tested material, they made the time to really get to know him. They provided reading materials at his own level and helped him improve. Then, the chance to choose subjects for deeper study made him suddenly care more about his learning. The idea for his graduation project in history, for instance, came from a discussion in his gender studies class that he wanted to explore more deeply.

"It really makes a difference, when you're learning something, to focus on something you really care about," he said. "It's really weird because before you know it you have this ten-page essay and you're like, 'Whoa, I wrote that?'"

Even the fact that Jameel got to take a gender studies class owes to Urban Academy's exemption from state testing. The consortium schools still teach history, but since they're not being tested on the mile-wide, inch-deep details the state requires, they can explore. Other options students can choose from there include a full semester on the civil rights movement. The range of subjects helped Jameel find what he wants to study in college: gender studies and Africana studies. And, with his grades much improved since freshman year, he had been admitted to Goucher and Hampshire colleges.

This time, he felt ready for the transition. "This school has really prepared me for college," he said. "The rigor of the performance assessments we do alone prepares you."

As we wrapped up, I asked Jameel and the students at ICE which learning experiences had made the most impact on them. They all named the work they did for their graduation requirements. Whoever said that about a standardized test?

Danville, Kentucky: A Challenge for Every Child

The New York consortium schools are hardly the only ones using performance assessments to support richer learning. There are other schools that use this practice even though their students still have to take standardized tests. Educators at these schools generally don't even try to cram in every piece of content that might be tested. Instead, they more or less ignore the state exams (though some still prepare kids for the SAT and ACT) and just keep the faith that, if students are learning deeply, they'll score okay.

The school district in rural Danville, Kentucky, is one such setting. In 2011, under the leadership of then superintendent Carmen Coleman, the district had lifted its dismal test scores and shot up to twenty-fourth in the state. "We were celebrating," Coleman recalled when I visited her a few years later, "but at the same time, less than 30 percent of our students were even meeting the minimum bar on the ACT. Those that were going to college were having to take remedial classes and were certainly not equipped for success."

So Coleman, along with several teachers and Bate Middle School Principal Amy Swann, traveled to New York to see what the consortium schools were doing. They came away amazed by what the New York kids could do, and they wanted their own students—70 percent of whom live in poverty—to have the same opportunities. Within a couple of years, they had Danville seventh graders doing original research projects, writing fifteen-page papers, and giving twenty-minute presentations to panels of judges that included university graduate students. One girl who loves swimming tested how two different types of pools, saltwater and chlorine, affected her timing.

Students with special needs (who often really struggle on fill-in-the-bubble tests) were able to do experiments, too, each one at a level of complexity that matched her abilities.

"The reason that we love the performance-based assessments is because they require kids to show what they know in different ways," Coleman explained. "Maybe with a public presentation. Maybe having to respond to questions just as they would in a defense of a dissertation. They might have to work in groups to solve a problem. So, not only can we assess content, but we can assess skills like perseverance, like leadership, like adaptability."

After Danville initiated the change, behavior incidents at the middle school dropped by 50 percent. Pointing to their success, the Danville schools boldly applied to the state for a waiver to opt out of state tests, even though no legal avenue for such a waiver existed. They were denied.

Danville has done another thing differently than most other districts. Not satisfied with the basic standards, Coleman and her colleagues created the "Danville Diploma," a set of aptitudes that each child should master by high school graduation. These include the ability to exercise creativity, persevere in the face of challenges, find reliable and accurate information, function well on a team, manage time, think critically across disciplines, and take initiative. (I'd note, again, that none of these essential skills could appear on a paper exam.) Starting in kindergarten, Danville students keep a digital portfolio of work that shows they're mastering those competencies. The children will show these portfolios to their panels of assessors at the end of fifth and eighth grades. When they graduate from high school, they'll be able to send their portfolio link to colleges and potential employers to show what they can do beyond a transcript.

In one girl's portfolio, Principal Swann told me, will be a series of dazzling animated videos on dance. This girl, socially isolated and withdrawn, was a poor test taker who hadn't particularly distinguished herself until she proposed an independent study to create the animations. "She can already talk about camera angles and physics and all kinds of things that we never would have known had we not said, 'Okay, follow your interests and let's see what you can do,'" Swann said. "We would have just thought she was an average student."

There's one more benefit to *nonstandardized* evaluation that's important to understand. Assessing students as the Danville and New York educators do—through a variety of modes and through personalized projects with real meaning—helps to shape kids' mindset about learning.

The reigning expert on this science is psychologist Carol Dweck, whose 2007 book *Mindset: The New Psychology of Success* became a surprise bestseller that shook up the status quo in schools, businesses, and family dinner-table conversations. Some of the schools I've visited have had their entire staff read it. Dweck's book distills decades of research down into a dichotomy between two visions of intelligence and learning: *fixed mindset* or *growth mindset*. When I met her in her office at Stanford University, she explained it like this:

> *In a fixed mindset, students believe their abilities are just these fixed traits. You have a certain amount and that's that. Some of us got a lot of math ability and some of us did not. But in a growth mindset, students understand that abilities can be developed. Everyone can improve, can cultivate their abilities through hard work and mentoring.*

The concept sounds simple enough, but it's actually incredibly powerful. "When you have a fixed mindset, as soon as you encounter something difficult, your interest wanes," Dweck said. "If the whole point is to look smart and feel smart and you're not, how much fun can that be? So we find students dropping majors or turning off to something they loved before as soon as they hit difficulty or have to struggle." In contrast, "Students with a growth mindset tell us they feel smart when they're working hard on something and finally making progress."

Dweck's research also upends the way many of us thought we were supposed to praise our children. She found that praising a child's innate qualities, such as intelligence ("Oh, look what you did, you're so smart!"), backfires. "It puts kids into a fixed mindset," Dweck says. "It tells them that deep trait of intelligence is fixed, and that's what we value in them." Instead, she urges parents and teachers to praise children's effort, progress, and thought process, and to place value on struggle, not just success.

Unfortunately, our traditional education system is stuck in a fixed mindset. It's common for children as young as six to be tracked according to an assessment of their aptitudes—placed in reading groups or math groups by ability, for example. These students quickly learn to identify themselves as "fast" or "slow," "smart" or "dumb."

Our test-driven methods make this kind of labeling worse. This institutionally fixed mindset celebrates academically adept students, rewarding them for their high scores and good grades and making them feel smart without ever really challenging them. And it leaves students for whom conventional testing is difficult feeling inadequate, which hardly encourages them to keep forging ahead.

It's hard to get kids to adopt a growth mindset when they spend their young lives in a fixed-mindset system. Yet it's crucial that parents and educators try, because—while our children's mindsets may partly be rooted in their natural temperaments—research shows that the experiences they have at home and in school also play a significant role. Performance assessments can make a big difference. They place the emphasis on a student's creative and analytical process instead of a one-shot display of a narrow set of skills. They're especially beneficial when paired with a school-wide attitude that failures are useful lessons, not defeats. In Danville, for instance, when students' work for a performance assessment isn't up to snuff, they're expected to keep revising until it is.

Dweck also recommends that schools and parents explicitly teach kids about the mindsets. "Kids are fascinated by the brain," she observed to me. "And teaching them that the brain actually forms new connections when they learn, especially when they learn hard new things or even struggle with new material, it's thrilling for the child."

Ending the Obsession

There's no sense waiting for the zombie apocalypse. Every child in America should have access now to the sort of stimulating, personalized learning that's going on in Danville and New York City.

One antidote to our testing affliction will ultimately be policy change. It is urgent that each of us who cares about children's health and quality education press our school board members, state lawmakers, and representatives in Washington, DC, to eradicate the creativity-crushing regime and instead adopt a program that encourages deep thinking and honors children's diverse strengths. The high stakes placed on exams have to go; no one's job or graduation should depend on a single measure. And instead of fixating on a single written test, we could evaluate schools on a host of outcomes with more meaning, such as college entrance and persistence rates, improved student health, and student engagement.

There are little glimmers of movement now. FairTest reports that by fall 2014, at least seven states had repealed or delayed their graduation testing requirements. (Rhode Island, finding itself under student-zombie attack, was one of them.) That same fall, state education secretaries and district superintendents from across the country got together and pledged to cut back on testing. The officials insisted that some testing is necessary, but told news outlets that many currents tests "are poorly designed, take too much time, [and] don't measure what schools really need to know." On a smaller scale, the whole district of Windsor Locks, Connecticut, is phasing out letter grades and instead using rubrics, which allow students to track their progress toward the skills they need to master. And high schools in Glastonbury, Connecticut, and Acton-Boxborough, Massachusetts, stopped publishing their honor rolls to relieve competition among students for grades and class rank.

As we undertake the campaign for change, we'll hear some skeptics contend that the new Common Core standards are already making things better. My answer: maybe. The standards were intended to replace eclectic and voluminous state requirements with a more streamlined national set that encourages critical thinking. Whether they actually improve learning remains to be seen; it will depend entirely on how they're implemented. "The Common Core, however dressed, shares the fundamental spirit with NCLB: standardization of curriculum enforced with high-stakes testing," writes Yong Zhao. Even if the learning goals are better, students' experiences will only improve if the means are better, too. Naysayers may also argue that doing deeper assessments on a national scale would be too time-consuming and expensive. That argument is a distraction. The fact is we *could* assess schools with better measures if we tested a smaller, representative sampling of students instead of every single one—which is the way science is normally done.

But—reality check. We all know how slowly the wheels of politics turn. It will take years to reform the testing regime in statehouses and in Washington. Fortunately, we can start to change children's experiences immediately by taking matters in our homes and communities into our own hands. We can begin, of course, by pressing districts to reduce standardized tests; some districts require double or even triple the number of standardized exams that states do. Beyond that, we should ask teachers to assess their students' daily learning in far more diverse and deep ways: through such endeavors as hands-on projects, public presentations, debates, and digital portfolios—the kind of work that actually resembles what students will someday do in the real world. If resistance is stiff, consider starting these innovations in a single classroom, where skeptics can see for themselves how students thrive.

"Whatever we do repeatedly is how we wire ourselves neurologically," explains Mariale Hardiman, director of the Neuro-Education Initiative at Johns Hopkins University. That's why it's crucial to give children a wide variety of experiences in school, she says, rather than "always teaching them and testing them in the same way."

Much of our work at the local level is not procedural but cultural. We need to teach our kids and our communities a growth mindset, and to broaden our shared definition of what learning looks like and what success in school can be. It starts with each of us shedding the belief that good test scores equal a good education. Without standardized tests, we'll still have ample evidence to gauge whether our students are learning well—just look at the essays they've written, the presentations they've made, the science experiments they've conducted, or the thoughtful discussions they're able to have. Yong Zhao also advocates for measuring a school's quality by the resources and opportunities it provides to every student, such as fair and equitable funding, a safe physical environment, well-trained teachers, personalized lessons, a broad curriculum including the arts, and support for innovation. In other words, assessing inputs, not just outputs.

Do not believe, either, in the "best high school" rankings that are invented by commercial magazines, and do not participate in the stampede to buy ever more excessively priced homes in "top-ranked" districts. Test scores are well known to parallel children's parents' income and education levels, so those rankings may not tell you any more about school quality than they do about local property values. (Dozens of high schools have already asked to be removed from such rankings, calling them "simplistic and misleading" and arguing that "communities deserve better.") As long as parents buy into these false measures, our schools will remain stuck in traditional education practices and test prep. Rankings keep schools focused on the wrong things.

Some of the cultural shift can start as simply as parents and teachers changing the tone of conversations at home and in the classroom. Allison Nelson, a mother of two in Potomac, Montana, says she and her husband have deliberately shifted the importance they place on their elementary-age daughter's test grades. They still urge her to do her best, but they don't pass judgment if a bad score comes home. "We just say, 'You know what? Maybe it was a bad day,'" says Nelson. And they look for a lesson to learn from it.

Changing our conversations with children sounds like a tiny tweak, but don't underestimate its power. I always think back to a particularly tough precalculus test my older daughter took. She got a D but took it in stride, knowing the test was tough and using the opportunity to see which concepts she'd missed. In earlier years, I had fueled her anxiety by fretting over every B and C, once even keeping her indoors all weekend to study for a fourth grade biology test. By this point, though, I'd learned to stay calm and just listen, to ask her what mattered to her and how she wanted to respond. Shelby, who loved math, decided that she wanted to learn what she'd missed, so she asked the teacher for extra help and worked hard to deepen her understanding.

Opting your children out of standardized tests can also send them an important message about what you value—in them, in their education, and in life. This is a message worth spreading to other parents, as well, to galvanize the community. Michele Gray, a mom of two boys in State College, Pennsylvania, was distraught when her third grader became so anxious about the state test that he started scratching his legs in his sleep. He knew his performance could have consequences for his school, yet Gray saw no educational benefit to the exams. So she called the state education department and learned that she could have her sons skip the tests based on a religious objection. She took it. Her boys did independent study during the two weeks (two weeks!) their classmates were undergoing exams. When Gray wrote a column in the local paper telling parents how and why to opt out, CNN aired a story about her. Suddenly, Gray was getting phone calls from as far away as Georgia from parents who hated the tests but never knew there was anything they could do.

Students, too, can take steps to reclaim their own educational lives and those of others from single-minded measurement. Zak Malamed, a student body president at Great Neck North High School on Long Island, had an epiphany sophomore year when he burned out after months of attempting to devote himself fully to everything—the school newspaper, student government, and a tough slate of AP and honors classes. Zak scaled down, still getting his work done but not trying to ace every test. In exchange for his well-being, he decided, a B-plus instead of an A-plus was fine. Friends started telling him he seemed happier. "As long as I do it my way and do my way really well," he believes, "I don't have to do everything, and I don't have to be good at everything."

The following fall, several of Zak's schoolmates were arrested in the Nassau County cheating scandal. He began to see how, even at his highly regarded, high-scoring school, our madness for measurement was hurting the whole system. His school sorely needed improvements, he believed. But as long as the scores were high and the college admissions were golden, everyone seemed content with the status quo. Frustrated, Zak and others formed a student organization to give voice to their concerns. Later, the group was formalized as a nonprofit organization called Student Voice, which aims to place students' input at the center of education debates around the globe. Zak is now a junior at the University of Maryland, pursuing an "engagement and media" major that he created, and Student Voice is still going strong.

Lillian Van Cleve came by her epiphany even more unexpectedly. She is a warm, open college student who grew up in San Francisco attending elite schools that put a premium on test scores. These schools required copious quantities of uncreative work—which took Lillian, a girl with ADHD, hours longer each day than her peers. By the time she reached high school, exhausted and uninspired, she was asking herself, "Where am I going to get the stamina? When is this going to end?"

One experience saved her. In the fall of her ninth grade year, Lillian's mom took her to Florida for a few weeks to work on Barack Obama's presidential campaign. She worked in the field office and became the de facto assistant to the local director. Handling phone calls, helping volunteers, and arranging logistics, she found something astonishing: her own value. "That experience was transformational," Lillian says. "It was the first time in my life that I can remember feeling good about myself, and feeling good at something. And I *was*." Suddenly, Lillian could see a world beyond the rigid confines of school, and she could see herself in it.

Back in San Francisco, she joined the Parents Education Network, an organization for parents of children with learning challenges, as a student adviser. And she transferred to a school that placed greater value on deeply exploring ideas. Now Lillian is a junior at a small liberal arts college in the Midwest. Some people treat her diagnosis with the gentle phrase *learning difference*, but she prefers the blunter term *disability*. "It is a learning disability not because of the way my brain works, but because of the system that I'm in," Lillian argues. "I'm disabled by the system, and if you think about it, everybody is, because it's set for a very narrow definition of a learner, and everybody's different whether they have a learning disability or not."

————

Since my own awakening I have struggled to help my children step back from society's measures of success and define their own. I've been opting my own Zak out of standardized tests since he was in fourth grade. Jamey opted herself out in tenth grade—and I understood why. I saw the need starkly one particular day, her first day of school that year. Here was Jamey standing in front of me, sweaty from cheerleading tryouts, flush with excitement for the new friendships she was making with teammates, full of determination to master the tumbling techniques she'd need to make the squad. And here, also, in that afternoon's mail, were the results of her California-mandated standardized tests. A row of good-but-not-great numbers, decontextualized and soulless on a sheet of paper in my hands. This is the vast divide our kids have to negotiate daily, between their *selves* and their *scores*. Will they or will someone else determine how their worth is defined?

Nowhere in those cold numbers will you see Zak Malamed's knack for leadership, Lillian's skillful activism, or Jamey's adeptness with animal science, which is now so apparent in the thriving preveterinary college student she has become. Let us join forces to end the testing madness and make it possible for every child to reach that state of self-determined success—to discover her own value and put it to great use—without having to fight such formidable obstacles all along the way.

CHAPTER 5

College Admissions:
Break Free from The Frenzy

I T WAS an overcast evening in late February when parents, students, and educators gathered for a *Race to Nowhere* screening in the auditorium at the Academy of the Sacred Heart in suburban Michigan. The 160-year-old school sits on forty-four wooded acres and is designed to be a nurturing place that focuses on the whole child, not just the Harvard application. After the screening, a panel of model students told the crowd that yes, the film raised serious issues, but no, this wasn't such a problem at Sacred Heart. They assured the community that they didn't feel as stressed as the kids in the film.

The students were doing what they thought they should—supporting their school. But junior Elle, another model student sitting in the audience, knew the rosy picture they painted was an illusion. She was a straight-A student, a field hockey and lacrosse player, poised, and bound for the most prestigious college she could test and transcript her way into, and she couldn't take it anymore. "They didn't speak the truth," Elle would later recall to me. "So I was sitting at my seat, and I just remember I was, like, fuming. And I was shaking."

Before she even realized what she was doing, she asked for the microphone. And then, her voice amplified across an audience of her teachers and peers, Elle uncorked the pressure that had been building in her for years.

Starting in sixth grade, Elle told the audience, she'd made it her mission to maintain a perfect transcript. She believed this was the necessary cost of admission to an elite college, and that ticket was priceless. "Going to a really great college that everyone sees as a really good school, that was success," she explained. Elle managed to sustain her taxing effort through sophomore year, when a British literature class had her reading and annotating fifty pages a night. The assignments took her five hours daily, on top of sports practice. She was so stressed that she started losing her hair; her ponytail shrank to half its normal width. But she didn't consider stopping.

Finally, junior year, an AP US history class pushed Elle over the edge. "It rocked my world," she said. "I had so much homework. I lived in my room, and a lot of times I would cry myself to sleep." She spiraled into a deep depression. "I would be driving down the road, and I would just be like: if only I could just turn the wheel a little, go a little faster, and just crash into something, it would be that easy." Elle confessed all of this, right down to her wish to die, to the assembled audience. Even her mother, sitting in the crowd, had never heard it before.

"I couldn't breathe," recalls Sister Bridget Bearss, the head of school. A devoted educator who believes deeply in the "heart" part of Sacred Heart's mission, she thought to herself: *This can't be happening.*

Elle's courageous act would trigger changes small and large, immediate and long-lasting, in the school community and in her own life. Right away, one of the girls on the panel "burst into tears onstage and started talking about how stressed she was," Elle recounts. Bearss convened a team of teachers that same night, staying at school until nearly midnight to discuss what they would do to make things better for their students. Bearss remembers asking herself, *Who else are the hidden Elles in our community?*

For Elle's part, she heard herself say out loud for the first time that her obsession with building the perfect college résumé was destroying her. "It woke me up," she says. "I realized that something had to change."

Many students and families I've met have taken the college admissions race to equal or greater extremes. What Elle realized that night—and what we as a society must recognize and embrace—is that the holy grail we're after is a mirage. A good life does not depend on a brand-name alma mater, nor is one guaranteed by an Ivy League acceptance letter. Either way, we're losing too much in its pursuit.

A Frenzied Nation

The Frenzy—capital *T*, capital *F*—is what Jon Reider, director of college counseling at San Francisco University High School, calls it. The college admissions process is a Darwinian and soul-bruising contest that represents nothing of the great leap toward autonomy, independence, and adventure that it should. The drive to *get in* spurs students to spend precious time on résumé-building activities that don't interest them, and their parents to spend precious money on test-prep courses that don't build meaningful knowledge. It demands that kids see their community of peers not as their safety net but as their competition. Perhaps worst of all, The Frenzy convinces many kids (and some parents) that admission to an elite college defines them; without an Ivy League acceptance or its equivalent, they are failures.

Eva Dodds, an independent college counselor in Michigan and board member of the Michigan Association of College Admission Counselors, sees the madness daily. From August through November, she says, "one of my lambs loses it almost every night." Intuitive and down-to-earth, Dodds tries to calm them; she does this work because she believes in her students, not in the system. Yet even outside the office, parents of her six-year-old son's classmates ask her what she thinks of certain schools, saying, "I know it's a little early, but . . ." and inquiring, "Is there anything we should be doing now to help our kids get into college?" Her answer is an emphatic, and rather horrified, no.

Yet Dodds understands where their worry is coming from. Acceptance rates at the most prestigious schools do indeed appear to be growing infinitesimal. For the class of 2018, for example, Wesleyan University admitted just 23 percent of applicants, Notre Dame 21 percent, Williams 18, Cornell 14, Vanderbilt 12, MIT 8, Harvard and Yale 6, and Stanford a mere 5 percent. Those odds may not be quite as impossible as they appear—more students are being courted to apply to elite colleges for which they're not qualified, effectively inflating rejections—but the numbers spread fear nonetheless. One client of Dodds's was so panicked that she came up with the idea of applying to her choice college via the art program, though she was not an artist, and using her friend's portfolio in the application. Plenty of others,

Dodds says, commit the less conspicuous fraud of pursuing nongenuine interests, cheating themselves above all.

Dodds's charges are suffering from the ailment that Philadelphia clinical psychologist Jeff Mitchell terms "Harvard-or-Walmart syndrome." On his website, he published a withering critique of the "academic extremism" driving the college race:

> *This is a societal disease, a virus of an idea that has spread through the LinkedIn generation and its children. It is a conviction, stark and unforgiving, that one's children will either (1) get into Harvard or (2) spend their lives working for Walmart. Infected with this idea, parents and children drive themselves far past the point of healthy ambition. Believing the odds are so poor, the stakes so high, and the degree of control over the outcome so tenuous, parents and children take extreme actions. No amount of pressure, no expense, no degree of sleeplessness or risk of humiliation is too high. And frankly, if one believes the choices are Harvard=success=security or Walmart=Dickensian=poverty, this extremism seems sensible and the only right course.*

The great fallacy is the belief that those ivory towers are the *only* place a student can adequately learn, grow, and embark on a good life. There's no certainty that those elite institutions are even the *best* place for every kid to do so. The *New York Times*'s Frank Bruni reported recently that he looked up the undergraduate alma maters of the CEOs of the top ten companies in the Fortune 500 and found only one Ivy (Dartmouth) among them. The remaining nine attended such universities as Arkansas, Texas, Nebraska, Kansas, Missouri, Auburn, and Saint Louis.

Eva Dodds herself attended the little-known College of Wooster in Ohio, where she honed her writing, research, and leadership and got what she considers a better education than she did later, in a master's program at the Harvard Graduate School of Education. "The reality of the situation is there are three thousand awesome, awesome, awesome colleges out there," she says. "And as cheesy as it sounds, there is a match for everyone." That match is a school whose offerings fit your particular academic and extracur-

ricular interests, and whose campus culture is suited to help a student like you succeed.

But the status anxiety fueled by American culture—not to mention the genuinely fearful vise grip of rising income inequality—makes an alternate path invisible to those in the throes of The Frenzy. "The stress is there," Dodds says, "because the culture says you're only successful if you go to these fifty colleges." The truth is that there is no surefire formula: some star students don't get in, while some students do get in with lower scores but unique qualities that help a college build a diverse class. Above a certain level of academic achievement, getting into elite schools is akin to a lottery. Nonetheless, many families mortgage the high school years trying to fatten applications and read admissions officers' minds. This panicked sense of competition even afflicts students with more modest goals as it fuels the misperception that perfect résumés are required to get into college, period, which is far from true.

Amid all the jockeying, the hurdles for low-income students can be especially hard to clear. A mom at another Michigan screening pointed out that the stakes of getting her kids into a university—and out of the cycle of poverty—were incredibly high. Yet for those whose families have no experience with college, there may be no one to tell them which high school courses to take or how to prepare for the SAT, and no one to help them with applications. Teachers in low-income communities tell me that the strain on these students tends to go unrecognized.

Meanwhile, The Frenzy has even spawned an entire sector of the economy devoted to helping both colleges and students (at least those who can afford it) play the game. The attendant army of marketing and recruitment consultants for colleges, application consultants for students, private test-prep tutors, essay coaches, and standardized test makers comprise what Reider calls "the admissions-industrial complex." Revenue among all these businesses runs well into the billions. Fear sells.

The craziest extreme I've ever seen is a hedge fund manager turned college counselor named Steven Ma. From his chain of ThinkTank Learning centers in the San Francisco Bay Area, Ma provides tutoring, test prep, and application coaching and guarantees that his clients will get into a "top" school, provided they hit certain minimum GPAs and SAT scores, or their

money back. How much money? His astronomical fees are based on a proprietary algorithm that predicts each kid's chance of admission to each school, *Bloomberg Businessweek* reported. The price tag for tough cases can reach $700,000. And some parents actually pay it. "Of course we set limits on who we'll guarantee," Ma told the magazine. "We don't want to make this a casino game."

Origins of the Arms Race

Today's college application process bears not the faintest resemblance to what this generation of parents experienced a few decades ago. My own applications in the late 1970s were a straightforward documentation of my courses and grades and a thoughtful essay about the career for which I hoped my college education would ready me. My volunteering as a candy striper in the local hospital, my work on the yearbook staff, and my participation in the math club were welcome breaks from schoolwork and chances to be with my friends—not credentials for college. I remember my applications not so much as a stressful hurdle to be jumped but as an exciting and empowering step toward my adult independence and stability.

So what's happened?

The former Yale professor William Deresiewicz sketches out the history of the slippery slope in his book *Excellent Sheep*. As Deresiewicz tells it, the origins of The Frenzy lie in an effort to expand private colleges from the exclusive clubs they'd been for a century or more, the province of elite Anglo-Saxon Protestant progeny groomed in private boarding schools. In the 1930s, a Harvard University president set out to raise academic standards and broaden access to the rising classes. He chose as his primary tool a then-obscure test called the SAT. In the 1960s, the Yale president did the same, and in short order other colleges followed. Yet this move toward meritocracy sparked a new arms race. Now applicants had to boast *both* the "character" and culture of an old aristocrat and the academic excellence of a modern technocrat—and look better than the growing competition while doing it. No pressure.

Since then the contest has only accelerated. Between 1970 and 2010, the number of students enrolled in four-year colleges more than doubled.

And the more grads that entered the workforce with a bachelor's degree, the more everyone else felt that they, too, needed a diploma to compete. "What was once an opportunity has become a necessity," Deresiewicz observes. "There is only one definition of happiness, and only one way to get it." In fact, over the past forty-five years the reasons students themselves give for going to college have drastically changed; whereas most incoming freshmen once said they sought meaning in their education, most today say they seek money.

Now the obsession with this one-and-only yellow brick road extends alarmingly far backward—into preschool, in certain communities. UC Berkeley psychologist and philosopher Alison Gopnik likens the resulting distortion of our children's "learning" to the famed plight of the Irish elk. The males of the now-extinct species earned a slight evolutionary advantage if they had bigger antlers. The result, Gopnik quips, was an antler arms race that produced bucks that could barely move under the weight of their giant antlers. "We've got something like that in the American system," she says. We all think it's crazy for high schoolers to pull caffeine-fueled homework binges every other night, but as parents, when it comes to our own child, in whose future we're so deeply invested, we can't help but fret that a slightly more majestic antler might get her into a better college and on the path to a better life.

It's all been intensified by the *U.S. News & World Report* college rankings, launched in 1983. The annual lineup purports to name the "best" colleges and universities in the country on sixteen measures of "academic excellence," including admission rates, graduation rates, class sizes, per-student spending, and—in a self-referential spiral—the reputation of each institution according to other college officials' opinions. So rich is this business that other media now publish copycat rankings of their own. (*Washington Monthly* deserves note as an exception. Its rankings are based on the refreshingly meaningful criterion of how much each institution contributes to the public good in terms of research, service, and social mobility for low-income students.)

These rankings generally do nothing to help students find an educational environment that fits them. Yet the list, however suspect its criteria, stokes students' ambitions and fears and fuels the myth that there is a "best" when it comes to the complex and personal art of education. Plus, it perpetuates a growing tendency among prospective college students to see college primarily as a stepping-stone to yet more prestige and "rank," rather than an opportunity for growth and learning.

Rankings also handcuff colleges that might want to demonstrate their success another way. Arizona State University psychologist Suniya Luthar, for one, has called on schools to systematically assess students' *well-being* and include that stat among their institutional credentials. Reed College, a selective and respected school in Portland, Oregon, stopped participating in the rankings altogether in 1995, refusing to send *U.S. News* its data. Reed argued that the magazine's methodology amounts to a "statistical charade" and that its lineup "takes a one-size-fits-all approach to institutions with radically different missions and character—a bit like asking whether the Beatles are better than Beethoven." The college paid a price for its stand: *U.S. News* kept on ranking Reed anyway, gathering its data from other sources, and the following year its rank plummeted to the lowest tier.

Some of the ingredients in the college panic are even more malignant. I was shocked to learn, for instance, that a lower acceptance rate earns a college not only a higher *U.S. News* ranking but also a higher bond rating. The more applicants a school rejects, the more generously Wall Street will lend money to it. A school's ranking also rises if it enrolls more students with higher SAT and ACT scores. So the more applicants a college attracts, the better positioned it is to skim those with the best statistical profiles, thus boosting its ranking and prestige and attracting even more applicants. It's no surprise, then, that I heard admissions officials on Jamey's campus tours urge high school students to take the SAT and ACT multiple times so that the colleges could "superscore" them, taking their highest score from each section even if it meant pulling from different sittings. This expensive and grueling exercise benefits the colleges and favors kids from families who can afford to pay for the test over and over.

In part for these reasons, colleges are increasingly deploying huge marketing machines that flood students' mailboxes with glossy brochures whether or not those students are qualified. The more applications they receive, the more they can reject, puffing up their statistics. Yet this numbers game can create a cruel, false hope for families. Eva Dodds routinely hears parents say,

"I know she has a 3.2, but look at what she got from Harvard. Should she still apply?" Dodds can't always dissuade them.

Moreover, the ever-shrinking admission rates spur students to apply to an ever-expanding number of schools. Using the Common Application, it's especially easy for anxious students to tick extra college boxes and thus hedge their bets. The National Association for College Admission Counseling reports that, in 1990, just under one in ten students applied to seven or more colleges; by 2014, more than three in ten did so. Applying to a dozen or more schools is now common. Dodds sees plenty of kids throw in five or six applications to schools they won't get into, against her advice. Their parents say proudly, "My kid has applied there," Dodds says, and then other parents think their kids should, too.

And so the growing flood of applications drives down acceptance rates still further, and the vicious cycle goes on. As we've seen, all this misery does not even produce the genuine learning we want for our kids. College professors widely report that too many freshmen arrive on their campuses profoundly averse to risk, not daring to try new subjects or endeavors that they can't be sure to ace. The traditional treadmill has stripped them of their spark. At UC Berkeley, for example, Gopnik told me her most interesting students are those who've transferred in from community colleges. They have "actually gone out in the world and done things . . . and now are coming back and bringing a degree of enthusiasm and exuberance and creativity to their schooling that we don't necessarily see in these very finely honed grade-getting machines that we are creating in our high schools."

Saddest of all is the self-doubt induced by our singular, competitive vision of college success. Kathleen, a high school senior from the Midwest, wrote to me that she'd built her life around getting into the same university as her older brother did. Aiming to be perfect in high school, she took almost exclusively AP and accelerated classes, participated in ten clubs, served as cross-country and track captain, and slept an average of four hours a night. As a result, she developed extreme migraines, scoliosis, and ovarian cysts, and longed for it all to end. Kathleen wrote:

> *The thing is, I was never as smart as my brother and the other girls in my class. I was the dumb girl in the smart classes. I hated myself.*

*Whenever I looked in the mirror I wanted to punch it so hard. . . .
I was 11th in the class and not in the top 10. And worst of all, I
was rejected from [my first-choice school]. I failed. The one thing I
wanted more than anything in my life was taken away. I let down so
many people. The day I found out, I walked into traffic hoping that it
wouldn't hurt, hoping that all the pain would go away. But the cars
stopped. I'm still here.*

*I want people to see that we walk around every day with the
world hanging on our shoulders weighing us down. Imagine what
would happen if it gets too heavy, and we crash. What would happen then?*

Steps at Sacred Heart

Bridget Bearss and the staff at Sacred Heart did not wait around to find out
what would happen if Elle and her schoolmates went on bearing that pressure without some help. Acting quickly after hearing Elle's testimony, they
launched a "curriculum think tank" to reassess what students truly needed
to learn and figure out how best to teach them. They asked, for instance,
whether summer reading really helps kids perform better. The answer, says
Bearss: "We don't really have any statistical evidence that more homework
and more summer reading equals higher achieving kids." So they eliminated
summer reading and tried to shift students' most challenging assignments
from homework to classwork.

Recognizing the importance of granting students a voice in their own
learning, the school also began building in more opportunities for children
to choose pursuits they're passionate about, culminating in a self-chosen
capstone project for seniors. Sacred Heart started a speakers series on
wellness, highlighting topics such as depression, suicide prevention, and
balance. And the staff redoubled their efforts to dissuade kids from overscheduling. "When you see a student who is just biting off way too much,
we're much more aggressive about saying no," Bearss says (though students
and parents can still override their advice).

To Elle's surprise, the school even changed the rules for what it takes to
be valedictorian. No longer did a student have to take the hardest course

load possible to become valedictorian or salutatorian. Elle stumbled on the change while looking through the student handbook at her senior year orientation. "It was kind of incredible for me," she said. "If I had just let the panel speak and say that everything was okay, nothing would have really changed because everyone would have thought that every student in our school was doing fine."

Bearss is watching to see what impact the reforms make. By fall 2014, a couple of years after the work began, Sacred Heart was seeing higher standardized test scores and fewer kids being referred for psychological evaluation, but it was too early to identify the reforms as the cause. Bearss, a onetime anti–Vietnam War activist turned educator, admits that there's some cultural quicksand her school still can't escape. "I have kindergarten parents who ask me for the college acceptance list," she told me. And for a small school that depends on its enrollees to stay in business, the pressure is real. Sacred Heart publishes the acceptance list on its website.

The Advanced Placement Illusion

Sacred Heart's move away from an insistence on the hardest possible course load is not an easy one to make. This is an issue dominated by the dreaded Advanced Placement class, one of The Frenzy's chief instruments of destruction. Originally designed to help capable students earn college credit while still in high school, the AP program is now touted as a way to prepare teens to succeed in tough college classes, expose poor and minority students to more rigorous course material, and reduce the cost of college by enabling students to graduate earlier. And the AP business is booming. *Politico* reports that the number of AP exams taken per year more than doubled in just a decade, reaching nearly three million by 2012. At the same time, revenues to the College Board, maker of the AP exams, surged to more than $600 million a year (prompting *Nonprofit Quarterly* to question whether the organization was a "nonprofit in name only").

Yet in 2012, students failed nearly half of the AP exams they took. The passing rates were even lower for Latino and African American students. The educators and students I've met across the country typically tell me the demands of AP classes leave them rushing through reams of rote content at the expense of rich, in-depth learning. Burned-out students cram before exams and quickly forget what they've learned. Rarely does teaching to the test leave time to cultivate the critical thinking skills that colleges claim to want.

Take the example cited by Jay Chugh, who teaches both AP biology and an elective, non-AP biotechnology class in the Acalanes Union High School District in California. In the elective course several years ago he started allowing more time for authentic research and open-ended exploration. As a result, two of his students went on to win the top prize at the Intel International Science and Engineering Fair. Ironically, the AP biology students would never have had time to do that—they often didn't even have time for labs because they were trying to cover so much content before the test in May. "Where is the time to do authentic science?" Chugh exclaimed. "It's not there."

The AP program doesn't necessarily, in fact, bolster college performance. A Harvard and University of Virginia survey of eighteen thousand college students in introductory science classes found that having taken AP science classes did not significantly boost their grades. And a study of more than eighty thousand University of California students found that once you factor in students' academic and socioeconomic backgrounds, AP courses had no significant relationship to how well they perform in the early college years. Middlebury College math professor Priscilla Bremser complained publicly in 2011 that more and more of her students who scored well on the AP calculus exam hadn't actually contemplated the important theories on which calculus is based. After hurrying through high school math to reach AP calculus, Bremser wrote, "a number of bright, hard-working students have shockingly weak algebra skills. At some point along the way the A.P. program has shifted from a way to meet the needs of a few students who are ready for a challenge to a de facto admissions requirement for many who may not be."

Besides, some private colleges—Dartmouth, for one—no longer offer credit for these exams because they are not seen as true equivalents to the college's own courses. As for the touted cost savings, it is possible for some students to enter college (at public institutions that *do* give AP credit) as second-semester freshmen, saving themselves a sizable chunk of tuition.

However, many private colleges charge by the semester for four full years, not by the course. So students there pay the same tuition no matter how many AP exams they aced. This is, ironically, the case at some of the nation's most prestigious institutions, whose students are most likely to have taken tons of AP tests (at more than ninety dollars a pop).

Still, frantic students are flocking to AP classes, and many high schools encourage this. Unfortunately, it actually boosts high schools' reputations to push more kids into AP classes, ready or not. The *U.S. News & World Report* "Best High Schools" rankings score schools entirely based on how many of their students take and pass at least one AP or IB exam. And schools whose students take the most AP and IB exams, regardless of whether or not they pass, rank highest on the *Washington Post*'s annual "America's Most Challenging High Schools" list. So we end up with sixteen-year-olds taking four "college equivalent" AP classes plus three regular classes simultaneously, whereas actual college students typically take just four courses at a time.

This is not to say that APs are all bad. There are some brilliantly taught AP classes out there, and some students who feel genuinely challenged and engaged by them. But that caliber of teaching and learning is possible in any class, perhaps more so in a course not driven by a standardized exam. What we lack above all in our AP mania, as in The Frenzy overall, is any shred of balance.

The pressure even gets to those who don't believe in it. Jon Reider, the San Francisco University High School college counseling director, is a self-confessed "curmudgeon" and "rebel" who spent much of our conversation deploring colleges' role in the admissions madness. (As a former Stanford admissions officer himself, he has the credentials to be a critic.) Reider complained that the hundred-plus college reps who visit his campus each year always tell students to take the hardest course load possible, leaving out the important phrase: *within reason*. Yet in the same phone call, he had to step away for a few moments to explain to a student who was considering dropping an AP class that it could hurt her college chances. "I hate that I have to do that," he said. "Maybe I'm a hypocrite."

At Irvington High, Assistant Principal Jay Jackson and the guidance counselors set out several years ago to discourage students from signing up for too many Advanced Placement and honors classes in their quest for a collegiate edge. Some kids were registering for courses far beyond their academic capacity, simply because they felt they should, and then struggling and failing. The counselors were starting to see serious psychological disorders among students as young as ninth grade, and the school's 5150s—police code for forcibly committing someone to a mental hospital, typically because of suicidal plans—seemed to be growing more frequent.

Wendi Bennett, an Irvington counselor with dirty-blond bangs and a tell-it-like-it-is demeanor, believes there are a few students who can genuinely handle all that work. The problem comes from the large number "who *think* they can do this, and they're the ones falling apart." Worse, she says, there are just as many beyond that who take the classes because their parents expect them to.

So the counselors created a special registration form for students to complete before they can register for an AP or honors class. Students had to fill out a table estimating all the time in their day, including homework, family time, free time, and necessities such as eating and showering, with eight hours already tabulated for sleep, and a maximum of twenty-four hours (yes, the school actually had to underscore that limit). They had to factor in added time for advanced classes. And the students and their parents had to sign statements including:

> *I understand that an AP class is extensive in content and requires additional time and work. The course load I am registering for is balanced and suits my ability level.*

And:

> *I understand that I should base my course choices on genuine interest and should NOT register for an AP course(s) because my friends/peers are registering for it or for the sole purpose of impressing a college.*

The form was a good effort, but it was no match for the achievement machine. The counselors found that when they sent the form home, students weren't giving it serious consideration. Bennett would laugh when students penciled in fifteen minutes for family time. "I had a couple that put zero for necessities," she recalls. "I'm like: please shower."

So, in a stunning act of commitment, in spring 2014 the counselors sat down individually with every single freshman, sophomore, and junior (about 1,700 students total) as they registered, to urge them to think carefully about their course choices. They pulled students out, one by one, during their English classes. The entire process took all four of Irvington's counselors a whopping one and a half months, every day, most of the day.

The school also put in place prerequisites for AP and honors classes. Students have to get good grades in the fall in a given subject area in order to register for an advanced class in the same discipline the next year. And, though it's not mandatory, the counselors enforce a very strong recommendation that students reach a certain GPA before they decide to increase their load.

Within a single semester, the Irvington counselors' intervention cut the AP class failure rate in half. Whereas the counselors used to be routinely called to tend to overwhelmed students having emotional meltdowns in class, only one student had that crisis the following year. There's still a long way to go to change the community's achieve-at-all-costs mentality—to get students, parents, and even some pressure-pushing teachers to reexamine their priorities. But students are clearly feeling some relief. And though it was too early to have comprehensive data on college admissions, the counselors were already seeing students accepted at great schools, such as Purdue, UC Davis, and UC San Diego, with only one or two APs. So Irvington made the decision to continue the one-on-one course registration again the next spring, despite the incredible investment it took. Imagine if every school did.

AP classes are, in fact, not critical to a college application. The Cranbrook Kingswood School in Bloomfield Hills, Michigan, restricts students to two or three AP classes a year yet remains a highly regarded prep school. Some of the country's most respected schools offer no AP classes at all. The Independent Curriculum Group, for example, includes about seventy-five schools nationwide that have chosen to liberate their teachers to create rigorous, deep, and challenging advanced courses instead of AP. Its participants have included many private schools, such as the Crossroads School in Santa

Monica and the Park School of Baltimore, as well as public high schools in performance-driven communities: Scarsdale, New York, and Marblehead, Massachusetts, to name two. In place of prescribed curricula these schools focus on fostering curiosity, creativity, and genuine engagement. The Carolina Friends School in Durham, for example, puts the money it might spend on APs into diverse opportunities to develop critical thinking, such as senior seminars in neuroethics and immigration and an entire semester course on the fall 2008 presidential election.

What happens when AP-less Carolina Friends grads go up against college applicants from elsewhere with oodles of APs? Nothing. Colleges know about the ICG schools' approach and thus don't penalize their students for it at application time. Having zero AP classes hasn't harmed their admissions. Nor has it hurt graduates of the New York Performance Standards Consortium schools. Nor of San Diego's highly regarded High Tech High, which worked directly with the University of California to develop an honors curriculum with more depth and flexibility than the AP regimen. The school offers the option for honors credit in any class instead of segregating students into separate AP courses.

It is possible for individual kids attending schools that are stuck on AP to opt out of those classes and distinguish themselves in other ways. Jamey took not a single AP class in high school but distinguished herself through community service that she cared about. She also chose certain courses to which to devote extra effort, once studying so hard that she set the curve on a math exam. Ultimately, she had multiple colleges to choose from. However, it's harder to convince colleges of the value of your choices when you have to go it alone, as Jamey did. Here again, our greatest power to end the race comes when whole communities work together to redefine what matters—and the success of groups like the ICG and schools like Cranbrook Kingswood and High Tech High is proof of that.

Colleges, for their part, must cop to their role in fueling the madness and cap the number of APs they'll consider on a student's application. The Ivies, especially, should recognize their powerful influence and limit the advanced courses that applicants may list. That would be a simple, responsible step, and other colleges would follow suit. High schools, too, should follow the courageous lead of those I've described in this chapter. Sacred Heart offers only three AP courses, total—a decision made years ago for the sake of learning. In rejecting AP biology, for instance, Bearss explains, "It was our assessment that our molecular biology course did a better job of teaching students how to think" because it's more about applying understanding than memorizing information. That is an assessment that many more schools should make.

The Elephant in the Room

The blame for The Frenzy falls on all of us: parents, students, teachers, college counselors, college trustees, *U.S. News*, the broader media, bond rating agencies, and the entire moneymaking admissions industry. Yet Reider considers colleges "the elephant in the room. And they get away with it, because nobody wants to criticize them." It's true: I've had seasoned, respected college counselors refuse to talk to me on the record about colleges' role in the madness because they don't want to anger admissions officers and jeopardize their students' applications.

It is high time that colleges acknowledge their powerful role in promoting The Frenzy—and work to ease it. University presidents, trustees, and admissions officers have the ultimate power to defuse the applications arms race. We parents and educators can help by teaming up with our own alumni associations to petition our alma maters to do so—perhaps, for those who can afford to donate, even threatening to withhold contributions until they stop the insanity. Besides capping the number of AP courses they'll consider, colleges should stop scaring kids into taking the hardest course load possible, and instead encourage them to follow their interests and develop as whole people. The fear-mongering messages that are delivered on campus tours and high school visits, driving students to sit for entrance exams multiple times and take excessive course loads, must stop.

Colleges should also put a ceiling on extracurricular activities they'll count in an application. You feel you need to run around to a dozen activities only because your classmates are doing eleven. Here, too, the Ivies could use their hefty influence to lead the way. To restrain runaway competition, Swarthmore College professor Barry Schwartz has even suggested that colleges simply set a minimum threshold for academic achievement and then admit applicants who meet that standard by random lottery. Alternatively, universities could consider a candidate matching system similar to that used by medical schools.

Reider would also like to see admissions offices get rid of all standardized testing requirements. "Everybody is aware that all these tests favor the people with what we call cultural capital"—families with the income, education, and experience to prepare well for tests and understand their protocols—he says. Families like his own. "It helps my kid get into college," he says. "But is it fair? No. Does it have any redeeming intellectual qualities? No." Indeed, SAT scores parallel students' parents' income so perfectly that the *Wall Street Journal* dubbed the exam the "Student Affluence Test."

The unfairness of it struck me hardest when talking with Isaiah, the Oakland Tech student, who had no test-prep courses before taking the SAT. "The first time I took it," he said, "they gave me twenty-five minutes to write an essay. I was like, 'Dude, that's like five paragraphs in twenty-five minutes, it's like impossible,' so I ended up just writing three paragraphs, and my paragraphs were only two sentences. I didn't even get all my ideas out." Then he talked to a fellow student who *had* taken SAT prep and found out that you're not supposed to write five full paragraphs. Rather, your first paragraph should be a one-sentence thesis statement, the next three short paragraphs supporting arguments, and the last one a two-sentence summary. Isaiah knew none of these arbitrary and unguessable tricks. Ruefully, he concluded that "SAT prep should be mandatory."

Even the National Association for College Admission Counseling agrees with cutting the cord on standardized tests. A NACAC report in 2008, led by none other than Harvard admissions dean William Fitzsimmons, urged colleges to consider dropping the SAT and ACT from admissions decisions, noting that test scores "appear to calcify differences based on class, race/ethnicity, and parental educational attainment" and "may not be critical to making good admission decisions."

Emory University president James Wagner has acknowledged that colleges' admission methods still miss many applicants with great potential.

His case in point is the program at Emory's Oxford College, a two-year residential college with automatic enrollment at Emory in junior year. At Oxford, Wagner explained, "We gamble more," admitting students with lower grades and SAT scores a hundred points below those at the main campus. Placed in small classes and taught partly through collaborative projects, these students flourish as well as or better than peers in the regular Emory program, and more of them go on to pursue doctoral degrees. "So I know for a fact that we're admitting students that we and our peers would otherwise reject, who are fabulous students," he said. "I don't know how to get that message out: Universities will not suffer [if we change our admission criteria]. We'll actually thrive. We'll be relieved, in fact, in many ways."

Plenty of admissions officers make their decisions just fine *without* those all-powerful scores, anyway. FairTest, a Boston-based organization that advocates for fairer measures in education, keeps a comprehensive list of all the colleges and universities that admit at least some freshmen without SAT or ACT scores—and it numbers well into the hundreds, and growing. The list includes more than 160 such schools ranked in the "top tiers" by *U.S. News*, including Wesleyan, Bowdoin, Bryn Mawr, Connecticut College, Wake Forest, and the California state universities. And how do their students fare? A 2014 study backed by NACAC and conducted by a former Bates College dean of admissions looked at a huge sample: more than a hundred thousand students at nearly three dozen of the colleges and universities that make standardized tests optional. The researchers compared the college grades and graduation rates of students who did and did not submit an SAT or ACT score with their application, and found no significant difference in their success.

Why does the reliance on standardized test scores persist despite so much evidence against it? David Hawkins, NACAC's executive director of educational content and policy, explains that it's partly because of history—"It was the very most elite institutions that were using these tests to begin with," he says, and where the prestigious schools lead, others tend to follow—and partly because there's a misperception that the tests provide what Hawkins calls "a common yardstick," an efficient way of sorting applicants and transcending variations in grading from high school to high school.

More universities must follow the test-optional schools' sensible lead. In place of standardized exams, they could allow applicants to submit digital portfolios, papers, videos, and other more personal demonstrations of skill. In a few places, this change is already starting. In 2014, Goucher College, outside Baltimore, began accepting a two-minute video, plus two high school work samples, *in place of* the Common Application. That is how Jameel, the student from New York's Urban Academy, applied. Bennington College in Vermont started offering applicants an even more flexible option: they can send in a portfolio of any material they want, including or not including grades and scores. This "dimensional" application is an invitation for creativity and independent thought. Admissions officers use the portfolios to gauge applicants' academic readiness and understand what each will bring to the college community.

Colleges that have made such changes say they're looking to capture more applicants with unique résumés who might be deterred by conventional measures. Since 2013 Bard College has been accepting what it calls the Bard Entrance Examination from those who don't want to take the traditional route. The instructions are to write four 2,500-word essays, chosen from twenty-one topics, to be graded by Bard faculty. Get at least a B-plus combined grade, and you're in—no tests scores, transcripts, or résumés required. Bard president Leon Botstein told the *New York Times* the new application was "declaring war on the whole rigmarole of college admissions," which is "loaded with a lot of nonsense that has nothing to do with learning."

Privately, admissions officers elsewhere admit they, too, want the system reformed. But colleges are infected with a Frenzy of their own—a senseless cultural panic about outcompeting other schools for applicants, stoked by the well-paid college marketing industry that makes it possible. Up against the juggernaut of the rankings, the other colleges' recruitment machines, and the directives of boards of trustees, individual officers don't see how they can be among the first to change.

Michael Beseda, the vice president for enrollment and communications at Willamette University in Salem, Oregon, is trying to buck the trend. After arriving at Willamette in 2013, he canceled the school's contract with Royall & Company, the enrollment-consulting behemoth that sells students on

easy, quick, and free applications, and set about doing recruitment and admissions his own way. Every message sent to prospective students came not from the marketing machine but from Beseda's own email address, and was written by Beseda himself to emphasize Willamette's particular offerings instead of the ease of application. Each acceptance letter contained a personal note about the candidate's qualities. In short, he cast Willamette as a unique school that suited particular students instead of a commodity.

The result: Applications, which had tripled to nine thousand under Royall, dropped to six thousand in a single year. But Beseda says the school got "a larger class, a much better class," because accepted students were more likely to actually attend. Wasn't Willamette afraid of losing rank as its admission rate ballooned? A little, but not much. Beseda's explanation centered on a startling fact: it turns out that a college's admission rate—one of the factors in the *U.S. News* rankings to which institutions seem most slavishly devoted—actually makes up a barely consequential 1.25 percent of its overall score. In other words, a school could theoretically admit every single student who applies and still score a 98.75 percent overall in *U.S. News*. (The portion determined by incoming students' SAT and ACT scores is more substantial, at over 8 percent.)

So why does the race for the ever more infinitesimal acceptance rate go on? Partly because extreme selectivity boosts the aforementioned bond ratings and conveys prestige in news stories, alumni reports, and other realms beyond the rankings. And partly, Beseda says, because the popular misperception about the rates' importance is self-perpetuating. Plus, both public and private colleges have grown more financially dependent on undergraduate tuition, driving them to recruit more "full pay" students who don't need aid and more out-of-state and international students who pay higher rates. "So both reputation and revenue really come down to who's in your entering class," says Beseda. "Those are the realities that have created this pressure, and educators haven't kept their wits about them."

So college officials, like young college applicants, seem to be sweating under some artificially created pressures. Yet as long as everyone else is doing it, it's scary to break away. Beseda hopes that by doing things his own way at Willamette, he can say, "There's nothing to be afraid of."

Reclaiming Success

The rest of us must not wait around who knows how long for more colleges to see the light. There is a lot we can do now. And most of it comes down to facing *our own* fears.

We need to remind ourselves, our students, and our children, as often as necessary, that education is not a badge to be worn. It is a deep and personal journey whose conclusion you cannot foresee, and the substance of that journey is far more important than the brand name in which it's packaged. Besides, it doesn't actually make *that* much difference where you go to college. Plenty of Yale students feel adrift and get little out of their time in New Haven; plenty of community college students are able to explore and grow along the way to their diplomas. The 2013 Chegg Student Skill Index, a survey of college students and hiring managers across the country, found that while 45 percent of students believed a degree from a prestigious college is "very" or "extremely" important to make them attractive to employers, only 28 percent of hiring managers thought so. The hirers cared far more about leadership.

So cast aside the rankings, the kid-to-kid comparisons, and the false gods of prestige. The greatest myth of all is that only a tiny handful of colleges are worth attending. And once you stop believing that, you can also stop believing that you have to kill yourself to get there—because the vast majority of schools out there truly want a diverse set of students, including interesting kids with Bs and Cs. Instead of competing for the same standard résumé builders as everyone else, focus on cultivating your own skills and passions. "Stop asking the question 'What do I have to do to get into <u>blank</u>?'" college counselor Eva Dodds advises. "Start asking: 'Where can I learn about <u>blank</u> and what will it prepare me to do?'"

Also frequently forgotten in the midst of the madness is that most students have to contend with practical questions, too. Outside of a very small, affluent minority of college-bound students, most future freshmen have to consider not only their own aspirations or passions but also family economics and geography. For them, a simplistic fixation on finding the "right" or "best" college obscures the more nuanced reality: that the "best" college may be, after all, the school that offers the biggest financial aid package or is close enough to home for them to help their family.

Sometimes, the answer to Dodds's question "Where can I learn about blank?" isn't even college. Abigail Baird, the Vassar professor, chuckles as she describes how she horrified her mother at Thanksgiving dinner by insisting that she didn't know if her six-year-old twins would go to college. "They're six!" she exclaims. "I don't know if they're going to go to college because I don't know what they're going to want to do." They might end up like Skylar Bird, who apprenticed himself to a local chef and opened his own restaurant in Buckingham, Pennsylvania, while still a teen. Or like the growing tribe of young college opt-outs working in tech in San Francisco.

There are important steps that each of us who plays a role in the college admissions race can take to escape. Here is where I urge you to begin:

Students, you can help yourselves by casting off convention and choosing learning over maximal prestige. Take advanced classes and join extracurriculars if they interest you, not because you think you should. Limit the number of times you take the SAT and ACT—or even opt out entirely, taking inspiration from Seattle high schooler Sylvie Baldwin, who refused to take the test because she didn't want to be boiled down to a number. Sylvie planned to apply to test-optional colleges as well as those that require scores, explaining her test choice in her applications. With the fifty-plus hours that Sylvie would have spent studying for the exams, she decided instead to write proposed state legislation to require drivers' education courses to address the environmental impact of driving.

It's also helpful to consider taking a gap year before enrolling in college to work, travel, or try something totally different; you'll benefit more from the education if you've first had time away from the academic race to reflect on your goals.

And relax: remember that there are hundreds of good colleges for all kinds of students. Consider, for example, the confident, blond-haired boy, clearly a student leader, who captivated the audience at a California *Race to Nowhere* screening by recounting how he'd forgone AP classes to spend

time with his family and then listing the multiple four-year colleges he'd been admitted to with his 2.4 GPA. Alison DeFiore, who grew up in suburban Massachusetts, is working full-time while earning her degree at the Woods College of Advancing Studies, Boston College's night school. She's enjoying the depth of life experience that her classmates bring and looking forward to graduating with minimal debt. And Elle, who, after her epiphany, took no more AP classes at Sacred Heart, enrolled at the University of Vermont. She planned to study psychology so that, as a therapist, she can help young people who struggle as she once did. More than seven million other students each year enroll in community colleges, where they can save substantial sums of money and potentially take more time to discover their interests.

"Just learn for the sake of learning," Elle advises. "Learn about what you're interested in and not what other people are interested in. That's what's really inspired me. . . . I focus on asking questions that are going to help quench my curiosity and things that are really going to help me understand the world better, as opposed to just get an A on the next test."

High schools hold plenty of power to defuse the race, too. And we parents, students, educators, and PTA groups can press them to do so. To displace competition and restore learning as the central aim of high school, they can limit the number of AP classes students may take and stop ranking students by GPA. Schools can encourage students to pursue classes and activities that truly interest them, and to apply only to colleges they genuinely wish to attend. They should also, like colleges, eliminate the GPA boost for AP classes and request to be excluded from the high school rankings. As the ICG schools demonstrate, it's possible for high schools to make dramatic changes and, by communicating their policy to admissions offices, not harm their students' applications at all.

Campus culture counts, too. High schools can ease their atmosphere by avoiding "college days," where students wear attire from the schools they plan to attend. Holding information sessions for parents that reframe college applications around personalized goals, not brand names, as Irvington High has done, can also help to lessen collective anxiety.

When it comes to equity, high schools should invest in more college and career counseling to help level the playing field between students with family resources and those without. San Diego's High Tech High, for example, serves its diverse students by hiring only college counselors who have worked in college admissions and who themselves are the first in their family to earn bachelor's degrees—thus ensuring that the counselors understand what some kids are up against.

And **individual educators** can take a cue from Esther Wojcicki, a legendary journalism teacher at Palo Alto High School. Every year on the day admissions decisions arrive, she makes sure to reassure her worried students with stories about kids who thrived at less fancy colleges. She underscores that acceptance or rejection letters neither seal anyone's fate nor represent their success or failure in life.

Parents, of course, probably hold the heaviest sway of all. Parental pressure can get bad: one Michigan dad made his fifteen-year-old daughter a "bible," a binder titled "Carly's Future" that listed the top-tier schools she should aim for, including his alma mater, Princeton. Eva Dodds routinely sees parents pushing their kids toward prestige and even writing college essays for them (which is perfectly visible to admissions committees). Most of us don't take it that far. But we still unintentionally influence our kids through the worried questions we ask or the kind of praise we bestow—or simply by failing to give our children a different vision of success from the overwhelming one that surrounds them.

If college is the right choice for your child, help her look for schools whose programs and campus activities actually suit her interests. Remind your child that college is what you make of it; the skills and lessons she gains by getting to know professors and engaging in the campus community will benefit her far more than the school name on her diploma.

One western Massachusetts dad named Jonathan Baum, a hedge fund lawyer, says he's seen enough of the fast lane to become "highly skeptical that the traditional path through law and finance bred anything more than the desire for more, a grinding inherent dissatisfaction." He made it a priority to frequently talk to his two kids about the importance of learning broadly and deeply, of meeting some basic standards but then pursuing what you enjoy. When it came time for his son to look at colleges, Jonathan underscored these priorities with a clever trick: he created a spreadsheet listing key qualities about each school, such as its size, its setting (urban or rural), its athletic options, its majors, and campus photos. The only thing he didn't include was the school's name. "To remove the name and prestige or lack thereof, and to really look at a school for what it is," he says, "I think that was the best thing that really happened in my choosing a college." He went to Bard.

What worked in my home was avoiding incessant dinner-table conversation about college applications. I let my kids take the lead in researching and applying to colleges because it was their journey, not mine. Our house was free of magazines that rank colleges, and our kids waited until junior year to take the SAT. The lessened pressure freed up Jamey to pursue what she loved, volunteering in a local veterinary clinic instead of loading up on activities. She searched for a school that would offer what she wanted: individual support, access to professors, and opportunities to learn the way she learns best, through hands-on experience and small-group discussions.

As I drove away at 1 a.m. after moving Jamey into her dorm at Denver University, I felt the pang of setting my second child free. The automated Bluetooth voice in my car kept repeating, like an echo of my heart, "searching for Jamey's phone, searching for Jamey's phone." But I had the comfort of knowing that Jamey was in the right place *for her*, a decision she'd made free from anyone else's expectations or definitions of success. And that she'd spent her precious years in my home building the real knowledge of herself, and the real-life skills, to thrive there.

––––––

Getting free of The Frenzy is fundamentally about defining your own values. Or, as college counselor Reider advises, "Refuse to get rattled. Be comfortable in your own skin. Don't listen to what other people think you should want. Realize that the most important thing about your education is what you put into it. The most important things that happen to you in college are the things that you could not have anticipated. A friend you made. A course you never expected to take. A professor you connected with. An activity. Some lead on life."

And finally, prepare yourself for the possibility that college will not be a life-changing climax after all. It might simply be a blend of fun, frustrating, interesting, and educational—one of many such learning experiences that our lives will hold.

CHAPTER 6

Teaching and Learning:
This Way Up

I T'S TIME to think bigger.

That became clear in the hundreds of *Race to Nowhere* screenings I attended, which at first left me feeling hopeful. In every audience, I found a growing awareness of the ills that undercut our kids' health and learning, the very ills we've identified in this book so far. The despotic grip of homework with questionable benefit. The depersonalizing pursuit of meaningless scores. The college admissions casino game, the padding of résumés, the deprioritizing of personal and family time, the perversion of values. And from that awareness sprang a new set of revolutionaries who refused to let themselves, their families, or their students get swept up in it all.

Still, something seemed missing. Our progress was piecemeal. Finally it dawned on me: we were trying to mend cracks when we needed to rebuild the foundation. All our discussions were based on the assumption that we were stuck with the current model, and we had to work around it. What we needed was a fresh vision of what education could look like if we cast aside outmoded practices and believe in our collective power to change the *system*, not just the symptoms.

So I set out to find schools in the United States that weren't just valiantly fixing the problems with the old model of education—reducing homework, dethroning tests, and defusing competition—but also pioneering something totally different.

What would the ideal school look like? A kind of school that goes deep instead of wide, that capitalizes on children's particular strengths and tends to their weaknesses rather than putting them all through the same paces, and that asks every student to cultivate truly original ideas instead of mere right answers? A school like that would value quality over quantity, encouraging students to persevere through challenging work that actually means something important to them. It would show high- and low-performing students alike that they can accomplish feats of intellect and creativity they never knew they could. It would frame learning as a rich and varied experience, not a transactional equation. Ultimately, a school focused on learning through vigorous, genuine inquiry would grow the kind of inventive thinkers and keen communicators that our children's futures will demand.

Such schools do exist in America. They are not, as you might guess, confined to wealthy enclaves where ample taxpayer contributions fund tiny class sizes and lavish enrichment programs. In fact, the reality is sometimes the reverse. Many schools in the affluent suburbs are constrained to conventional methods and perfectly content to remain that way, delivering their graduates to the doorsteps of Dartmouth and a formulaic life, few questions asked. The pioneers, it turns out, are found in a wide range of communities and include public schools serving diverse populations. These schools are led by teachers and administrators, and supported by communities of parents, who understand that the old ways of education don't work for most kids and that the modern world demands something different. Their methods are driven by the belief that our educational system should modernize its purpose and work to unleash the true potential of every child.

I have spent countless days in these groundbreaking schools, marveling at the excitement on kids' faces, the near-professional quality of their creative work, and the confidence and pride with which they described their learning to me. Every time, I've wished my family lived nearby so that my own kids could go there. And every time, I've asked myself: Why can't every child have an education like this?

———

That is what superintendent Travis Hamby was asking himself when he took the helm of the Trigg County Public Schools in 2010. The entire K-12 district is housed on a single campus in rural Cadiz, Kentucky, three hours southwest of Louisville and more than an hour northwest of Nashville. Cadiz (locals say *KAY-deez*) is a sparse, sleepy place where the whole community comes out to cheer on the high school football team on Friday nights. It has a two-block downtown of brick storefronts, including a salon, a bank, the county courthouse, and a disproportionate number of antique shops. A big draw to town is the annual Country Ham Festival.

Hamby, a chatty former math teacher with a cheerful Kentucky twang, took the job in the midst of a tough time for Trigg County. A car seat factory that employed hundreds of residents had shut down, sending many into unemployment. More than half of the district's two thousand students already qualified for free or reduced-price school lunches based on their families' low incomes; the plant closure only pushed that number higher. And though Trigg students' test scores were good—at one point the district ranked twentieth out of the 170-plus districts in the state—the outcomes for graduates were not. More than 20 percent of the Trigg grads who entered a four-year college were not returning for their second year. Among those who went to a two-year college, the rate of those not returning was nearly 30 percent. For Hamby, the writing was on the wall: the former factories weren't coming back, and his students weren't well prepared to thrive in a new kind of economy. In this new world, he understood, good old reading, writing, and 'rithmetic aren't nearly enough skills to succeed.

Plus, when he peered into classrooms, Hamby saw students sitting inertly and unhappily at their desks, bored and disengaged. As a father of three, Hamby could see in his own home how traditional schooling was extinguishing creativity and passion instead of sparking it. In the early years, all three of his boys were curious, imaginative, and enthusiastic about learning, as most children tend to be. His kindergartener would still come home and immediately open his backpack to show his mom what he'd created that day. But the older two had stopped showing that kind of excitement years ago. Every night in the Hamby home became a homework battle, unraveling the family's cohesion. "I want our school district to continue to tap a child's curiosity, imagination, their creativity," Hamby said. "I want my kids to come home with that enthusiasm every single day, because they've been engaged, because someone's cared about them, because someone's really tried to pull out the greatness that lies within my child."

When I met Hamby in early 2013, he was preparing to make a dramatic change in the way teachers taught in his district. A courageous change, in fact, for someone working within a system that still prizes conformity. He knew he'd have to take a hundred risks to create the kind of inspiring education that he wanted for his own children—but he was ready. "We've got to do something different for the sake of our kids," he said to me. "The greater risk is that we do nothing."

The Greatness Within

Hamby was entirely right. We are the inheritors of an outmoded education system, designed for an age when most decent students could anticipate a lifetime of reliable industrial or agricultural work. The world that today's graduates enter is entirely different, demanding not regimentation but invention. To thrive in the modern (and unknown future) economy, where work is increasingly creative and service-oriented, today's students need to develop the kinds of adaptive skills that can make them successful in any role. Besides, the old ways have *always* confined kids to narrow modes of learning and narrow opportunities to find success. There's no evidence that that traditional model was great for our generation, either.

The technological revolution in the world economy has, at last, focused public attention on this problem. "What was considered a good education 50 years ago is no longer enough for success in college, career, and citizenship in the 21st century," wrote the National Education Association, the country's largest teachers union, in 2012. "The new social contract is different: only people who have the knowledge and skills to negotiate constant change and reinvent themselves for new situations will succeed."

You'll find all kinds of different names for these evergreen skills. A group of leaders in education, business, and government joined together in 2002 to define them as "twenty-first-century skills" and work to position them at the center of American education. The partnership included executives from Apple, Cisco, the National Education Association, the US Department of Education, and more. They interviewed leaders across diverse industries and found broad consensus on the most crucial skills. And they summed up these core aptitudes as the Four C's: critical thinking, collaboration, communication, and creativity. Tony Wagner, an educator at Harvard University's Innovation Lab and author of *The Global Achievement Gap*, then traveled the world conducting interviews and expanded and adapted the list to seven:

- critical thinking and problem solving

- collaboration and leadership

- agility and adaptability

- initiative and entrepreneurialism

- effective oral and written communication

- accessing and analyzing information

- curiosity and imagination

"Literally, from Taiwan to Singapore to Thailand to Bahrain to Finland, Spain, England, from West Point to Wall Street," Wagner told me, "I've seen total agreement about the importance of these skills."

However you count them, it's evident that these kinds of creative and collaborative abilities—and the vibrant learning experiences that foster them—are what people have always needed to succeed. They form the foundation of an engaging life. Yet when the American Management Association in 2012 surveyed hundreds of managers, directors, and executives across a wide range of public and private industries, more than half said their workers needed to improve on the Four C's. The bosses called their workers' competency average, at best. Three out of four predicted these skills would become even more important in the near future. "In the world of business, you see a premium on novelty, nuance, customization, experimentation," says Daniel Pink, author of *Drive* and *A Whole New Mind*. "In our schools, we see a premium on routines, right answers, and standardization. That ought to alarm us very deeply."

Our schools, steeped in tenacious traditions, have been far too slow to adapt. Walk into a classroom today, and it's likely to look pretty much the same as when Hamby was a student himself in Hopkins County, Kentucky, in the 1980s. He earned good grades but never felt especially challenged or engaged, and he's frustrated that so little has changed. "Students are still primarily sitting in rows," he observed. "They are primarily listening to a teacher, for much of their day, talk. There's a lot of rote types of learning still going on."

One study published in the journal *Science* states the problem in hard numbers:

Researchers observed elementary classrooms across four hundred US school districts and found that fifth graders spent more than 90 percent of their school day in their seats, either listening to the teacher instruct the whole class or doing seat work on their own. They spent a negligible amount of time learning in small groups, and received five times more instruction on basic skills than on problem solving or reasoning. No ten-year-old is going to be inspired to creative leaps by this kind of system.

No one I know—not Hamby, or Pink, or Wagner, or me, or any of the hundreds of folks I've interviewed—blames teachers alone for this stagnation. It's natural to teach the way one was taught. Besides, the education system itself is inflexible. Teachers are tethered to a heavy bureaucracy, stacked up all the way from the principal's office to the halls of Congress, which insists they cover more material each year than is humanly possible. Then it tests their students on this, and publicly praises or shames their schools on the results. Teachers of English, for example, "are often asked to teach 120 or more students a day a simplistic formula style of writing that will enable the students to pass standardized tests," writes Wagner, a former teacher and school principal himself. "And they have very little time to do anything more." Even the new national Common Core standards, much touted for reducing the number of required bullet points and emphasizing skills along with facts, may prove too wide, too tested, or too standardized to fix the problem.

As educator, author, and speaker Ken Robinson points out, this stifling paradigm has even infiltrated our language, in which educators widely describe teaching lessons as " 'delivering the curriculum,' like dropping it off

like FedEx," he says. Instead, learning should be seen as an active process, a form of growth fueled by experience. This is true for learners of all ages. A 2014 study at the Universities of Washington and Maine compared undergraduate college courses in science, technology, engineering, and math that were taught through traditional lectures or through more participatory learning. In an analysis of more than two hundred studies on the subject, the researchers found that students in active-learning classes scored higher on exams. Students receiving lectures, in contrast, were one and a half times more likely to fail the class. To break those unhelpful old traditions, Robinson suggests excising the word *delivery* from our educational vocabulary entirely.

To be sure, students still need some basic knowledge: strong literacy, numeracy, and an essential understanding of our social and scientific world. But the great realm of granular information is now available at their fingertips, through technology. What they will need to succeed as adults in this century is not piles of information in isolation, but rather practice in how to use it well. They need to understand how to access information and apply it to new situations, and how to be good citizens of an interconnected global world (essential life skills that are, in truth, long neglected but not really new). The continued fixation on informational knowledge to the exclusion of genuinely meaningful experiences produces disengagement and narrow thinking, even among star students.

"I'm a straight-A student, but I think a lot of my As in the past have been because I did my homework. I don't think I retained all the information," says Alexandra Carr, a poised and confident recent graduate of Trigg. "A lot of teachers would be surprised to know how bored I was in their classes sometimes." What actually prepared her for her mechanical engineering studies at the University of Kentucky, Alexandra says, was a hands-on high school engineering class where teams of students created their own original product and built it, setting their own deadlines, over the course of a year. (Alexandra's group made an award-winning safety latch for a cattle gate.) Outside of that, she said, her traditional high school classes gave her no major challenges that students had to solve without hand-holding by teachers, "and that's a huge part of what college is."

What pains me most as a parent is how much raw talent and passion we are losing in our devotion to such limited—and limiting—modes of learning. The students who drop out, or who spend their school years feeling bored or unsuccessful, or who simply never realize there are broader ways to think than the tests demand: theirs are bright minds squandered. The same is true for straight-A students like Alexandra, whose other talents languish in a system stuck on right answers. There are inventors, artists, craftsmen, and entrepreneurs among them. Some will eventually find their way despite their schooling, and some, discouraged and disillusioned, will not. "Typically what you see in schools is a preoccupation with a certain conception of intelligence," Robinson observes. "It's a capacity for a certain type of propositional knowledge, a certain type of deductive reasoning. It's very important, but there's much more to human consciousness than that."

As this generation of children grows up in a world grappling with a booming population, a changing climate, a widening income gap, and an ever-evolving technological revolution, the stakes are too high to cast the whole universe of indispensable other human capacities aside. The stakes are too high for even a single schoolchild, one whose experience might help her discover the power of her own imagination or, conversely, determine early on that she's a dud with little to contribute. Says Robinson:

> *If you incarcerate kids for eight hours a day, if you give teachers no creative freedom, if you treat them like data points or points on an assembly line, don't be surprised if they don't enjoy it very much. You wouldn't either. . . . If we start to treat students as human beings and schools as living centers of imagination and creativity, then you get a completely different result.*

In Students We Trust

When Hamby looked around the Trigg County schools in his first years there, they didn't look anything like "living centers of imagination and creativity." So he and a handful of other administrators and teachers went looking for more innovative models.

The Trigg team's quest ultimately led them to an inspiring, innovative charter school half a country away in California. High Tech High occupies a sprawling campus of old US Navy training buildings near the San Diego airport. What started as a single high school of two hundred students in the year 2000 has been so successful that it's grown to a network of twelve schools spanning grades K-12 and serving five thousand students. Co-founders Larry Rosenstock and Rob Riordan opened High Tech High with one primary mission: to improve equity in education. So the school has no tracking system and groups students in mixed-ability classrooms. The teaching here is based on the philosophy that students (actually, all people) learn best by working collaboratively on real-world projects with impact beyond the classroom, coached but not spoon-fed by mentors who know them well.

When you walk into the original high school, you see students working together in clusters, both in classrooms and around couches and tables in the wide halls. The warehouselike space is filled with light from skylights. The walls between classrooms are actually windows, creating a feeling of openness and fluidity (there's nothing strange about collaborating widely when you can literally see one another). And as in the real world, the disciplines here blend: social studies is not separate from English, nor English from science, nor science from math. The atmosphere conveys something akin to a thriving office: calm but not quiet, focused but not constrained. There are no textbooks or bells. Kids are working mostly under their own direction, with guidance when they need it. No one is riding or haranguing them. If they need to go to the bathroom, they go, like adults do, no need to ask permission. And by and large, given genuine responsibility for their time and an engaging purpose, the teens put it to good use.

Some of the projects that students here have produced will defy the imagination of almost anyone who's spent most of his or her time in traditional schools (which is almost everyone). A biotechnology class worked with the Port of San Diego and the San Diego Zoo to research, write, design, illustrate, and publish an absolutely professional guidebook to biomimicry and sustainability around the San Diego Bay. Following the massacre at Sandy Hook Elementary and the shooting deaths of two boys in San Diego, eleventh graders ran a successful Kickstarter campaign to produce a documentary film on the causes of gun violence in America and what young people can do about it. And, on a day when the Trigg team and I visited, a ninth grade class showed us a visual and intellectual gem: Apocalypto, a huge, beautiful wooden diorama, suspended on the wall, combining mechanical gears, artistic carvings, and the principles of physics to visually represent the social, environmental, and political reasons for the cyclic rise and fall of civilizations.

So, rather than generating formulaic assignments (what Ken Robinson calls "low-grade clerical work") or writing research papers only ever to be seen by their teacher, these kids are asking original questions and producing projects that mean something to the world. They present and defend their work to classmates, teachers, parents, and community members at periodic exhibition nights. Knowing their work will face a real audience, students feel motivated to do their best. If their product isn't polished enough, a teacher coaches them to revise it until it is. Students still learn lots of content, but they acquire it as needed while they're passionately pursuing important projects. The ultimate assessment of their learning is the quality of their work itself.

"We have found that the more we trust young people," says cofounder and CEO Larry Rosenstock, "the more trustworthy they become."

What most struck Hamby on his early visits to High Tech High was the students' confidence in explaining their work to adults. When they showed Apocalypto to the Trigg team and me, a self-assured freshman named Sharon explained, "In humanities, we started out by studying ancient civilizations and how they rise and fall, and every individual group created a theory. And then in physics, we had to take our theories and create a mechanical representation." A boy in her work group continued, describing how his group's theory hinged on five different states: "The first one is trust, which was represented by this cam, which slowly declines over time, and the last one is rebellion, and we represented this with civil unrest, which slowly rises over time." We had to work to keep our jaws from dropping.

"It was evident through that conversation that there was a really deep level of learning that had occurred, which was in every conversation," Hamby said. There was no " 'Okay, I've taken a test, and now I can forget it,' " he observed. "It meant something to them."

Visitors to High Tech High tend to assume that these are exceptional students enjoying the benefits of a school with deep pockets, but that's not true. Admission is by random lottery. More than one in three students qualify for free or reduced-price lunch. Moneywise, nearly all of the schools' operational funding comes from California's per-pupil allocation, the same budget given to every public school in the state. Much of the dazzling work the school achieves is facilitated by collaborations with local businesses and organizations, and by the passion of a faculty that is, unlike teachers in so many schools, given true freedom to teach. The outcome: 98 percent of graduates of all the High Tech schools go to college, and 86 percent graduate from college (compared to a national rate of just 59 percent). About one in three High Tech grads are the first in their families to go to college.

"You walk away from visiting this high school and you think, why can't we do this?" Hamby said out loud after one trip there. "Why can't a public school in western Kentucky do this for our kids?"

Learning by Doing

What's happening at High Tech High is called project-based learning (or problem-based learning), and it's not really new—it's based on the sort of educational inquiry pioneered by Socrates. It is, fundamentally, *learning by doing*, and doing so with provocative questions and appropriate supports in place. Project-based learning is only one model of personalized, inquiry-based learning; there are many. But it's the one I'll focus on here because it's well established and documented, and because it's what I've seen practiced most clearly.

"Imagine if we taught baseball the way that we teach science," says UC Berkeley psychologist Alison Gopnik. "We would tell kids about baseball in the first couple of years. By the time they got to be in junior high, maybe we'd give them a drill where they could throw the ball to second base, over and over and over again. In college, they'd get to reproduce great, famous baseball plays, and then they'd never actually get to play the game until they were in graduate school." High-quality project-based learning is, essentially, playing ball.

There are also some important things that project-based learning is *not*: It's not total unstructured anarchy. Nor is it a recipe with an expected outcome. It is, significantly, not the shoebox diorama or poster-board "project" or canned science experiment that you and I probably did in school. Daniel

Pink calls these sorts of assignments "terrarium problems," self-contained and clearly defined and thus wholly unlike the real world.

Another thing innovation in learning is not: technology for its own sake. Digital technology is a tremendous tool, and one that kids need ample guidance and practice to use well. But it's not a panacea, and it doesn't replace the human relationship in education. (Don't let High Tech High's name fool you: technology enables some of the work kids do there, but the machines themselves are not the point.) I've seen students use computers to create captivating videos and conduct complex data research, and I've seen rooms full of students staring at screens doing math practice problems in a kind of robotic test prep. Like any tool, digital technology can be used for exciting invention or mind-numbing monotony—in other words, for good or ill. As Hamby said to me once, voicing lessons learned firsthand, "Technology plays a critical role in supporting twenty-first-century learning, but you can have twenty-first-century learning in the absence of a lot of technology. . . . Don't mistake that we're doing something great just by giving everybody an iPad."

Inquiry-based education is tricky to study scientifically because it's so complex. There are countless different ways to do it, plus different teachers, students, and settings, so it's hard to compare apples to apples. On the whole, though, the research shows that an inquiry approach doesn't hurt test scores, and sometimes it helps. More importantly, it reveals that test scores are not at all the point. Students learning this way build skills that are not easily tested on Scantrons—problem solving and self-reliance among them. And studies show that they have higher attendance and more excitement about learning, which naturally helps them learn better.

One study of five thousand Detroit middle schoolers in low-income communities found that those learning science through a well-developed inquiry curriculum scored higher on a standardized exam than those learning science the traditional way. A US Department of Education study tested more than four thousand high school students in Arizona and California learning economics through project-based or traditional modes. The project-based group edged out their peers on a test of economic literacy, and substantially outperformed them on problem-solving skills and application to real-world economic dilemmas. Other studies have found similar impacts in elementary school. In other words, if the projects are well designed (and that's an important *if*), students studying through inquiry still learn the facts, and they also learn essential skills for life and work beyond the classroom.

Fundamentally, this sort of learning springs from the belief that children flourish when we support them in asking open-ended questions and solving problems for themselves. Thus, they cultivate their creativity, which Ken Robinson defines as "the process of having original ideas that have value." "The argument for creativity in education is all-encompassing," says Robinson, who contends that it's just as important in science, math, and language as in art. "It's not some exotic addendum that we can squeeze in on a Friday afternoon when all the serious work's finished. It's about the whole character of education."

Trigg's First Try

Hamby and the Trigg team took what they'd seen in San Diego back to Cadiz and decided to try it. In preparation, a handful of administrators and teachers attended more trainings at High Tech High (which runs its own graduate school of education and provides professional development to teachers from around the world) and at the University of Kentucky. They visited model schools in Kentucky and Ohio, including Danville, Kentucky, where students were already blossoming in the district's first year of using performance assessments. Crucially, the school board supported them. The district formed a committee of twenty people to guide the change, including three high school students—youth input that Hamby considers essential. For the new approach to take root, it couldn't be a mandate issued from above; it had to become a part of the school culture at every level.

The change makers set the Four C's as their goals. And they braced for mistakes. "It's like jumping into the pool," said Hamby. "We're going to take a risk."

To stave off community skepticism, the high school held a meeting in the school theater before the semester started, where Principal Shannon Burcham gave a packed house of freshman students and parents this message: "We're trying to provide you with opportunities that maybe your brothers or your sisters or your mothers or fathers didn't have. We want you to start connecting school to your life and to the passions you have."

Trigg started small, in fall 2013, with just the teachers who were game to try something different, in grades five, eight, and nine. This is just what High Tech High's Rosenstock recommends: "You're going to have some horses at the gate who are ready to move, and you know who they are," he says. "Get those people running, and give them as much freedom to run as possible."

The school reworked its class schedule to give ninth graders a longer block of time for projects. The ninth graders, many of them just a year away from earning their driver's licenses, began with a project on distracted driving. Working in small groups, they were to use math to research local and national safety statistics, and then use language arts to create an awareness ad campaign for their community. The teachers started the students out with some direct instruction and then remained as guides to help them along the way. Meanwhile, the fifth graders followed a similar process to investigate why birds were congregating and nesting on campus and how to kindly encourage them to live elsewhere.

I visited that October to see how the experiment was going. In Amy Breckel's freshman class I met Summer, one of the students on the district's change committee. She was a broody teen with a bubbly voice, a puff of dark brown hair, and bright blue-green eyes. Summer didn't like the new kind of learning at first, and she wasn't shy about saying so. "The teachers pushed you," she said. "I didn't want to be pushed. So I really didn't like them." Plus, she resented being assigned to work with classmates she didn't know well.

Breckel affirmed that the experiment started shakily. When she suddenly gave kids more independence to direct their own learning, perhaps for the first time in their school careers, many of them didn't know what to do with it. "When you give them that kind of freedom, wanting them to be creative and come up with solutions to problems, they look at you like, 'Where's my rubric? Where's my step-by-step process of how I do this? How many points is this? How long does it have to be?'" Breckel said. And opening up the classroom to unscripted discussion and questions, "The first day I did that it was like crickets chirping in my room." Some of her typical "good students" struggled with the new methods.

What turned Summer's views around was the close connection she began to forge with her teachers. When the Trigg team had visited High Tech High, they saw that strong relationships were central to the school's success. The ninth grade teachers they observed there work in teams of two, one covering humanities and one covering science, and keep the same group of students most of the day. Plus, each adult in the building serves as an adviser to ten students, meeting weekly and sticking with the same kids for all four years. "What makes problem-based learning work for them is they have a system in place where they can make every kid successful in that environment," Breckel noted. "If a kid is falling, they have somebody there to catch them, to find out what's going wrong."

Each Trigg teacher had a much larger caseload of students rotating through her classroom, but even so, they had started to see deepening relationships that fall. Rather than weaving projects into the core academic classes, the high school had placed them in a separate class called Fusion, designed to draw on all the other disciplines. Over the first month of Fusion, the teachers came to know Summer better than they had before. They discovered that while Summer had been on the honor roll in sixth and seventh grades and intended to be the first in her family to go to college, she'd hit a major obstacle in eighth grade. The Saturday after Christmas that year (she remembers the day), Social Services had taken her away from her mom, split up her siblings, and sent her to live with her dad, with whom she had very little connection. Her grades crashed.

"I felt like the world was going to end," Summer told me of her eighth grade year. "I didn't take school seriously. It was boring, and I stopped caring." As teachers lectured at her and assigned what seemed like busywork, she felt she had no control over her world, neither at home nor at school.

When I visited her ninth grade class in October 2013, though, I saw what a difference a new year—and a new teaching model—had made. Summer and her project partner were busily designing a billboard to read, *If you want to survive, don't text and drive.* She was engaged and excited to make a good product. Other kids in the class, too, seemed far more alive than the glassy-eyed bunch that Breckel had sometimes seen before. As the students worked in small groups, the teachers could circulate the room and assist them one-on-one. That's what Summer says allowed her to bond with them, to feel cared for, and to reconnect with school. "School is way better this year," she said. "It's not all just sitting in the classroom listening to the teacher and doing worksheets. It's you having a voice with your fellow peers."

In early November, all the freshmen presented their work at Trigg's first-ever exhibition night. Parents, community members, and fellow students poured into the high school's halls and classrooms. They watched fourteen-year-olds, dressed in their Sunday best, describe what they'd created and why. The visitors pressed the kids with questions. The kids, bubbling with a mixture of nerves and pride, answered from the expertise they'd gained.

To be fair, the product of Trigg's first foray into a more vibrant kind of learning wasn't perfect. But it was a beginning. The teachers had struggled to let go of their typical direct instruction, ingrained over so many years, and spent too much time trying to deliver to kids everything they'd need to know before they started. Summer and her project partner had nearly come to blows over disagreements about how the product should look and how equitably the work was being shared. Many others had run into trouble just finding enough time in class to work together on such a complex endeavor. In a single semester Trigg hadn't matched the sophisticated work they'd seen at High Tech High, but neither Hamby nor anyone else expected them to.

What they *had* done was given kids a taste of a new kind of school. The experience showed Summer how reliant she and her classmates had previously been on their teachers, and she wanted more. "It's extra work, yes, but it's good work. It makes you want to try harder," she said to me. "I want the teachers to teach more interactively, not just standing in front of the room and telling you that you have to do this and this. I want it to be us coming up with the answers, and I want it to be us finding good and new ideas to put forward."

Learning Is a Process

Stanford University professor and IDEO founder David Kelley says people often ask him if today's college students are creative. At first blush, he responds, you could say they're not. But in reality, "They're wildly creative, just like they were in kindergarten. It's just been blocked. And our job is to figure out how to take those blocks away."

Fortunately, there are many variations on richer, more exploratory kinds of learning going on around the country. In the Reggio Emilia approach, for example, young children lead their own learning, with parents and teachers as collaborators, and cultivate thinking and creativity through art. The Big Picture schools, a network of more than fifty in the United States, provide teens a customized curriculum based on each student's interests and goals and reinforced by real-world internships. And, inspired by innovation hubs like IDEO, a growing number of classrooms are integrating Design Thinking—a collaborative problem solving method where student teams design products and solutions with a real-world user in mind.

Whichever kind of innovation you might try, key principles apply. Wherever I've seen schools improving students' experience, I've found that learning is:

- led by the student, with support, rather than spoon-fed by the teacher

- guided by a teacher who has the autonomy and trust of her supervisors to make critical decisions about each child's education

- personalized to tap the strengths and interests, and to address the needs, of individual students

- geared toward depth of understanding, not breadth of information

- blended across disciplines, allowing for the natural overlapping of science, math, language, history, art, technology, and other subjects

- purposeful and meaningful to students beyond the goal of a mere grade, a kind of purpose that typically derives from a connection to the real world

- strengthened by collaboration: among students, among teachers, between students and teachers, and between schools and the community

- free from the arbitrary confines of traditional school schedules

- equitable for all students, providing an appropriate challenge for each one without segregating (or "tracking") them by ability

One of the key lessons that the Trigg team took from High Tech High—and something that conventional education frequently forgets—is that deep learning is as much about the *process* as it is about the product. Ron Berger, a teacher in rural Massachusetts for forty years and chief academic officer of the nationwide network of inquiry-based Expeditionary Learning schools, explains this aptly.

"When I was in school," Berger says, "we were on a treadmill of turning in final-draft work every day, every assignment. We were given an assignment, we filled it out, we turned it in. We were given an assignment, we filled it out, we turned it in." When the assignments came back, graded, kids typically threw them away. The work didn't mean much. Though Berger attended what were considered to be good public schools, he says, "Nothing I did in the thirteen years I was in school is something that I still own today and would show you as an example of beautiful work."

The work students do at the 160-plus Expeditionary Learning schools (and High Tech High, among others) is quite a contrast. There, the first assignment that a child hands in is only a starting point. The students' work, often conducted over the course of weeks, is to reconsider, revise, solicit feedback, and improve what they've done—much like I do when polishing rough cuts of a film, or editing drafts of this book. The teachers' job is to provide the resources and supports that individual students need and to show them how much more they can actually achieve. Children learn to give one another rigorous, constructive critiques—and to take them. They might make half a dozen drafts or more. The final product, as Berger has seen over and over again, is a work of "extraordinary quality, something of beauty and value for their community and for themselves."

Why go through this laborious process instead of just churning through worksheets? Because it's more meaningful and motivating for everyone, adults included, and because human beings learn so much better this way. Since school is an experience that shapes a child's identity, a process like this can even shape how she learns and works for life. "High-quality work is transformational for kids," Berger says. "When a student does a piece of work that's way better than he or she thought they could do, they're never the same person again. It changes their sense of who they are and what they're capable of." Simply put, it's the growth mindset set in motion.

Psychologists support Berger's observation. "Piaget, the father of child development, was super clear: people learn from their own experience," says Vassar College neuropsychology professor Abigail Baird. "Think about the stuff you know really well. You know it from trial and error, from your own experience, not from being told."

When implemented well, this approach allows all kinds of students to find success. One boy had grown frustrated with the repetitive lessons in elementary and middle school. He felt apathetic. He didn't shine. Then, in ninth grade at High Tech High, he undertook a project on the history of rock music posters. Preparing for his presentation, he researched the history of twentieth-century America, found the connections between the music and the culture, read books, and regaled his family with all he learned. "It was the first time where he did something of that magnitude all by himself, and the outcome was just gorgeous," said his mom. "That is the project he looks back on and says, 'Wow, if I've done this, I can do whatever the next challenge is.' . . . He discovered his capabilities in a way that he hadn't before."

Berger, who works as a carpenter outside of class, offers further examples of what happens when you turn schoolwork into an act of craftsmanship. His own classroom is constructed like a workshop, with movable project tables instead of desks. There, seventh graders once collaborated with a local college laboratory to collect samples and test the town's homes for radon gas. Students prepared surveys, kits, and information packets for residents, learned to use Microsoft Excel to analyze their results, responded to press inquiries, and made a final report to the town government. The state and federal radon commissions ultimately requested copies of the students' report. And in Portland, Maine, Berger recounted to me, King Middle School students studied the civil rights movement by finding local residents who'd been active, but unsung, participants in that history. The children interviewed these people and told their stories in a four-volume book, *Small Acts of Courage*, which they presented at a public ceremony alongside their interviewees.

If the Portland students had been told to study the civil rights movement for a test, some would have done so and some would not. Most wouldn't have remembered many of the details for long. This way, though, Berger noted, "They all studied it deeply because they knew that pretty soon they would be going out and meeting with a person whose story was never told by anyone, and they would be interviewing that person, an unsung hero, and it would be their job as a journalist and an historian to really tell their story in a way that would honor them." As he wrote in his book *An Ethic of Excellence*, "As every teacher knows, you can mandate tests and standards and curricula all you want, but it means nothing if you can't inspire kids to care."

Starting Small

Let me pause for a moment to acknowledge that the prospect of wholesale, whole-school change might look a little daunting to many communities. The Herculean effort and humility required of the change makers in Trigg County is evidence of the challenge. Yet there are many examples of communities that have made an impact with more bite-size (which is not to say *easy*) reforms.

David Ackerman, principal of Oak Knoll Elementary School in Menlo Park (whom we met in chapter 3), has made bold moves to reduce homework. He's also taken some unusual steps to deepen teachers' relationships with their students and provide more personalized attention.

In 2008, having pulled off his homework revolution with relatively few scars, Ackerman decided to try looping—keeping children with the same teacher for more than one year. Without looping, he explains, school ends each spring "and everything you've learned about that kid . . . it doesn't pass easily to the next teacher. The new teacher spends the entire month of September figuring out who the students are as learners and how to approach them. That seems so inefficient." Moreover, when teachers keep the same students for longer, he says, "The accountability for their progress is much deeper."

Ackerman pointed out to me that looping should hardly be considered revolutionary. The practice is at least a hundred years old and is commonly used in Europe. However, he took the change a step further by combining it with two more innovations: multiage classrooms and team teaching. In his new program, children in kindergarten through second grade would share the same classroom, and they'd stay with the same group of peers for all three years. Their kindergarten, first, and second grade teachers would teach the whole group together. This one-room-schoolhouse kind of setting would help students learn at their own pace. An advanced kindergartener could read with second graders, or a struggling first grader could pair up with a younger reader. (Some experts advocate for looping or multiage approaches in middle and high school, too.)

For an administrator like Ackerman, making the change wasn't so complex. He was a seasoned principal with a solid track record, so he simply decided to do it. But he also employed some wise strategies to help his innovation work well. First, he gave teachers a choice, starting his reform only with those who were enthused about it. Second, he presented scientific research to parents and staff showing how looping helps. Third (and most uncommonly), he gave *parents* a choice. They could pick whether their child would be in the multiage, looped class or a traditional class.

When I saw Ackerman several years later, he told me the program had grown so popular that it had twice as many applicants as spots, and the school had to hold a lottery to determine who got in. Plus, Oak Knoll had added a second multiage program for grades three through five. All told, 260 of the school's 760 students were in a multiage, looped group. And Ackerman had instituted regular looping (staying with the same teacher for two years, though not combining multiple ages in one classroom) for the rest of the school in grades four and five. Starting innovations as opt-ins "is a way to get what you want," Ackerman told me. "Give people the choice, and if they're skeptical then prove it to them."

At Monument Mountain Regional High School in Great Barrington, Massachusetts, an innovative solution for student engagement came from the most important (and obvious) source: a student. In his junior year, Sam Levin was growing frustrated with what he saw around him. "I felt my friends weren't engaged, that they weren't learning, that they weren't happy," he recalled. His mom issued him a challenge: to start his own school.

Sam thought about this, and realized he'd seen the same classmates who fell asleep in class and begrudged homework get up at six a.m. on a Saturday to tend to the school's student garden. They earned no grades or extra credit for this work. But students themselves had created the garden, so they cared about it. Sam proposed to school leaders that they bring that level of passion and ownership to the classroom by creating a school-within-a-school led by the students themselves. Principal Marianne Young, who recognized the same problems with traditional methods that Sam did, went for it.

The high school's Independent Project is now in its fifth year. Students who choose to participate spend an entire semester in a class with no periods or bells. Instead of following a prescribed curriculum, students come up with their most burning questions in English, history, science, and math and spend their mornings researching them and presenting their findings to classmates. They discuss, debate, and offer one another critical feedback. A teacher is there to guide, support, and challenge them. In the afternoon, students work on a semester-long project of their own design. One boy composed his own portfolio of musical pieces. A group of students collaboratively filmed and edited an original documentary. A girl who had previously pushed herself to a near breaking point to earn top grades studied photography and produced a book of images illustrating human connection.

Matt Whalan, who was diagnosed with ADHD and had long hated school but loved creative writing, wrote his own short novel. Before the Independent Project, Matt would write for hours every day after class, but "most of that work went unrecognized by anyone at school," he said. Besides giving him the opportunity to apply his passion in school, Matt says the experience helped him focus and taught him to see "what was important to me . . . and the ways in which I can be important in the world."

Some teachers and parents worried at first that the program's unconventional model would harm students' college applications. But so far, participating has only served to distinguish them. Matt, for one, enrolled at Marlboro College with a generous merit scholarship. Since the Independent Project started, schools across the country have approached Principal Young for guidance in creating their own.

Successes and Setbacks at Trigg

I keep going back to Cadiz, though, because I feel so compelled by the courage of their efforts—the sweeping scale of the change they're seeking and

the persistence they're applying to it, despite obstacles. Change takes time. As Trigg expands its reforms, piece by piece—it extended projects to more grade levels and added performance assessments in its second year—it continues to straddle two systems. The educators are pursuing inquiry-based learning on the one hand, while still having to serve the master of standardized testing on the other hand. Teachers don't yet have the time built into the day for the collaboration and planning that complex projects require. And the state, like many others, still credits the school based on the old metric of "seat time" (literally the number of hours students have spent in each subject, not what they've learned). Trigg could choose to switch to a competency-based credit system, but then it would lose funding for every student who fails the competency assessment.

Still, Trigg soldiers on. By year two, in the fall of 2014, the tenth graders were now doing project-based learning, too, working on a cross-disciplinary assignment to solve a water-quality problem at Land Between the Lakes, a forested National Recreation Area straddling the Kentucky-Tennessee border nearby. The students had visited the park, where each small group had chosen its own problem to tackle: some investigated how to combat invasive mussel or lotus species, others how to tame algal blooms from agricultural runoff.

This was a much meatier, more effective project than the year before, where the effort looked at times like an arts and crafts exercise, with final products that didn't reflect all the research students had done. One exceptional group of three students, Autumn, Kaylin, and Brayden, had decided to address beaver dams that were flooding a road in the park, where cars contaminated the water that then flowed back into the watershed from which residents drink. "We visited there and we saw that this was a huge problem, and so we immediately said, 'How are we going to fix this?'" explained Autumn, her round face framed by brown hair spooled into a wide bun. The three teens described, with obvious depth of knowledge, how they'd interviewed park staff about previous failed solutions, tested water samples for contaminants, and considered local laws. They'd divided the labor according to each kid's strengths: Autumn writing, Kaylin designing, Brayden building. Their solution: beaver pipes, the ends covered with metal mesh to prevent beavers climbing in, set up to drain water quickly from the road back into the waterways. The group said Land Between the Lakes staff liked their idea and might implement it.

That was the high point of my visit. Low points were in evidence, too. It felt a bit scary, as a parent, to see the semichaos of students who weren't yet used to this method working on their own with only occasional guidance. I could tell that teachers hadn't yet mastered how to guide kids through the iteration process that Ron Berger described. And understandably so: Breckel still had to handle a caseload of nearly 150 students at a time, compared to the High Tech High teaching teams' fifty. Consequently, the teachers themselves were unsatisfied with the quality of some kids' creations. Breckel said, "I had one student say to me, 'Ms. Breckel, this is the most work I've ever done in my whole life, and you're still telling me I need to do more.'"

Summer, for her part, was taking two math classes, playing clarinet a dozen or more hours a week in the marching band, and trying to earn the straight As she felt she'd need for a college scholarship. She said Fusion class this year was "way better" than the year before. They were getting the hang of it. Outside of Fusion, however, most of her classes remained the same as ever.

Hamby would be the first to admit that Trigg still has a long way to go. "We might have a failure or two or three or four in our experiences in implementing this change, but we're going to pick up the pieces," he said. "We're going to figure it out, regroup, and go back to the drawing board, and we're going to implement again."

He, Breckel, and others had visited High Tech High again that fall to get more help (pursuing their own process of iteration and improvement). As Hamby ambled in and out of classrooms there, he exclaimed in frustration about how the trappings of tradition—especially school schedules and physical spaces—constrain innovation. He'd like to literally move walls in Trigg County, to carve out a "makerspace" for group project work in the library. And he's doing it—but it took him eighteen months and an expensive engineering contract to finally get the approval. He's also trying to convince his high school site council to obliterate the traditional bell schedule, which keeps students cycling from one isolated subject area to another (English happens over here, science over there). "Just throw it out the freakin' window," he exclaimed while exiting one High Tech classroom. "I mean, there's no reason." His ideal schedule would give half the freshman class over to four teachers (English, science, social studies, math) and let the teaching team use the day as they see fit. In other words, he would trust teachers—which our educational bureaucracy rarely does.

The Trigg team toured High Tech's elementary school, as well. Inquiry-based learning can fit fairly naturally into the early grades, with simpler projects tailored to children's ages (Montessori and Waldorf methods are, after all, based on inquiry). Honestly, what we saw there didn't look as dramatically different from a regular school as the high school does. The teachers at High Tech Elementary still spend the mornings on direct instruction in reading and math, then turn to projects in the afternoons. But the work was of excellent quality, and the kids weren't afraid to describe their learning.

The day we visited, students in a fourth grade class had just received copies of a book of adventure stories that they wrote. They'd researched their stories by rock climbing, kayaking on a local bay, and hiking up a nearby mountain, while holding bake sales and other fund-raisers to cover the cost. They planned to sell the books at the next exhibition night and donate the proceeds to charity. Hamby asked the children how they felt when they saw their books. "I was yelling," said Andreas, a small boy in a backward cap, excitedly. "And I felt so happy. Like: I'm an author!" Meanwhile, in a nearby room, fifth graders were using Chromebooks to write proposals for the robots they would create.

For all their dazzle, the High Tech schools also have their imperfections. A handful of students each year find that the student-driven format doesn't work well for them, and they leave. Some parents of conventionally "successful" students worry that the hands-on work at High Tech High will derail their kids from the traditional track to college. Yet one mom, an engineer, expressed great gratitude that both her creative, unconventional son and her book-smart daughter got to go there. All schools talk about putting individual children's needs at the center of their work, she said, but this one actually does it. "They are learning to work in a group environment, which is very important," she observed. As in the real world of work, "They're learning to plan, they're learning to scope, and I think they're learning more from their mistakes than they're learning from their successes. . . . It's pretty awesome when a kid at ninth grade experiences this."

Pick Your Metric

Foremost in Hamby's mind that day at High Tech High was one big worry: test scores. His district's scores on state tests (which are not given to ninth graders, one of the classes piloting project-based learning) had dropped slightly the first year of the change. Hamby had a firm faith that deepening students' engagement and understanding through meaningful projects would ultimately translate into better test scores. But he worried his teachers might defect if the marks didn't go back up. "They fear that somebody's going to take out a big stick and beat them over the head if they take this risk," he said. Besides, he told me, the school board has been supportive so far, "but after this year I have three years left on my contract, and then it's one election away for me." If Hamby goes, so, too, could the momentum for change. All the more reason to make a whole set of students and teachers, not only the superintendent, the leaders.

Larry Rosenstock, the High Tech High CEO, answered Hamby's concern by arguing that just because you can measure a thing doesn't mean that it's what matters. He urged the Trigg team to pick a metric that they *do* believe matters and stick with it. "We pretty much ignore standardized tests, and we get away with it because our four-year college graduation rates, for the population we have, are very high," Rosenstock said. "So I urge people who want cover to pick your metric. Don't assume the metric they gave you is the right metric." (High Tech High also gets away with it, it should be noted, because its students test in the 80th percentile statewide, which is pretty good for a school that does no test prep.)

Rosenstock's argument might be harder to sell in Cadiz, where the accomplishments in San Diego are half a continent away. So Hamby hoped, at least, that the exhibition nights would demonstrate what sophisticated skills this effort is all for. "Come in and see," he pronounced. "The scores might not show it yet, but look at what our kids can do."

By the second year of Trigg's transformation, the exhibition nights had indeed come closer to convincing one skeptic: Trigg County High's own PE and health teacher, James Shelton. A towering man in a blue Fellowship of Christian Anglers Society sweatshirt, he told me he worried about whether the students were really learning all the required content in the midst of the projects. Shelton had skin in the game. His daughter was one of the sharply dressed students lined up along the hallways beside their posters and dioramas, ready to explain their work. Fewer than ten freshmen were absent that night—a level of attendance matched only by athletic events.

Despite his concerns, though, Shelton indicated that he wouldn't ask his school to turn back. "I saw [students] presenting in front of a group, public speaking, research, standing up for your position, and then trying to explain it," he said. And he expects those skills to bolster them in college and beyond.

I have deep admiration for the brave change the Trigg team is undertaking, flaws and all. Shelton had said, "We're going to get there, I have no doubt," and I fervently hoped that he was right—that they would ultimately arrive at the kind of transformation they were aiming for, despite the hurdles.

If we are going to grow more schools as creative as High Tech High, as engaging as the Expeditionary Learning schools, and as courageous as Trigg, the change will happen at the local level. We needn't (and shouldn't) wait for shortsighted politicians in Washington or misguided college admissions gatekeepers to recognize that they're leading a generation of youth in the wrong direction. Starting now, we can begin to change children's everyday experience in school. Teachers can experiment with inquiry-based projects and invite students to pursue their own questions, gauging their learning through the quality of their work. "You are, for [your] students, the education system," says Ken Robinson. "And if you change your practice, you have changed the education system for your students."

Parents can inform educators about alternate models, advocate for local change, and support schools that are willing to do it. Principals and superintendents can create the conditions that facilitate deeper learning: assessments that support diverse, hands-on lessons; schedules that allow time for teachers and students to collaborate; a culture of experimentation that gives teachers freedom to innovate and students the space to make mistakes; and flexibility in the way the school day runs and the classrooms are arranged.

Students, too, can make an impact by speaking up for what they want and how they learn best. Everyone has the power to help tear down some (literal and figurative) walls.

As I left Trigg and turned south toward Nashville, the nagging question on my mind was the same one Tony Wagner, the high school teacher turned Harvard professor, had put to me when we met. We were discussing the ways that education can (and can't) cultivate young innovators. "The best and brightest of this generation are succeeding in spite of, not because of, their schooling," Wagner said. "We should not leave the future success of our kids and our schools up to what I would call random acts of excellence. We need to create a system that is about intellectual and moral excellence, a system that is humane and vibrant and exciting. And we know how to do that. The question is, *will* we do that?"

CHAPTER 7

First, Be Well

Z OOM OUT.
        We've seen that fixing the runaway stressors that are sickening our kids is essential. It's imperative that we revolutionize our approach to homework and testing, reimagine success, and reclaim our families' frayed time. We must invent new school policies and practices, local and national, that encourage risk and innovation. And we must collectively decide, as stakeholders in our school communities, to meet children where they are, instead of prodding them continually toward a prescribed credential. As the preceding chapters have illustrated, all of these changes—attacked singly *and* taken together—are crucial to safeguarding our children's health and fostering true learning.

Which brings us to one final, important piece of our work: the deliberate promotion of children's total well-being—extending beyond the realm of academics—above all. Just as the new vision for great schools casts them as hubs of deep and personal learning, it must also frame them as centers for fostering lifelong wellness. Unless we place that priority first, all of the practical and policy changes will not be quite enough. Nor is simply ensuring our children's basic health a sufficiently high bar. Beyond healthy, we need to strive toward happy. Stable. Self-possessed. Equipped to embrace meaningful challenges, forge strong relationships, tap inner resources, and make good decisions. These are the hallmarks of true success: the qualities that will empower young people to become thriving students and, later, thriving adults, and that will enable them to flourish in any realm they enter, long after they have left our care. And these are the skills cultivated by schools, families, and communities that support the whole child—social, emotional, physical, spiritual, and cognitive—and not just the one-dimensional student.

This is, in the end, what this entire book is about: rising to the challenge of raising and teaching children to become whole people, ready to genuinely thrive. This essential aim calls on schools and communities not only to immediately address the issues we've examined in this book but also to proactively place children's well-being at the center of every decision they make. The cultivation of resilient hearts and bodies must be as much a part of our core mission as cultivating lively minds. This is an especially profound responsibility when we consider the tremendous physical and emotional growth that takes place during childhood and adolescence, which sets the stage for a child's whole life. When we truly put wellness first, the question "How will this affect students' well-being?" becomes inseparable from the question "How will this affect students' learning?"

The task is considerable. Many times, as both a parent and filmmaker, I've found that wellness ranks last among considerations in school. Historically, the demands of athletic leagues, bus companies, testing regimes, teachers unions, and traditions—calcified by our fear of questioning the status quo—have come before the goal of nurturing happy, healthy students. Health, as a discipline, is merely a one-semester high school class. Balance is absent from the syllabus entirely. Wellness is too often addressed only when something goes wrong.

"It's very strange not having any acknowledgment that we're human beings in this," says Erin, a California high schooler who stayed home nearly her entire freshman year with severe depression. Erin remembers ruefully how, even as her family and friends supported her, the school made recovery hard. There was no letup on the amount of work sent home to her, despite her fragile state. A biology teacher flunked her on several assignments because she couldn't attend labs. When Erin finally felt ready to return to school, she was forced, despite doctors' notes, to take an anxiety-provoking test to prove that she needed accommodations (extra time, a calm space in the library) to, of all things, take tests. In the contest between Erin's well-being and the inflexible demands of that system, the system won.

And yet the value of structuring schools to support holistic well-being is obvious to most of us. The skeptic will insist that schools' focus should be academic alone, or that all nonacademic skills are "soft." But most of us know implicitly that wellness is no fluffy frivolity; it is a necessary ingredient for other good things. Our children can do their best only when they are physically and emotionally well.

Science backs up our instincts. Studies have found that the brain actually works better when it's in a good mood. In a positive state of mind, doctors make more accurate diagnoses. Happy job candidates are more likely to get a second interview. Optimistic businesspeople make more sales. And students who were told to think about the happiest day of their lives before taking a math test scored higher than their peers. Shawn Achor, a researcher and author, calls this the "happiness advantage." In his much-watched TED Talk, he explains, "Your brain at positive performs slightly better than at negative, neutral, or stressed. Your intelligence rises, your creativity rises, your energy levels rise. In fact, we've found that every single business outcome improves."

So, too, do outcomes in other realms of life, such as friendship, marriage, and health. One study, published in *Psychological Bulletin* in 2005, synthesized more than two hundred scientific papers on the link between happiness and success. The authors' conclusion: that positive emotions don't simply happen in concert with successful life outcomes—they come before. They wrote: "Study after study shows that happiness precedes important outcomes and indicators of thriving, including fulfilling and productive work, satisfying relationships, and superior mental and physical health and longevity."

I find it telling that the best businesses are already figuring this out. Silicon Valley firms routinely offer mindfulness lessons. A new management book by international business leader Margaret Heffernan touts the great benefits of learning to listen, of avoiding mind-numbing overtime, and of treating employees humanely, letting them leave the office and take a walk. The data analytics firm SAS Institute even caps its employees' workweek at thirty-five hours. And as we learned in chapter 3, years of research on human expertise shows that people who excel in all kinds of fields typically devote themselves to highly focused work no more than about four and a half hours a day. For health, productivity, and creativity alike, less is more. It's striking that billion-dollar corporations, the very destinations some hope their kids can reach someday, have recognized this before our education system has.

Our kids' miserable state is not some inevitable modern norm. UNICEF, in a 2013 report, ranked the United States twenty-fifth out of twenty-nine affluent countries on overall child well-being. Poverty and income inequality account for some of this dismal record, but not all. American adolescents rated their own life satisfaction lower than their peers did in two-thirds of the other countries. And the United States came in second to worst on children's ratings of their own relationships; kids in most of the other countries were more likely to say that their classmates were helpful and kind, and that their parents were easy to talk to. I'm reminded of the many times students at film screenings have said they can't turn to one another for support because they are in competition.

The moral is not that we should spare our children from the least discomfort or displeasure—that's unrealistic and unhelpful. It's that we must provide them with the environment, in school and at home, that will teach them to find satisfaction in their everyday lives. In place of exaggerated demands out of step with children's natural development, we must provide the support and learning experiences that give kids the skills to cope with life's challenges and to reset their moods to positive once the trouble is gone.

An entire field of research and educational practice has arisen around the cultivation of resilience. What makes one child bounce back from disappointments and setbacks while another child crumbles? Researchers have found that, even in the most terrible circumstances, beset by poverty and neglect and violence, at least 50 percent of children rebound and succeed. Children with the capacity to tap into their resilience possess certain essential strengths—empathy, communication skills, problem-solving skills, confidence in their ability to affect their own circumstances, and a sense of identity and purpose. They are typically flexible, optimistic, self-regulated, and internally motivated. The potential to embody these strengths lives within all of us.

"The question of whether we believe an individual possesses the capacity for resilience is no longer appropriate," says Sara Truebridge, author of *Resilience Begins with Beliefs: Building on Student Strengths for Success in School.* "Everyone has the capacity for resilience. The appropriate question is whether it has been tapped—and if not, what can we do to tap it?"

That challenge is ours. Research has clearly established that a child's capacity to access her resilience often hinges on three main supports from the adults around her, Truebridge notes: caring relationships; opportunities to contribute and participate; and high expectations that are not about the end product but rather about the qualities that sustain learning and growth, such as effort. Ed Hallowell, psychiatrist and author of *The Childhood Roots of Adult Happiness*, explains: "If parents and schools would promote these qualities"—such as optimism, self-esteem, a feeling of control over one's life—"with the verve and ingenuity they promote getting good grades, the emotional health of children (and the adults they become) would sky-rocket."

A Strategy from Saint Louis

So how do we do that? How do we, in the midst of the competitive firestorm that childhood has become, cultivate in kids a sense of joy and worthiness and the capacity to cope with hardship?

These were among the questions troubling Stuart Slavin when he witnessed the simultaneous undoing of two groups of people he cared about deeply: his medical students at Saint Louis University and his own two teenage daughters. Slavin is the pediatrician and medical professor who emailed me after seeing my first film. He has become one of Jay Jackson's close collaborators in the campaign for wellness at Irvington High. But before I introduced him to Jackson, Slavin had already carried out his own quest to restore young people's well-being.

About eight years ago, he saw some articles on medical students' poor mental health. "I really was struck by how awful the statistics were," he recalls. "It was not just one study. It was multiple studies that showed a serious problem." Yet all his students at SLU appeared to be happy, so he thought perhaps his school didn't have the same problem. Or were they just good at hiding it? To make sure, he anonymously surveyed students. "The results were just as bad as everyone else's," he says. "We had very high levels of depression, very high levels of anxiety." So Slavin did the right thing, the thing we all must do when facing the reality of our students' distress; he put health first. He said to himself and to his colleagues: "This can't be. We can't allow this to stand."

Like a good scientist, Slavin went back to the medical literature to see what solutions had been tried. "And again I was kind of shocked by how little had been done," he recalls. So he and his colleagues at SLU, a Jesuit school, undertook their own kind of mission. Their first action was improving students' access to mental health care, which is critical. Then they launched a variety of wellness initiatives, including team-building activities and optional seminars on how to eat, sleep, and exercise well—which "was nice but didn't seem to fundamentally address the issue," Slavin observes. The meat of their work came next. SLU took twin approaches: one, change the academic environment to reduce stress, and two, build students' capacity to cope (because, as Slavin says, we can't control their environment forever).

To reduce the fuel for unnecessary stress, SLU gave students a half-day off every other Wednesday and converted preclinical classes for students in their first two years to pass/fail grading. The school strengthened its social fabric by creating student-led learning communities that convene students with common interests and plan activities. These learning communities, in turn, sponsored new electives that would bring students a deeper sense of meaning, on subjects such as violence prevention, global women's health, music therapy, and the intersection of spirituality and medicine. And, in the second year of the effort, the school began requiring a course of resilience training.

"The results have been unbelievable," Slavin says. Depression rates among first-year medical students, which hit 27 percent when Slavin first measured them in 2009, have plunged to 8 percent. The portion of students suffering from anxiety plummeted from 55 percent to 23 percent during the same time. Simultaneously, students reported that they felt more connected to each other. And their scores on early medical boards exams improved. (After seeing those statistics, can you doubt that schools exert powerful influence over students' mental health?) "The cost is virtually nonexistent, and academic performance has gone up," says Slavin, rather amazed himself by the results. "So you kind of go, 'Oh my God, why isn't anybody doing this?'"

We might go further and ask: If a medical school can do this, why can't our high schools and middle schools?

Slavin wondered the same thing. As his daughters entered middle school and then high school, their homework loads became ever more absurd. His older daughter began showing signs of anxiety and distress, breaking down crying, staying up until midnight finishing assignments when she was already exhausted. The stress spilled over onto the whole family, as Slavin, his wife, and both girls became edgy and short-tempered with one another and could no longer find time to do fun activities as a family. "Ninth grade," he recalls, "felt like just a complete breakdown of our family's structure." As a pediatrician and educator, he could clearly see the harm being done to his daughter's mental health and well-being.

So Slavin, who sat on the board of his older daughter's high school, gave his fellow board members a detailed presentation showing all the relevant research on teen health, the limited effectiveness of homework, and more. He got nowhere. He kept pressing, but the board made no movement toward meaningful change. As is so often the shameful case, all kinds of other concerns came before health. Finally, exasperated, Slavin pulled his daughter out of that school. "It was really frustrating," he remembers. "This is my work. I'm a pediatrician. I know more about child development than 99 percent of the people in the country, and that's not because I'm smart, that's because I've studied it. And I have this mountain of evidence. But ultimately I couldn't get the evidence to win."

Slavin is hoping to have better luck at Irvington, where he has a devoted ally in the main office. And his successful strategy at SLU provides a kind of blueprint for other schools working to improve students' mental health. His lessons for reformers are fairly simple: prioritize wellness by (a) resetting policies and practices, both academic and extracurricular, to relieve excessive stress, (b) directly caring for students' mental and physical health, and (c) teaching them how to care for themselves. These primary actions, in turn, promote a general *culture of wellness*: a shared belief among educators, students, and parents that health and balance are the first priority and are a prerequisite to true success and learning.

Tackling part (a)—the tweaking or even overhauling of polices—entails everything this book has addressed so far. This is the work of taming runaway homework and testing, defusing college admissions anxiety, and reclaiming the shared definition of what makes a person a success. A key aspect of part (b)—the direct care of children's well-being—is ensuring that our schools have enough counselors to give adequate individual attention to the students who need it. In Slavin's case, this was SLU's first priority. Irvington High, as well, expanded its counseling staff in fall 2014 through a partnership with the local youth and family services department. The new counselor devoted all her time to ninth graders who were struggling in their classes, meeting with families, providing extra supports, and trying to help them stabilize before sophomore year. This was an improvement over most American high schools, where the average ratio of students to guidance counselors is nearly 500 to 1, and where those counselors are disproportionately occupied with college applications rather than genuine psychological care.

Another essential element of part (b) is, of course, physical. A slew of scientific studies establish the importance of exercise for physical and mental health and optimal brain functioning. That's why the wisest schools are making time for it during the school day. A high school in Naperville, Illinois, bucked the trend to cut back on every subject that's not tested and made PE a daily requirement. Naperville Central High even arranged for struggling students to have PE immediately before their most challenging classes. And it helped: students showed dramatic improvements in those subjects. Bishop O'Dowd High School in Oakland created space during lunch for games like Ping-Pong and Frisbee, to promote play and socializing rather than working through lunch. And at the college level, Berklee College of Music professor Kathleen Howland, who teaches neuroscience and music therapy, pauses in the middle of her classes for a dance break. Howland turns on music, and she and her students dance and laugh, "which allows us to decompress from the curriculum and oxygenate," she says. The exercise also contains a lesson: afterward, Howland prompts her students to reflect on how the dancing affects their attention, mental processing, and energy, and how that compares to drinking coffee or eating a candy bar.

The Power of Connection

It's important to recognize one critical part of caring for children's wellness that requires no new staff or special programs and costs next to nothing. The approach is simply to create more opportunities for kids to forge deep personal *connections*—with adults at school, with other adults in the community, and with one another. (This is what Slavin achieved with his medical school learning communities.) Research demonstrates that connections are critical both at home and at school. In fact, studies have shown that strong relationships with caring adults are among the most powerful forces for building resilience in children. One study in New Zealand monitored a thousand residents over more than thirty years and revealed that social connectedness in adolescence was more closely linked with adult well-being than was getting great test scores and doing well in school.

"In resilience research, the biggest predictor of doing well in the face of adversity or pressure is good relationships, love, feeling connected, feeling warm support," says Suniya Luthar, the Arizona State University psychologist. "Teachers are very often cited by youth as the people who saw them through very difficult times. . . . If [you do] not feel that kind of acceptance and love, you can be the person with the most perseverance and grit and toughness, eventually we all crumble."

That kind of connection doesn't necessarily happen on its own. It's not sufficient for schools simply to leave teachers and students to their own devices and expect that they'll forge the bonds they need. The school day is busy. Teachers in high schools with traditional schedules might see 150 students in a day. In order to truly serve children, schools must make connectedness a part of their core educational practice.

Nadia Lopez, the Brooklyn principal who became suddenly famous when the Humans of New York blog featured her appreciative student, fosters connection through sheer force of energy. When I spoke with her to learn more about her approach, it was spring break, yet she was nonetheless in her office with a student who had asked for help with his studies. Her school serves middle schoolers in gritty Brownsville, a poor neighborhood rife with drugs and despair. Lopez's whatever-it-takes approach derives in part from her training as a nurse, where she learned to look at a patient's entire wellness picture instead of just diagnosing a narrow problem. Then, as a young teacher dealing with distressed, distracted children, she told me, "I found that the most powerful thing I could do was just sit and talk to kids, and once I knew about them, management wasn't an issue, because they knew I cared about them."

So Lopez, a Brooklyn native herself, arrives at Mott Hall Bridges Academy at six a.m. and stays until evening. She observes classrooms daily, and deeply reads the file for every one of her two hundred students. It's crucial to her that school be a place where each child feels seen for her unique gifts, not branded by shortcomings. So, if a child voices an interest in a particular sport or field of study, she tries to create opportunities for him to pursue it. Outside of class, Lopez calls parents and visits their homes when she has concerns about a student. "I'm just relentless," she said. When Lopez asks parents and students what's different about this school, she added, "Ninety-nine percent of the time it's: 'Someone cares about me here.'"

Lopez's superhuman dedication creates the conditions that can give rise to resiliency. It is admirable, amazing, and, in her view, necessary to serving students who face so many obstacles in the rest of their lives. It is also hard to replicate Lopez's energy. She's an outlier. Yet the fundamental values that underlie her approach apply everywhere. It takes only one relationship to make a difference for a child, and it's incumbent on all of us, educators and parents alike, to help put in place the structures that support that. Any adult at school can create a culture of care.

Educators do, however, need the opportunity to foster connection with kids within the hours of a normal school day, and I see more and more schools making this possible. Block scheduling, for example, which gives teachers and students more flexible time for one-on-one interactions, can help. So can smaller class sizes. Also beneficial is team teaching, where pairs of teachers share all the same students, or looping, where students stay with the same teacher for multiple years. Creating small schools within schools can be another effective way to strengthen community.

"What resilience research offers advocates," writes Bonnie Benard, author of *Resiliency: What We Have Learned*, "is well-documented support for an educational approach based on meeting young people's basic needs—for belonging and affiliation, a sense of competence and meaning, feelings of autonomy, and safety."

Of course, the adults working in schools need the same things, too. So collaborative approaches such as team teaching are effective not only because they build bridges between students and their teachers, but also because they create a network of relationships that support *everyone* in school—including teachers and staff. Schools do well by widening the ecosystem of connection still further to include parents and neighbors. Maryland's Gaithersburg Elementary, for instance, has done this by inviting local residents in to use school computers and take adult classes, and by hosting evening events where families share meals and learn educational games. The national movement for community schools promotes this, casting schools as community centers where local kids and adults alike can find resources and opportunities on weekdays, evenings, and weekends.

The net result is a good kind of climate change—a school that becomes less like an assembly line and more like a community, where children and adults alike feel known and supported and thus able to thrive. Parents, in addition to benefiting from this kind of connectedness, can encourage it. Beyond advocating for new policies, I've urged my own kids to seek out one teacher or counselor whom they trust so they have someone to turn to with concerns at school. I've tried to build a little village of caring friends and mentors around our family, knowing that my children may sometimes need support from people besides me. Now I see Jamey building her own community and making a point of getting to know her professors in college, perhaps helped by that early experience.

A world away from Brownsville, in Palo Alto, dad and newly minted school board member Ken Dauber is trying another promising tactic to build connection. The cries for reform in his affluent community are poignant. Three local students killed themselves in the 2014–15 school year by stepping in front of commuter trains. A Palo Alto High School junior, Carolyn Walworth, wrote in March 2015 in a local paper that she and her peers are "gasping for air." Revealing that she has missed menstrual periods, had silent panic attacks in the middle of class, and landed in urgent care due to stress-induced pain, Carolyn went on: "We are not teenagers. We are lifeless bodies in a system that breeds competition, hatred, and discourages teamwork and genuine learning. We lack sincere passion. We are sick."

I heard about Dauber because of the grassroots group he started in 2011, as the community reeled from an earlier string of teen suicides. His organization, called We Can Do Better Palo Alto, champions students' mental health and proclaims to any potential skeptics: "We reject the false choice between lowering stress and high achievement. We believe that lower stress and achievement go hand in hand." For Dauber, a sociology professor turned Google software engineer, this work is a matter of principle. It is also personal; his oldest daughter, the firstborn of his five children, suffered from mental illness and took her own life at age twenty-six.

Relentless in his own way, Dauber has ruffled feathers. He used public records laws to access internal school documents and refused to take no for an answer on his reforms. He lost his first bid for a seat on the school board in 2012, then won his second run in 2014 with the endorsement of the *Palo Alto Daily News*, which wrote that he "has forced the district to take a closer look at itself." Dauber advocates loudly for reduced homework, and also wants to see the schools change their schedules, complete finals before winter break, provide lessons in social and emotional skills, and more closely align the standard curriculum to individual students' needs.

His biggest push, though, is for an advisory program. The idea couldn't be simpler: the school sets aside one period a week (or more) for a small group of students to meet with a teacher or other staff member to discuss issues of importance, academic or otherwise. Over time, the advisory group becomes a little community, where students feel known by the teacher and supported by one another. "It's a way for kids to have a connection to an adult at school," says Dauber. "Teachers are probably the most valuable connection kids can have."

I've seen advisories work beautifully at San Diego's High Tech High, where each teacher-adviser sticks with the same students for all four years. Advisers there make home visits to get to know families well. Each advisory group includes students in all grade levels so that younger teens can watch the older ones weather important milestones and learn from their experiences. The impact is powerful. I saw one High Tech High student turn to her assignment on the same day is "fair," are finding it hard to shake that tradition. So Herrmann says she's working with them, sharing relevant research, and letting them know that it's okay to make time flexible because, after all, "We're after learning."

An Ounce of Prevention

As to the final aspect of Slavin's strategy—teaching students how to care for themselves—I can already hear the chorus of critics clamoring that emotions are the domain of the family and schools should keep out. Or that the responsibility for teaching greater well-being resides with physicians and counselors, not educators. Which would be fine if learning happened in a vacuum, hermetically sealed off from children's inner and outer lives. But that is not reality. "Schools have no choice but to teach character," observes educator and author Ron Berger. "Because the very experience of school imbues character in students. You either do it poorly by paying no attention to it and instilling poor character values in kids, or you do it thoughtfully and make sure that your school is making kids more respectful, more thoughtful, more kind, more studious, more courageous."

Besides, we parents need schools' support in this critical piece of child development. In our family, I strive to teach emotional and physical health, offering my kids vocabulary to talk about their feelings. I pointed out early to Zak how cheerful he was after exercising outside, yet how grouchy he got from playing video games, and he ultimately chose to avoid them. I make sleep, family dinners, and time outdoors a top priority. We take walks together, and we unplug from devices as a family at meals and certain times on the weekend. It *is* my job, as a parent, to take these kinds of proactive steps. Still, Zak still spends seven or eight hours a day at school—and more if you count band, tutoring, and other activities. Many of his life lessons occur there.

What's more, there are explicit kinds of instruction that we will examine below that can help children build the skills for happiness, wholeness, and resilience, and schools should play a role in teaching them. Before I did the research, I might not have believed that emotional intelligence can be taught—coaching kids to manage their own emotions, take setbacks in

adviser for help improving a relationship with a core teacher, and anotl
receive great support from her adviser after the loss of a family member.

In Palo Alto, Dauber backs up his argument for advisories with eviden
from student surveys at the district's two high schools, Palo Alto High (a.k.
Paly) and Gunn. Their ratings of school counseling services differ widel
In the 2012 survey, 88 percent of students at Paly said at least one adult a
school could support them if they were struggling academically, while onl
57 percent said that at Gunn. And 84 percent at Paly said they'd have a sup-
porter if they were struggling emotionally, compared to just 43 percent at
Gunn. To what does Dauber attribute the disparity? To the fact that Paly has
an advisory program and Gunn does not.

Of course, the success of advisories is all in the execution. They miss the
mark when used for impersonal school logistics or tab keeping, becoming
just another forum for herding kids along the academic track rather than an
outlet for emotional support. The program must be about authentic personal connection, and teacher-advisers need solid training to respond to
serious issues that may arise.

Dauber's demands for change, which ran aground on institutional inertia
for years, may stand a better chance of succeeding after this second wave
of tragedies. Gunn High's new principal, Denise Herrmann, is a transplant
from a Wisconsin high school where she took steps to relieve excessive pressure. She is enthusiastic about advisories, observing that "students say the
teachers they feel most connected to are their band teachers or their football
coach, someone who they're with for four years who has really seen them
grow and change." Advisories could be part of a package of reforms she's
developing.

Meanwhile, Herrmann is working immediately to rein in extreme
homework loads as another means of caring for students. She's also pressing for a simple little thing that's anathema to public education: flexibility.
"The idea of not having four or five tests to study for the next day, the idea
that they can postpone a test so when they do feel stressed there are releases that they know will be there for them," Herrmann explains. "That's
the thing that students are asking for as the most immediate relief." Some
teachers, schooled to think that requiring every student to turn in the same

stride, and relate in healthy ways to themselves and each other—but it's true. And these emotional and social skills, once imbued, stay with kids as they grow.

Important caveat! These lessons are valuable, but they can never, ever be an excuse to avoid systemic change. Just like a business defeats its own wellness efforts if it still expects employees to clock eighty-hour workweeks, we'd be doublespeaking to say, "Our kids are breaking under the weight of our impossible demands, but they've got relaxation classes, so they'll be okay!" Equipping kids for resilience is good medicine, but we must still cure the societal sickness that ails them.

With that caution in mind, I'll describe three well-established educational practices (among many) for teaching children how to maintain healthy minds, hearts, and bodies. These work best when they're not simply an add-on—a separate program delivered in forty-minute chunks once a week—but a reflection of the way we teach children every day, putting our humanity first, whether in class, on the athletic field, in band rehearsal, or at home.

Social and emotional learning is, in essence, a set of tools and strategies for managing the self. It equips children with the skills to be good friends and collaborators, committed learners, and stable individuals—skills including self-awareness, self-regulation, empathy, communication, and thoughtful decision-making. As SEL expert Janice Toben explains, "It allows students to solve their own problems," to weather mistakes, to accept and support one another, and to manage their own moments of boredom or disappointment. "The social and emotional skills are not fluff. They're not touchy and feely; they actually create an environment so that real academic learning can happen."

At the WINGS after-school SEL program in low-income North Charleston, South Carolina, teachers weave social and emotional skills instruction into crafts, games, and homework help, five days a week. The strategies they've studied then become an integral part of teachers' discipline methods when skirmishes break out. "You're worrying about his choices when you need to be worried about your choices," they remind kids who get upset about others' behavior. "Make the choice that's best for you." These sorts of easy-to-remember sayings, echoed and enacted day after day, eventually embed themselves in students' own social and emotional tool kit.

Toben, who ran the SEL program at the Nueva School south of San Francisco for twenty-seven years, explained to me how the lessons typically evolve as children move through the grades. They'll start in the early grades by teaching children a vocabulary for emotion: this is *sad*, this is *frustrated*, this is *lonely*. Next, as children become more adept at noticing their shifting emotions, they start to learn assertive communication strategies and problem solving. By fifth grade, they're studying how conflicts escalate and how to prevent escalation. "Students tell me all the time they go home and say to their parents, 'Hey, that's escalating,'" Toben says. In fact, parents, staff, and other adults at school are very much a part of this approach. By sharing the principles of SEL with all, it becomes not just a program, but a set of values shared by a whole school community, reinforced in every arena.

Finally, in middle school and higher, kids begin to examine their own ways of interpreting setbacks and talking to themselves. Negative thinking patterns (e.g., "I failed the math test because I'm stupid, and I'll always be stupid") are powerfully linked with depression, while positive thinking patterns (e.g., "I failed the math test because I misunderstood some things, but I can learn") protect against it. Armed with these skills as they enter the cauldron of adolescence, Toben says, "They're better off at being an individual, at holding a boundary, at pushing aside groupthink and pressure."

The earliest SEL programs emerged from Yale University in the 1960s. Now SEL is practiced in thousands of schools around the United States and included in nearly a dozen states' education standards. Some entire city districts, including Austin and Nashville, are integrating SEL into their K-12 approach. A landmark 2011 study gauged the results of more than two hundred in-school SEL programs serving hundreds of thousands of students. It found that, compared to peers who got no SEL, students in these programs showed significantly better behavior, better social and emotional skills, and a substantial bump in academic test scores. Another study looking at dozens of *after-school* SEL programs found similar benefits. The WINGS after-school program, for one, has a real impact during the school day. Despite the destabilizing effects of poverty and crime in many WINGS children's lives, after two years in the program students demonstrate significantly better school attendance and higher test scores and grades. Doesn't it stand to reason that kids who feel socially happier and steadier within themselves are more able to take advantage of their studies?

For communities looking to adopt SEL, the Collaborative for Academic, Social, and Emotional Learning (CASEL) in Chicago is the online hub for resources and guides to proven programs.

Positive psychology is an entire field of science as well as an educational method. Its mastermind, University of Pennsylvania professor Martin Seligman, spent decades studying depression and helplessness before arriving at a dramatic turnabout in his thinking. Psychology "has been sidetracked," he wrote as he assumed the presidency of the American Psychological Association in 1998. Rather than focusing narrowly on fixing disorders, psychologists should also dedicate themselves to fostering strengths, he argued. "Treatment is not just fixing what is broken, it is nurturing what is best within ourselves."

The ensuing research produced a practice called positive education—a set of methods for nurturing the traits that are known to act as buffers against mental illness, such as honesty, optimism, and perseverance. In practice, positive education programs have a lot in common with SEL. They use stories, skits, and examples from students' own lives to teach healthy communication, relaxation, and other coping and problem-solving skills. The results so far are hopeful: studies of Seligman's Penn Resiliency Program, for example, have found that it reduces depression, anxiety, and behavior problems, and that its benefits last at least two years.

The skills for happiness *should* be woven into the fabric of education, Seligman and colleagues assert, because so many young people are already depressed, because wellness also leads to better learning, and because "we want our teenagers to be healthy and vibrant, not merely free of disease; optimistic and exuberant, not simply 'non-depressed'; intimately connected to others, not just part of the crowd; . . . and passionately engaged in activities that excite them, not just 'occupied.'" Amen.

Finally, there's **mindfulness**—which was trending in education even before it made a 2014 cover of *Time* magazine. The practice began in schools on a small scale a couple of decades ago and then mushroomed over the past five years into an educational movement. You can now find dozens of mindfulness programs in hundreds of schools in a majority of US states. At Saint Louis University, for instance, Stuart Slavin opted for a resilience course that includes mindfulness. Kevin Wehmhoefer, coordinator of mental health services and outreach at Harvard, started offering mindfulness classes in student dorms and found it to be the "single most effective tool" he's encountered in his work so far. At Gunn High, Principal Herrmann plans to weave the practice into her reforms.

It's clear why: not only do the lessons provide kids a little oasis of quiet and calm in the midst of the school day, but studies show the training actually improves students' behavior and attention. If your brain is abuzz with agitation over the latest playground skirmish, or anxiety about an upcoming test, or distress about a painful situation at home, you're not likely to be fully tuned into today's fractions lesson. Plus, the basics of the practice can be taught and put to use in very little time, while the benefits can be lasting. Mindfulness is often confused with a religious practice, but it's actually just a method for noticing one's own mental and emotional state and calming it down. Parents can learn it and model it for their kids, too. (As a chronic overthinker and rat racer in recovery, I've experienced the benefits firsthand.)

I had the chance recently to witness a mindfulness lesson in Richmond, California, in an impoverished neighborhood where children routinely come to school upset about neighborhood shootings. The instructor was Tim Scott Jr., a mindfulness professional and hip-hop artist who goes by the name JusTme. He stepped to the front of a fifth grade classroom, sporting short dreadlocks and a gray hoodie and exuding compassion and enthusiasm, and twenty-eight heads turned toward him. "I got my feet on the floor, my spine in a line, my hands in my lap, and my heart to the sky," the children sang together as they settled into a "mindful sit." Then, with JusTme reminding them to notice the sensations in their bodies and to let go of any judgments about themselves, the classroom fell into silence.

The sit lasted just a few minutes, but it seemed to release the frenetic energy that had buzzed among the students moments before. Afterward, they acted calmer and more focused. JusTme's lesson today was on mindful test taking. He asked the kids what changes happen in their thoughts, emotions, and bodies when they're taking a test. "I feel nervous and stressed," one boy said. Other students added on: "I feel pressure." "I feel sleepy."

What could they do about this? To keep calm, he said, they could take five mindful breaths (they all practiced one, inhaling deeply). They could send themselves and their classmates some compassion, saying things like "I'm going to give it my best" instead of "I'm not good enough." And they could notice the emotions in their bodies, in a tight stomach or a tapping foot, and "name it to tame it." When JusTme left after his twenty-five-minute lesson, he had trouble crossing the playground as every few steps a child ran up to hug him.

The Bay Area–based nonprofit that trained JusTme, Mindful Schools, also trains teachers to practice and teach mindfulness in their classrooms. Training for teachers is crucial, as the practice can sometimes surface past traumas for kids that instructors must be prepared to handle. A UC Davis study showed that Oakland elementary students who received Mindful Schools lessons demonstrated significantly improved behavior—especially in paying attention—compared to peers who didn't get the lessons. Studies of other mindfulness programs have found benefits including better attendance, lower suspension rates, and even improved grades. My favorite stat: according to a state survey, a San Francisco middle school that adopted a transcendental meditation program posted the highest happiness levels in the city.

Demand for mindfulness in schools is rising accordingly. Enrollment in Mindful Schools' online introductory class had multiplied nearly tenfold in just two years as of early 2015. The practice suits diverse students and communities, as it can help one child cope with family turmoil and another child cope with academic performance pressure. I know for myself that even simple breath work can help me untangle the tension in my mind. When I've shared this technique with my kids, it has helped them, too.

Digital Detox

Speaking of serenity, and the lack thereof, one other potential thwarter of well-being that deserves special scrutiny is digital technology. I've wrestled mightily with the merits and perils of technology for myself and my family. I've despaired whenever I've noticed that my kids just spent half an hour texting when they could have been outdoors, or that I just squandered forty minutes on email that could have been spent with my children. I've gasped upon seeing groups of teens at school sitting "together," staring at their phones. Seeking guidance, I read all the credible research and commentary on the subject that I could. And what I found is that with screen time, as with everything, the key to well-being is balance.

Some amount of tech time for kids is healthy. They need to learn to use today's tools, and to use them well. They should have the chance to unwind with digital entertainment if they like to, and to socialize in modes that match those of their peers. "It *is* the way this generation communicates, and anyone who worries that tech is isolating our kids should just look at one of the 'stories' their kids tell on Snapchat or Instagram," says Brigid Schulte, the reporter and author of *Overwhelmed*. "Some are hilarious and sweet."

Still, the growing science on screen time confirms our gut parental sense that caution and supervision are required. Digital devices can play on our brain's reward system, releasing the neurotransmitter dopamine and making it hard to resist a tweet or a text message. When we're hooked on that hit, our screen obsession sucks us away from ourselves and the people around us, and it habituates us to a distant, disembodied kind of human exchange. "Science is showing that tech works on the same brain structures as addiction—the basal ganglia—which means it's incredibly seductive, if not addictive," Schulte explains. "We as adults have a hard time managing it. I would argue it's using *us* more than we are effectively using *it*."

The danger lies in that lack of control. In an interview with journalist Bill Moyers, MIT professor Sherry Turkle argues that seeking that "neurochemical hit of constant connection" actually leaves us with a face-to-face-connection deficit. Absent are the intimate, important subtleties of a facial expression or a tone of voice, the meandering path of an in-person conversation. The loss affects all of us, but the implications are especially troublesome for children, who are still forming their social selves. Turkle, the author of *Alone Together: Why We Expect More from Technology and Less from Each Other*, explains that our smartphones and Snapchat accounts promise us that we'll never have to be alone. And this is powerful because "the capacity for solitude is terribly important to develop. I even believe that if you don't teach your children to be alone, they'll only know how to be lonely."

School communities, likewise, could use a dose of digital-communication restraint. In some schools, it is increasingly routine for teachers or coaches to email students and families about assignments late in the evening or on weekends—or vice versa. Even if it's not explicitly demanded, many kids, parents, and educators feel the pressure to promptly read and respond. This late-night communication is not malicious on anyone's part—it reflects the inherent temptation technology creates to blur the line between school and home, just as it has blurred the work-home line for businesses that reach their always-on employees at all hours. But it is nevertheless an invasion of private time. It is appropriate and important for us now to set limits, asking schools to contact students and families—and families to contact educators—only during normal business hours. Companies including Volkswagen have already done the same for their workers.

If we want to give our children all the opportunities they need to grow a full set of social skills, we need to teach them to how to resist the constant digital connection fix. And if we want to preserve the precious time our families have to be in the same room and actually engage with each other, we have to set limits. But spotting the problem is one thing, and knowing how to solve it is another. How do you safeguard your kids from the downsides of technologies that are ubiquitous and somewhat necessary, or tell them to put down a device that you yourself are holding in your hand and compulsively checking every ten minutes?

I've found that the experts' advice for parents so far generally comes down to this: pay attention. Families need to be mindful of how they use tech—taking care not to let it use them—and keep ever vigilant about maintaining a balance. "Create sacred spaces in your home," Turkle advised Moyers. "Places that are device free: kitchen, dining room, and the car. You can't introduce this idea when your child is fifteen that the car is for chatting. From the very beginning, kitchen, dining room, and the car are places where we talk." Saying "no" to phones and computers in the bedroom, while tricky to sustain in our hyper-connected world, is another sound way to set limits and safeguard children's sleep. For her part, Schulte and her family have built in a kind of autocorrect mechanism for each other. "There are some times that I look up and my husband's on his email and I'm on my email and our kids are on their phones," she says. "We say, 'Phones down! Everybody be where you are.'"

As to the confounding question of how much is too much, the American Academy of Pediatrics recommends zero screen time for children under age two and a maximum of one or two hours a day of entertainment on screen for older kids—which sounds, I confess, too permissive on some days and too restrictive on others. I take comfort in the message from the organization Common Sense Media that the *quality* of kids' media diets matters as much as the quantity. "The reality is that most families will go through periods of heavy and light media use, but, so long as there's a balance, kids should be just fine," the group writes. The sweet spot for each child and each family will look a little different. The key is to make a media-use plan that suits your family and to talk with your children about your values. And, sometimes, to join them in consuming the media they enjoy! In my house, Zak and I have lots of fun watching *Modern Family*, whose all-too-relatable characters often lead us into meaty conversations.

You Count, Too

Now we come to the trickiest part of prioritizing wellness, the part that demands we pair our dedicated advocacy with deep introspection: modeling healthy living ourselves. This is true not only of monitoring our own technology use but also of moderating the pace of the entire way we lead our lives. As someone who has at times preached better than I practice, I know how challenging, and how important, this part of our work can be. Children learn their priorities not only from the structure of their experiences in school and at home but also, quite keenly, from the role models around them. In other words: us.

When I was at my most balanced, Zak was in middle school and the girls in high school. I was making my first film and putting into practice the lessons I learned in researching it. Our family had pulled back from overcommitment. Shelby and Jamey were playing just one school sport each. Zak played in the school band but exercised on his own, always on some kind of board (skate, surf, snow). For myself, though I had film screenings to attend and a growing grassroots community to nurture, I made time to exercise almost daily. I turned off my computer in the evenings, read books, and took hikes with my friends. When the kids saw me going to yoga class every week, they asked if they could come along. My wellness set the tone for the household. And, revelation of revelations, I found that—just as research would suggest—when I felt well and rested the quality of my work improved.

Nonetheless, maintaining balance is an ongoing challenge. When I started making my second film, I slipped back into familiar patterns, sleeping too little and sending emails at eleven p.m. Old habits die hard—especially when breaking them is an act of cultural defiance.

I have come to see that this problem, like every problem we've examined in this book, stems from twin plagues: our twisted vision of success and, related, a culture of busyness that has become synonymous with success itself. In the American lexicon, "success" is defined by publicly visible achievements: career, income, property, influence. It is the man who climbs his way into the corner office, the woman who leads a high-tech design team while raising perfect kids, and the child who plays state-level soccer and earns a 4.5 GPA—all of them dashing around to do so. Nowhere on that list would we typically think to put the man who simply makes time to meditate each morning, the woman who enjoys gardening with her neighbors, the young adult who feels rewarded by mentoring a struggling kid, or the child who sleeps amply and has time to stare at clouds. Why couldn't those be the markers of a successful life?

As we begin to redefine success—for our kids and for ourselves—we must place wellness at its core. That doesn't mean we need to quit all commitments and retreat into monastic stillness—though doing just that, at least occasionally, would likely do us all good. The key is to reset the balance. When I set about reclaiming my family's own runaway schedule, I began by asking myself what mattered most to me, and by asking my children what topped the list for them. I let go of believing that peace would come when I made it through my to-do list—an eventuality that, of course, never came. Instead, peace had to take precedence.

As parents, it is also time we reclaim the definition of successful parenting, with wellness ranking first. Half a century ago, success as a parent in America meant raising responsible, respectful citizens who stayed out of trouble and grew up to be gainfully employed and start families of their own. Now it seems the measure is how well your children perform, from school to sports to sparkling alma maters to high lifetime earnings. As the culture has tilted more toward materialism, so has the definition of excellent mothering and fathering. The focus is too often on what your child does, instead of on who she is. Let's tilt it back. Success ought to be raising a healthy, wholehearted child who cares for herself and others, appreciates everyday joys, and believes in her own ability to handle life's ups and downs.

For example, as Erin, the California teen, recovered from depression, her mom started a local support group for parents of kids dealing with mental health problems—thus bolstering children's and parents' wellness at once. Her mom also became a strong advocate at the school, convincing officials to add mindfulness lessons in PE classes, distributing suicide prevention information, and pressing the administration to appoint a liaison for students with health problems. I'd call that successful.

Young people today need to see more adults acknowledge health problems openly and place them before every other concern. In fact, experts urge us to talk honestly with our kids about our own stresses and struggles, and about the roots of and treatments for anxiety and depression. Schools and parent groups can play an important role here, by organizing events and campaigns to educate the community about mental illness and the effects of toxic stress. We should even discuss the realities of suicide, and we parents should ask our teens, directly and compassionately, if they've ever thought about it. The honesty doesn't scare them; it strengthens them. It also does not put the idea of suicide in their heads; psychologists are clear on that. Rather, it empowers young people to tend to their own hearts and prioritize their inner goals. It shows them that it's okay to ask for help. Most of all, it telegraphs to them, as they strain against the impossible expectations around them, that *they* are not the problem. As Erin observes, "There's all these kids who don't know that what they're living through isn't normal."

A final word on adults' wellness: like children, we, too, need strong personal connections in order to thrive. This always reminds me of a moment related to me by psychologist Suniya Luthar. After a lecture she gave on student stress in a privileged, high-pressured community, she spoke with a mother in the audience. The woman was beautifully, impeccably turned out, but Luthar recognized a look of despair and anguish in her eyes. That conversation awakened Luthar to the loneliness and isolation that so many mothers feel. And, I would argue, many fathers, too—all kinds of parents from communities across the socioeconomic spectrum. "Why? Because there is no time," Luthar says. "You're caught up in doing so much for so many people and doing it so well that there is absolutely no time or space left over for you to be connecting."

In a study she conducted of more than two thousand mothers, Luthar told me, a single question emerged as a strong predictor of our well-being: "Do you feel seen and loved for the person you are at your core?" In the midst of all our accomplishing and achieving, we often forget to make time for those everyday moments, with family or friends or strangers, where we give and receive love. "Little exchanges where you feel a true warmth from somebody do so much to inoculate you for the next several days or even weeks," Luthar says.

So as we begin to place our own wellness first, perhaps hauling it up from fifth or sixth place, where it has languished, we need to make *connection* a part of it. We thrive best when we each take care to create our own network of supportive friends and family. Friendship, love, and companionship are essential to our well-being. Let us grant ourselves the time and space to be well. We deserve it. "Once we get there," says Luthar, "we're going to be that much better able to do it for our children."

Irvington Strides On

Irvington High School is trying to get there, too. When I checked in on the progress of the school's wellness effort in mid-2015, the status was: slow—but determined.

Jackson and the Edjoycation Task Force students were preparing to hold their second Community Night Off, ideally with local elementary and middle schools on board. The Edjoycation students had handed out leaflets on sleep and tabled at the school health fair. The action that was making the most impact at Irvington so far, though, was a structural one: the new class

registration routine, which requires a one-on-one meeting with a counselor for every student and limits overloading on honors and AP courses
(as explained in chapter 5). "Even a lot of hard teachers who you'd think
would promote taking as many as you can, they're going, 'Oh, you should
only take three,'" said Edjoycation leader Aneesha. And some of her fellow
students were voluntarily reducing their course load to have more time for
themselves. The new registration process, no longer a free-for-all, she said,
"got them thinking."

It seemed that Jackson and the Edjoycation crew had achieved an important first step: awareness. At least Irvington students, teachers, and parents
were starting to recognize the problem, even as the pressure continued to
boil around them. And boil it did. Jackson said a half dozen kids had already
forged teachers' signatures to get into more AP classes. The yearbook was
still publishing its annual "Top 10" list of seniors with the highest GPAs,
and the student newspaper was fully funded by tutoring center ads.

Jackson's hopes for further wellness reform currently center on two ongoing strategies. One: embedding happiness lessons into students' regular
classes (Jackson is delivering many of these short teachings himself, visiting
English classes to provoke students to consider the true purpose of their
learning and remind them that happiness hinges not on our accomplishments but on our relationship to our goals). And two: his work with Stuart
Slavin, modeled on the successful process at Saint Louis University.

Slavin and Jackson were nearing the moment of revelation with a tactic
they'd been working on for months: a detailed scientific survey of students'
mental health. Unlike the informal survey Jackson had run before, this
one would reach almost every student in the school. It would use scientifically verified measures to gauge the teens' anxiety, stress, and depression. It
would link their ailments with factors such as sleep deprivation, homework
loads, AP courses, parental and peer pressure, and college admissions. All
told, it would reveal precisely how unwell Irvington students were and the
likely causes of their ill health.

What could possibly be so powerful about a survey? Proof. Jackson and
Slavin were after hard evidence that the epidemic of student distress is oc-
curring right here in *this* community, with *these* children. Such proof is what
Slavin possessed at Saint Louis University, where he enacted swift and ef-

fective reforms, and what he lacked at his daughter's high school, which refused to budge. What Slavin learned from that experience is that generic
stats about miserable teens across America aren't enough to conquer cultural and institutional inertia. "It has to be *your* kids," he observes. In fact,
measuring students' well-being is actually a practice that all schools should
do annually, whether they're considering reforms or not. It's just as important as any assessment of learning.

By the summer of 2015, after some number crunching, Slavin and
Jackson expect to have a scientific analysis of the real state of Irvington
students—including irrefutable data on the severity of their stress. And
they intend to use that evidence to get the community's attention. Forget your traditions, assumptions, and standardized tests, they might say.
Forget the *U.S. News & World Report* college rankings, the Common Core
standards, and Race to the Top. *Our kids are sick.* This problem is here, and
it is real. And as any parent knows, when your child is sick, nothing else
matters.

The data will also help them tailor new reforms directly to Irvington
students' real needs, based on the prime sources of stress that the survey
reveals. If the data-first method proves effective at producing real change,
and that change proves effective at improving children's health, then Slavin
wants to help many more schools apply it. "As a pediatrician and educator,
even though my younger daughter is now a senior in high school, this is part
of who I am and what I need to fight for," he said. "That's why I'm still here."

My own hope is for all of the above. I hope that Irvington and others can
restore health and wellness to their rightful place as our first priority. That
our shared definition of success comes to reflect integrity and joy instead
of status and frenzy. And that, even as we gather local evidence to provoke
broad change, we don't wait on the data to begin.

I know personally how much courage and tenacity the task can take.
My commitment to the cause has ruffled feathers at my children's schools,
where I've made more than one request for a meeting. It has made for awkward conversations in the pickup line, as other parents raised eyebrows at
my kids' empty schedules. It has also branded me as a bit of a renegade
among my friends. I hear the same from others—the Anne Robinsons, the
Stuart Slavins, and the hundreds more who contact me every year—who

have taken up the daily charge against the cultural inertia that says there's little we can do to hit the emergency "stop" on the treadmill.

We continue, though, because it is precisely this multitude of persistent actions that ultimately adds up to transformation. Many of the change makers we've met in this book have already shifted policy and moved public opinion, through organized actions with their schools, school district boards, and PTAs. Less visible but just as essential is sustaining the daily churn of change: the quiet, dogged, everyday decisions that we each constantly make to champion our kids' holistic well-being and safeguard the precious few years that make up their childhoods. It is through such actions that we dare to disrupt the status quo. This effort, at once individual and communal, is ultimately about healing our culture. And we will know we are successful only when our children are truly well.

CHAPTER 8

Action:
How You Can Replace the
Race to Nowhere

THIS IS what we've learned, in a nutshell.

Education and childhood should not be a race. Yet our achievement-obsessed culture has turned them into one. For too many children and families, the school years now feel like a sprint. Students race against what feels like a ticking clock, striving to burnish the best résumé and outcompete other kids on the path to college. From privileged enclaves to low-income communities, students, parents, and educators across the country feel relentless pressure to compete, achieve, and perform. Crowded out is time to genuinely learn, discover, and grow.

In homes across America, nightly homework marathons have replaced family dinners. High-stakes tests have turned ten-year-olds into clinical anxiety patients. Parents have converted into chauffeurs and taskmasters. And in classrooms, the mountain of content required for standardized exams keeps students and teachers in a mad scramble just to get through it, rarely pausing to consider questions deeply or develop creative skills.

Against this backdrop is the mounting expectation that children should zip through back-to-back music lessons, soccer practices, tutoring sessions, and other enrichment activities—forsaking sleep, health, family time, and play. The ironic result of it all is that our children are sadder and sicker, not smarter, and they're leaving home less prepared to thrive.

There is a better way, a way that cultivates the kind of genuine intellect, happiness, and integrity that is beyond measure. Many parents, educators, and students are already working to create it. We can all join them. Here are some simple truths and basic steps to guide us.

(Note that these tips apply to everyone. The "actions at home" are written toward parents, but students also could take the initiative and ask their parents for support. The "actions at school" could be spearheaded by anyone—student, parent, teacher, counselor, or administrator—and any community member could contribute. Suggested actions in each section appear approximately in order of difficulty, with the simplest starting points listed first.)

1. You govern your home.

Somewhere along the line, parents granted schools authority over what our kids should do *outside* of school. The result: countless hours of excessive homework and extended school activities, starting at an ever-younger age, all coming at the expense of sleep, family time, and the myriad kinds of learning that happen outside of classrooms. After-school hours belong to us. It's up to us, as guardians of our children's welfare, to gauge the healthiest, most important uses of their time. It's time to draw the line.

Actions at home

- *Look at your child's school-to-life ratio.* Keep track of the amount of combined time that homework and school activities take after the last bell, and how that affects your family. Just recognizing when the ratio is imbalanced is a first step to righting it.

- *Urge your child to go to bed at an age-appropriate hour,* regardless of homework. If homework assignments are consistently incomplete because they interfere with play, family time, or an appropriate bedtime, schedule a conference with the principal or classroom teacher to discuss the mismatch between assignments and your child's well-being. Children should be going to bed before, not after, working adults. The National Sleep Foundation recommends nine to eleven hours of sleep a night for children through age thirteen, and eight to ten hours for older teens.

- *Don't require your child to do schoolwork when she's sick.* Schools, under pressure to stick to a strict content schedule, tend to send home thick work packets to sick kids, which only mount into a homework pileup. Send your child a message that if she needs to rest, she can—and should. The work can wait. When asked, teachers are usually able to offer creative ways for students to combine or skip assignments if they've missed more than a day of class. Besides, the appropriate place for schoolwork to happen is in school.

- *Resist the push for private tutoring.* One-on-one support is worthwhile for some students and not for others. Yet in some communities, tutoring is practically standard fare, seeming necessary just to keep up with everyone else who's doing it. Ask yourself if it's really best for your child. Even better, encourage whole groups of parents to stop along with you, while calling on schools to bring lessons in line with students' actual developmental needs. Pricey private tutoring deepens inequality, extends the school day, eats up essential time for other experiences, prevents teachers and schools from truly seeing what kids understand, and sends the message to kids that we don't think they can do it themselves. Children who need extra help can ask their teachers—which also helps teachers keep better track of what students are and are not learning.

Actions at school

- *Ask your school to create a shared calendar* with teachers and coaches to track major assignments, events, and exams. This enables educators and mentors to check the combined demands on students and avoid accidental pile-ons. You can also ask your school to assign set days of the week to specific subjects for homework and tests to ease bottlenecks of out-of-school work.

- *Press your school district to set developmentally appropriate curriculum,* personalized for each child, so we can stop sucking up afternoon hours with outside tutors. There's no sense expecting all six-year-olds to read sentences and seventh graders to master algebra—or requiring those who are ready to learn more to wait. Each child reaches these kinds of milestones on her own schedule. Schools should also build time into the regular school day when teachers can offer students individual help, as Chicago's Walter Payton College Prep High School and the K-8 Potomac School in Montana have done.

- *Petition your school to set a no-homework policy on weekends* (aren't they supposed to be weekends?), holiday breaks (aren't they supposed to be breaks?), and over the summer—and to cap outside-of-school hours that may be directed to homework, sports, and clubs. Ultimately, petition for one evening each week to be free from all school obligations. Well-rested minds work better.

2. Homework doesn't work.

We tend to take it as a given that homework helps kids learn and develops their self-discipline. The trouble is, that's not necessarily true. Research shows little to no academic benefit to homework before high school, and diminishing returns in high school when take-home assignments last longer than an hour or two. Besides, homework exacerbates inequalities for students whose families don't have the resources to help them with it, or those who need to care for younger siblings or hold down after-school jobs. Moreover, once students are in departmentalized schedules with five to seven teachers assigning thirty to sixty minutes of work each, we're relegating them to a second or third daily shift. Excessive homework eats up the time kids need to grow in all the essential ways, not only academic. Exercise, socializing, downtime, and sleep all optimize children's brain functions and are essential elements of their growth. Homework shouldn't trump all.

In accordance with our Healthy Homework Guidelines—detailed in chapter 3—I recommend the following.

Actions at home

- *Let your child know your priorities from a young age* so that when she gets older she's already comfortable putting health and sleep before finishing every last assignment.

- *Avoid asking about homework the moment your child walks in the door.* A warm conversation or a bit of playtime between you and your child is more meaningful than being a taskmaster. It's important to honor the break that a kid needs after a full day at school.

- *Resist the impulse to do your child's work for her.* Doing so deepens inequities between kids and reinforces the message that kids can't handle their own education. Plus, parents' intervention keeps teachers from seeing how well students actually understand the assignment. If the work is negatively impacting your child, address that with the teacher.

- *Experiment with replicating your child's homework for a week,* as writer Karl Taro Greenfeld did for *The Atlantic,* to get a sense of what's truly expected of students and what, if any, benefits it might confer. "Memorization, not rationalization" was his thirteen-year-old daughter's advice to him. The experience left Greenfeld exhausted and doubtful about homework's merits.

- *Consider opting your child out of homework entirely in elementary and middle school.* Meet with your child's classroom teacher, guidance counselor, and principal to explain your stance at the beginning of the year, and encourage other parents to do the same. Change comes with critical mass.

- *Help your high schooler factor in homework overload when choosing classes.* It may be possible to prevent excessive after-school work by resisting the temptation to overschedule academically. Encourage your child to limit AP and honors classes to subjects she truly enjoys and wants to pursue and support her in advocating for herself if she needs to change her schedule.

Actions at school

- *Survey students school-wide to determine how much time they're actually spending on homework* and publicize the results. Ask them which kinds of work are helpful to them and which are not. It's surprising how frequently we forget to go straight to the source for feedback. Also consider surveying teachers on how much work they assign and compare their estimates to students' actual reports; teachers may be surprised by the realities.

- *Launch a community-wide initiative to have teachers and parents all do homework for a week,* as Greenfeld did in his home. Opinions may shift once adults have walked a mile in modern students' shoes.

- *Create study periods during the school day* where students can put new skills to work in the presence of a teacher who can help as needed. Doing so narrows the gap between affluent and poor students, provides teachers with valuable opportunities to offer individual attention, and supports a better school-to-life ratio.

- *Urge individual teachers and whole schools to stop grading homework.* As Virginia teacher Mike Miller found, eliminating the superficial goal of a grade can free students to think creatively and take risks. And research shows that grades diminish motivation. To grow and improve, learners need more feedback than a single letter, anyway.

- *Organize with fellow students, parents, and educators to make homework assignments at your school the exception, not the rule, and to allow any family or student to opt out.* One parent's preferences about how her child spends the after-school hours shouldn't dictate another's. It is through collective action that we can press effectively for this ultimate cultural change.

3. Just because you can measure it doesn't mean it matters.

In our test-obsessed education system, schools are under so much pressure to post good scores that they speed through tons of tested content while pushing aside deeper, more engaging ways to learn. The march toward uniformity leaves little room for attending to children's individual talents or needs. Tests now drive what and how we teach, when what we need is the other way around. When the tests are high-stakes—meaning teachers' jobs, schools' budgets, and students' diplomas are on the line—this structure does even more harm. The people in the best position to evaluate what students know and what they still need to learn are actually the teachers who know them. By placing so much weight on just one limited measure of student knowledge, we're dismissing entire other realms of important skills (creativity, cooperation, critical thought) and missing opportunities for much more meaningful learning driven by teachers and students themselves. Ironically, test scores aren't even a predictor of life success.

Actions at home

- *Remind your child that she is more than a test score.* Explain to her that standardized tests measure only one narrow set of skills in one limited way, and there is far more to human intelligence and value than that. It's important for her to hear this when even her teachers are stressed about the exam.

- *Opt your child out of standardized tests* if you find the exams are doing harm. Strengthen your action by organizing other parents to do the same. Parents have done this effectively even outside of the eight states—Utah, Wisconsin, Colorado, Pennsylvania, Minnesota, Oregon, Washington, and California—that explicitly allow it. Refer to the organizations FairTest and United Opt Out National for more information.

Actions at school

- *Remind your teachers that they are more than a test score.* Teachers, like students, need to know they're supported if they break the mold and strive for student engagement and deep learning instead of simply scores. Parents might take the time to send a positive note to school with your child thanking the teacher for a thoughtful assignment; administrators could celebrate great inquiry-based lessons at staff meetings.

- *Urge your high school to request to be removed from school rankings,* such as those published by *Newsweek* and the *Washington Post.* These rankings perpetuate the false notion that quality learning can be quantified and keep schools focused on the wrong goals.

- *Reserve more time for self-directed and open-ended projects* while spending less time on students passively listening to lectures. This is a crucial part of a shift toward making education student-centered. To develop creativity and collaborative skills that will be essential in work and life, students need time to explore complex questions without expected answers.

- *Call for an end to the publishing of student honor rolls, rankings, and test scores,* which promote the notion that scores matter most and prompt students to compare themselves to one another. Academic marks are a private matter. Experiment with ways, such as gallery shows and project exhibitions, to recognize and celebrate young people for a wide range of skills and contributions, academic and otherwise.

- *Encourage your school to use performance-based assessments* in which students demonstrate their skills by performing meaningful tasks (such as original research and design) and presenting them in various formats (such as visual depictions, oral presentations, written stories, or digital portfolios) rather than simply answering prescribed questions on paper. Capstone projects can replace final exams. Students at San Diego's High Tech High, for example, have published compilation books of their short stories, created a documentary film about gun violence prevention, and worked with the local port and zoo on sustainability for the San Diego Bay.

4. Learning is a process, not a product.

Education, likewise, is an experience and not an equation. Our educational system is stuck in churn mode: children crank out assignment after assignment, rarely getting the chance to receive deep feedback, refine their work, or reflect on what they have learned. Productivity takes precedence over improvement. The drive for perfect performance eclipses actual learning. And students often remain passive recipients of content. The classic bell schedule is another impediment; it cycles students to a different class every fifty minutes, leaving no time for depth or focus and little chance to have a say in what they learn. It also stacks up simultaneous homework assignments for as many as eight classes a day and prevents teachers of different subjects from collaborating. As a result, our children lose opportunities for rich learning daily because they're sleepy, hurried, and disengaged.

Actions at home

- *Cultivate a growth mindset in your home by praising effort, not outcomes.* A growth mindset holds that skills grow with practice and perseverance. Effort counts, and mistakes are opportunities to learn. Process and persistence are more important than perfect performance. Vocally observe your child as he tries, struggles, and improves, and don't lavish praise for specific grades or honors.

- *Change the focus of your conversations from grades and homework* to interests, efforts, and discoveries. Find opportunities to ask your child what she's interested in or excited about at school. What you talk about sends a message about what you value.

- *Allow your child to make mistakes and learn from them.* Ease performance pressure by talking with her about your own missteps and how they helped you improve.

- *Resist the temptation to constantly check grades on School Loop* or other online tracking systems. Everyday grades are not the most important part of kids' learning. And no one, including children, thrives when micromanaged.

Actions at school

- *Cultivate a growth mindset in your classroom and school.* This applies to adults' development, too. Make your school a safe place to innovate. Encourage teachers and students to take risks, and see the opportunities for growth in failure. Celebrate process and progress, not output.

- *Change the schedule to allow depth, foster relationships, and support personalized learning.* Block scheduling, in which classes meet for longer chunks of time and not all classes occur every day, is one model for doing this. A growing number of schools are making this switch and finding that it allows for deeper study.

- *Create opportunities for personalized and inquiry-based learning* in which students explore questions that they generate themselves on subjects with particular interest to them. This means creating flexibility in schedules and requirements so that teachers and students may shape their own experiences. Honoring students' own voice and choice in their studies helps to engage them. And the inquiry process—finding and vetting information sources, experimenting, and asking further questions—is just as educational as the answers students find.

- *Make constructive critique and revision an integral part of your students' work.* Otherwise, as educator Ron Berger says, you're just on "a treadmill of turning in final-draft work every day." The richer learning comes in the revision. Reducing the total number of assignments and projects will allow more time to go in depth on each one.

- *Provide teachers more time to work together and plan cross-disciplinary projects.* Old traditions keep teachers siloed in their classrooms, even though science, history, math, art, and language are intimately connected with each other in the real world. Supporting more staff collaboration can yield livelier projects, invigorate teachers themselves, and help students see deeper meaning in their work.

- *If it's tough to overhaul the whole school, try testing your innovations in certain classrooms where teachers, parents, and students can opt in.* Creating a little laboratory school within a school allows you to demonstrate the benefits of different methods without scaring those who are reluctant to change. The same strategy can be effective for many innovations, such as classrooms that are non–test driven or are homework free. Once they see the caliber of teaching and learning happening in this "lab," many more people may want to participate.

5. Brand names are for clothes, not colleges.

The college rankings, invented as a marketing technique to sell magazines, have mixed with other societal shifts to produce utter madness around college admissions. Your child's school years become an arms race, and their classmates become their competition. Even if your student isn't aiming for a top-ranked college, she is nonetheless swept up in the misguided sense that every school wants a superstar's résumé. It's all a shell game. There is no such thing as a "best" college—different students thrive in different settings—and colleges actually seek a diverse set of students. If you think about it, you probably know graduates of all kinds of schools who have gone on to be happy and well suited to their careers. The right college for your child might be one you've never heard of. Or a community college. Or, for some students, no college at all.

Actions at home

- *Emphasize with your child that the point of high school isn't simply to get into college.* Likewise, the point of high school and college isn't strictly to prepare for a career. Important learning happens for its own sake, and leads to paths and successes that cannot be prescribed. Discourage overscheduling and explicit résumé building. Encourage your child to make his or her choices about classes and activities with the present—and not just the future—in mind.

- *Help your child seek a "best fit"* rather than a "best" college. Your mantra: "Be yourself." No one but your child herself can determine the best path for her.

- *Boycott paid test-prep courses.* Like private tutoring, this is one of the "extras" that exacerbates social divides but that parents and students come to feel they need to do to keep up. You don't. The SAT and ACT are exams of limited value that mainly mirror family income and indicate little about a child's potential for success in college or in life. Not all colleges require them for admission. If, however, they are unavoidable, your child can prepare on her own with books and practice questions for a fraction of the cost. Then, take the exam itself no more than once or twice. Encouraging a teen to approach the tests this way will help her build self-efficacy, goal setting, and confidence. The time (and money) saved can be used for more nourishing purposes.

- *Refuse to buy magazines or read websites that rank colleges.* The rankings are a numbers game that says little about the educational experience. (Assessments such as *Washington Monthly*'s, which rates schools based on their contribution to the public good, are a notable exception.)

- *Based on your child's own priorities, help make a personal, anonymous assessment of colleges based on the schools' merits beyond brand name.* Together with your child, list the attributes of the colleges that interest her, such as campus setting, course offerings, and clubs, then compare them without the colleges' names. One Massachusetts dad I met did this with his son, who said he found it eye-opening.

- *Encourage your child to consider taking a gap year* to reflect on her goals and strengths and experience new endeavors away from school. Even the Harvard admissions office encourages this as a way to reduce stress, discover new interests, and arrive at college better prepared and ready to benefit. Information and resources are available through the American Gap Association.

Actions at school

- *Bust the myths about college admission.* All sorts of false ideas (that you need to take the SAT over and over again; that a kid with a B average can never get into a good college; that where you go to college will determine who you become) swirl around schools and add to students' and parents' anxiety. Information from the non-profit Education Conservancy can help dispel these myths. Go out of your way to spread the truth.

- *Refrain from publicizing lists of the colleges that admit students from your school.* These lists fuel the misperception that there are "best" schools and that status, not education, is the purpose of admission.

- *Invest in more college counselors* to provide personalized guidance to students seeking to scratch beneath the headlines and find the right college fit. This resource will also help level the playing field for students whose families can't afford private consultants.

- *Petition college admissions officers to cap the number* of advanced classes and extracurriculars they will consider on applications. They have the ultimate power to end the résumé arms race, and high schools (a.k.a. their recruiting centers) might influence them. High schools can also set caps of their own, as explained below.

6. Time is a mirror.

The way we use our time is the truest expression of our values. That means that, if we pay attention, our schedules can show us whether we're living our most important values or not. We need to constantly consider our children's school-to-life ratio and strive to help them keep it in balance. As the writer Annie Dillard famously said, "How we spend our days is how we spend our lives." Your child only gets one childhood.

Actions at home

- *Keep a log of your activities, and your child's activities, over the course of a few days.* The record will show you what you're truly prioritizing.

- *Safeguard time for what matters most* to your family. Sleep, exercise, family meals, and time to connect with friends and community don't come after you've checked off everything else on your to-do list. Often, much of the list can wait.

- *Choose one midweek day when your family schedules nothing.* No afternoon lessons or social engagements for kids, no evening meetings or events for adults. This is the moment in the middle of each week when your family is automatically set to pause, rest, and reconnect.

- *Model healthy use of technology.* Consider whether you own your technological devices or they own you, and ask your kids the same question. If tech is taking over, create tech-free zones for family interaction, such as the dinner table, the car, vacations, and the hour before bed, and call a regular tech-free evening (e.g., Tech-Free Tuesdays) when your family can connect in person. You might even create a weekly technology Sabbath: an entire tech-free day. Kids need our help learning to tame the tug of technology.

Actions at school

- *Keep a log of how much time in a day students spend* doing certain activities: listening passively to lectures, losing minutes to passing periods and attendance checks, using more minutes checking and assigning homework—or engaging deeply and actively in learning under their own direction. The imbalance you find may convince you to restructure your schedule and your methods (see guideline 4, above).

- *Ensure adequate breaks for kids of all ages.* Fears about high-stakes tests have prompted some schools to curtail recess, despite the mountain of evidence that rest supports learning and play is an essential part of cultivating happiness and creativity.

- *Plan community nights off* when teachers assign no homework, coaches cancel practice, and families are encouraged to turn off their technology at home. It'll give everyone a little glimpse of what it's like to rest, play, and reconnect with family without obligations hanging over our heads. If it works well, make it a monthly or even weekly occurrence.

- *Advocate for an appropriate school-life balance.* Document the daily hours your child spends on school demands and let teachers, coaches, and club directors know how all the lessons and activities assigned by many adults add up. Often they are unaware. Question how many after-school hours the school should own.

7. Less is more.

We want the best for our children, so when we see other kids loading up on Advanced Placement classes, dazzling audiences at the dance recital, or crossing the state to play soccer, we fear that ours are falling behind. In fact, we're more successful when we choose to focus on just the few things that matter most. Research shows that happiness lends itself to greater success (better work, health, and relationships), not the other way around. Even a bit of idleness itself is essential; neuroscience confirms that our most important and creative thinking and growing often happens when we're at rest.

Actions at home

- *Urge your child to limit the number of Advanced Placement and honors classes she takes at one time.* This choice affects homework, health, and everyday life in your home for the whole year. It may or may not affect her admission at the most competitive colleges, but wherever she goes, she'll be healthier when she gets there.

- *Help your child choose just a few activities that genuinely interest her,* not gobs of them that she feels obliged to stuff on her college résumé. Encourage her to fill in the blank: "Above all else, I want to do . . . with my free time." Colleges still appreciate applicants with strong character and real interests, and prioritizing her passions will help your child with time management, too.

- *Put a premium on play.* Not the structured kind, where kids appear at appointed times on soccer fields to take instructions from adults, but genuinely free and unplanned time, no adult direction allowed. Research shows it's essential for children to spend some time inventing activities for themselves.

- *Reclaim control of your family's school-to-life ratio*—and empower your child to do the same for herself. Like Berkeley sports mom Emily Cohen, try banishing the word *mandatory* from your home. Teachers and coaches are free to make requests for your kid's time. But if your child has a cold, a big exam the next day, or an important family event, you decide.

Actions at school

- *Limit the number of AP and honors classes any student can take at one time.* There's no proof that students learn more or better in AP classes; in fact, the huge quantities of required content tend to crowd out time for deeper learning. Yet students competing for college admission feel compelled to take more than everyone else, even at the expense of sleep, health, and learning. Colleges evaluate students' applications in the context of what their school offers; if there's a school-wide cap on AP classes, there's no penalty for not taking more.

- *Cap the number of mandatory hours students must spend on a sports team or school activity each week.* Research suggests that the benefits of athletics and activities diminish beyond about ten hours per week, total, for all commitments combined. Schools should set limits to preserve students' well-being and keep the proverbial playing field level among activities.

- *Consider shifting from semesters to trimesters* in which students take the same number of classes over a year but fewer each term. This schedule affords greater focus and allows more time for depth and independent work. Taking fewer, yet deeper, courses at one time also more closely resembles how students will learn in college.

8. Wellness is worth as much as academics.

Without physical and emotional well-being, no student can embark on a happy life or achieve his or her full potential. Research shows that stressed and sleep-deprived brains can't learn optimally. Yet young people's health is often an afterthought in an educational system that's sprinting to satisfy standardized-testing pressures and stubborn traditions. We need to put students' well-being in the place it deserves, as a foremost priority all its own.

Actions at home

- *Learn about the long-term effects of sustained stress on the mind and body* and share what you know with your kids and their teachers. Research shows the potential harm is profound.

- *Teach your children that their health is more important to you than their achievements.* That message too often gets lost in all our running around to meet expectations and obligations.

- *Model balance for your children.* We know the keys to well-being are sleep, good nutrition, exercise, play, purposeful work, time outdoors, and time to connect with friends and community. Make wellness a priority for yourself, as well, and explain to your kids what you're doing and why.

- *Know the signs of depression and talk with your teen about suicide.* Watch for the signs in the young people (and grown-ups) you know. California's Know the Signs campaign, available at suicideis preventable.org, is a helpful resource.

- *Start a support group for parents or families* dealing with stress and mental health concerns, as one California mom did. This way, you bolster the well-being of both kids and their caretakers at once. If the members agree, the group can also become an organization advocating for changes at school.

Actions at school

- *Campaign for later school start times.* Science has clearly established that kids' sleep chemistry changes in their teens, making them sleepier in the morning and more alert at night. The American Academy of Pediatrics recommends starting middle and high schools at eight thirty or later.

- *Elevate young people's voices by creating a student group, supported by school staff, to discuss and address excessive stress.* Irvington High's Edjoycation Task Force, which organizes fun stress-relief activities, and Ridgewood High School's Principal's Advisory Group, which works with teachers to tackle homework overload, are different examples of these. Kids need to know they'll be listened to if they speak up about the support they need.

- *Offer mindfulness lessons at school.* Besides reducing excessive stress on students, we also need to equip them with coping skills for stress they can't avoid. Mindfulness lessons for schools are rapidly growing, and research is finding that they can reduce depression and help improve children's attention, participation, and care for others. What's good for hearts and minds is good for learning.

- *Educate the school community on the signs of depression* and the ways in which our education system fuels it (e.g., marching students through repeated defeats and constant measurement, with no sense of control over their time or circumstances).

- *Measure stress, depression, and anxiety among your students.* An anonymous survey can help illuminate the real magnitude of the problem, which kids are often adept at hiding. Be sure to ask about the root causes of stress, and then design interventions to address

them, as Saint Louis University Medical School has done and Irvington High School is doing.

9. Relationships are the foundation of health and learning.

Humans are social beings, and strong connections with others are critical to the healthy development of children and to happiness at any age. Connections for kids are also a key to developing resilience, that all-important capacity to navigate challenges and overcome traumas that research shows is nourished by a strong bond with a caring adult. Interpersonal connections are critical to learning and motivation, too. It's the lessons connected to our personal interests and done with guidance from a teacher we know and trust that most often light up a mind. Unfortunately, our educational tradition tends to prevent personalization and erode the chances for kids and adults to get to know each other well. Important connections exist not only between and among teachers and students, but also between what young people are studying and what they care about. We have too much content to cover, too many testing requirements, and too many changings of the guard (switching teachers every year or even every hour) to make learning personal or connections deep. Clever schools are finding ways to fix this.

Actions at home

- *Know your child.* Inquire about her genuine interests. Avoid the temptation to become another constant measurer in a kid's life, asking continually about grades and scores; this way, she knows she still has your support even when she stumbles.

- *Prioritize kids' social time.* Time with friends—play for younger children, and hanging out for teens—is as essential to healthy growth as food and water. Protect social time from the myriad other "productive" obligations that would crowd it out.

- *Develop a village of supporting adults in your child's life.* Encourage kids to interact with teachers, coaches, fellow parents, clergy, and other community members. Each adult may offer something different: an interest, an interpersonal style, a life perspective. There will be times when kids need to turn to someone besides you.

Actions at school

- *Urge your school to schedule a weekly advisory period* where a small group of students and one adult meet to support one another and discuss important issues in school and life. Keep the same adviser-student group together for as many years as possible. Besides teachers, school counselors, nurses, and principals can lead advisories, too.

- *Offer ample opportunities for students to exercise voice and choice in their school experience.* Students who have a say in how their classroom runs, and a choice about what books they read or what topics they study, are more engaged. Schools in the New York Performance Standards Consortium, for instance, typically teach a whole class about a general topic (e.g., World War II) but allow individual students to choose which aspect (e.g., war propaganda, Rosie the Riveter, or the roots of the military-industrial complex) to study deeply.

- *Encourage your school to shift its academic schedule* for the sake of relationships, not just academics. The classic bell schedule makes teachers' caseloads too large and class time too quick and impersonal. Longer, deeper classes can create stronger teacher-student bonds and a calmer campus.

- *Ask your elementary school to consider looping*—keeping students with the same teacher for more than one year. Middle schools and high schools can create a similar closeness through team teaching, keeping fifty or sixty kids together as a unified group, with just two teachers (typically one for English/history and one for science/math) sharing all the same students.

10. Cultural rebellion is better with company.

It can be lonely diverging toward sanity and humanity in your child's education when every family around you appears to be marching straight ahead. Sometimes you wonder if *you're* the crazy one. You are not. Plenty of other parents out there share the feeling that the Great Résumé Race has no place in childhood. They, too, are wondering what to do about it. You'll gain crucial support—and amplify your calls for change—if you find them.

Actions at home and school

- *Talk about your values.* Talk about them anywhere (in private conversations and public forums, at birthday parties and youth sports meetings), with anyone who'll listen. By voicing your thoughts you'll empower others to listen to their instincts, too.

- *Build a support network.* When you meet others who share your values, stay connected with them. It's easier to break with convention when you're not the only one.

- *Arm yourself with reliable research* on the real benefits and costs of homework, the impact of test obsession, and the long-term effects of unchecked childhood stress. Solid knowledge will support your conversations. Understand what makes for *good* research. You'll find relevant studies cited throughout this book.

- *Listen to young people.* Ask kids how they're feeling and what they need. It's a simple but often overlooked step. Their voices matter, and their answers will inform your actions. Give students a real voice and a place at the table.

11. Society doesn't know everything about success.

When well-meaning adults ask kids the dreaded question "What do you want to be when you grow up?" we all know there are certain acceptable answers. The same is true when a fellow parent asks, "Where does your child go to college?" Name an unknown state university or say your child is not in college at all, and an awkward silence is likely to ensue. There's no sense blaming these people, since the assumption that status and money are the measures of success infects us all. TV shows and advertisements only reinforce the illusion. But we don't have to believe it—or participate in it.

Actions at home and school

- *Redefine success for yourself and your family.* Challenge your own assumptions. Ask your children (or students) about their views, too. If we look deep inside, tuning out the cultural noise, most of us will find that our hopes for our children are this simple: health, happiness, and the ability to support themselves and contribute something to their community.

- *Be explicit about your values.* Your children (or students) may get the message from everywhere else that anything less than a top-ranked college admission is inadequate. They need to hear, convincingly, from *you* what really matters, and to know they will be loved, valued, and respected no matter what.

12. Children's health and preparation for the future ultimately hinge on school change.

However much we do to cultivate healthy homes and prioritize meaningful learning instead of the collection of credentials, schools still have a lot of impact. We'll be swimming upstream until we help schools undo old traditions that hurt students' health and education and adopt new practices that tap children's individual talents and fulfill their needs. And we will only effect this change through a groundswell of grassroots action that begins with you. It is by engaging everyone that we begin to spark a cultural shift in our communities—a change deep and pervasive enough that it will outlast any one leader. You, along with your fellow parents, students, educators, and community members, are the advocates the next generation needs.

This last principle is crucially important—it is the ultimate aim of this book. It is also complex and tricky to execute effectively because it entails organizing diverse stakeholders, dealing with the historic and top-heavy

institution of education, and asking people to question assumptions they hold dear.

Fortunately, parent-advocates before us have found strategies for doing this effectively. I devote the rest of this chapter to presenting their advice.

How to Advocate Effectively for School Change

- *Gather your community together for a discussion of concerns and priorities.* This is what turned out to be so powerful about *Race to Nowhere*; the film screenings were an opportunity to bring communities together, raise awareness of the problems and potential solutions, spark discussion, and galvanize people to action. At screening after screening, I saw how the emotional testimonies of people in the audience shook others out of their complacency with the status quo and moved them to make change.

  "I was sitting here thinking about my son, who's only been in the first grade for, what, five or six months," said one parent in Castro Valley, California. "And he has already come home and asked me, 'Do you think I'm doing a good job? Are you proud of me?' This is my seven-year-old!" Feeling the power of her community assembled around her, this parent went on, "We need to mobilize, we need to do something. At what point are we just sick of it? What are we going to do about it? Can we join together, not just in Castro Valley, and get up there to the White House?"

- *Organize with like-minded parents and educators.* Every community possesses the power to set new priorities and organize for action—and the collective wisdom to know what it needs. All it takes to begin is to convene. "It's not a top-down change, it's a bottom-up," says High Tech High CEO Larry Rosenstock. "It's like community organizing. You go out and you individually connect with people." A parent meeting or film screening can be a starting point. Then, ask those who share your concerns to help you reach out to more people, speak out at school meetings, conduct research, propose new school policies, and orchestrate petitions.

Alicia Vanderhyden, a mom who supported reforms in Potomac, Montana, explains, "It takes a community. Change starts with one person, but the most powerful part of any change is not the leader, but actually the followers. It's that second and third person that have that faith that the change can happen, and that support it and practice it, that are the most critical."

- *Involve students from the get-go.* Students are, ironically, the most ignored voice in education reform—even though they are the most profoundly affected by school practices and the most intimately familiar with what works and what they need. You could solicit their input through informal conversations, formal surveys, or, as Trigg County, Kentucky, superintendent Travis Hamby did, by asking them to sit on the committee that would guide his schools' change. At Monument Mountain Regional High School in Massachusetts, educators even took a student seriously when he suggested starting a school-within-a-school for independent studies, with great results.

  "It was probably the very best thing that we did, to engage our students in the conversation," says Hamby. "If you want to think about what you want to create, let students talk about what it is that would more deeply engage them in learning. Students know the kind of learning experience they would like to have."

  Ron Berger, a Massachusetts teacher and chief academic officer of the Expeditionary Learning schools, adds this perspective: "The hard thing about changing school is that what we're familiar with is hard to step away from. We're in habits of how we teach. We're in habits of what we think school should be, so change feels a little scary to us, not just to parents, but to teachers, too. The only people who aren't afraid of that change are students themselves, because students grow up today in a changing world. They're ready to take on those challenges."

- *Partnerships between parents and educators are especially important.* As any mom or dad knows who has tried and failed to work through a school bureaucracy on an important matter, disconnection be-

tween home and school leaves parents feeling disempowered. It's also a wasted opportunity for a powerful collaboration. So parents, find someone at school who shares your goals (a teacher, an assistant principal, a counselor, a curriculum director), and join forces. Educators, reach across the home-school divide and do the same. The greatest potential for change comes when parents and schools work together.

Anne Robinson, pediatrician and parent-activist in Ridgewood, New Jersey, says a key to her success at starting reforms was finding one sympathetic administrator (Assistant Principal Jeff Nyhuis) and then sticking with him. "This is how you begin to create change: through conversation," she says. "The only way to create change is to open up lines of communication."

Her collaborator, Nyhuis, agrees. "I get very busy with other tasks," he says. "If I didn't have the parents helping me in pushing me in the right direction, we wouldn't be where we are today."

- *Use social media to expand your support network and amplify your message.* Create local networks to stay connected with people within your community who share your goals. Or connect with other reform-minded parents and educators, even those across the country or across the world, to find fresh research and resources and exchange experiences and ideas with others in the movement. The Race to Nowhere pages on Facebook and Twitter can be a starting point for finding these comrades.

It was in part through a Facebook group, for example, that New York State's testing opt-out movement mushroomed from one Long Island mother to the parents of more than 175,000 students statewide. Social media also played a central role in the Race to Nowhere network's successful campaign for homework-free holiday breaks. Ridgewood and Walter Payton took the lead. Then we shared their stories and called on everyone in our network to advocate for this symbolic change, placing a map on our website where schools could add a pin when they joined. Hundreds of schools and thousands of individuals ultimately participated.

Sometimes, the greatest benefit of participating in such communities is simply knowing you're not alone. One member of our Facebook community, Renee, wrote that the "daily doses of sanity...swim upstream in an onslaught of get-ahead-academically-at-all-costs-and-by-all-means messages." Another, Marianne, rallied fellow members to action with this cry: "Jump off the hamster wheel and start speaking up, there is strength in numbers!!"

- *Start with a realistic goal.* Traditions, even outdated ones, are sticky. You may need to spread awareness and win allies by starting with smaller steps that don't send skeptics away panicking. For instance, you could try homework-free holiday breaks on the way to making homework assignments the exception, not the rule. Begin with one hands-on, student-directed, cross-disciplinary project per semester. Or pilot your innovation with one class or teacher and then expand. A few small victories will fuel bigger ones. Be patient and persistent.

- *Gather data to support your case.* Resources in this book and on our website can provide general hard data. But beyond the general science on stress and school, you'll need local statistics to show that the problem affects your own community. Saint Louis University pediatrics professor Stuart Slavin found this out the hard way. He presented a host of general research on excessive homework and student health to the board of his daughter's Saint Louis school. Despite his credentials as a medical professor and pediatrician, he couldn't get the board to budge on easing students' pressure. Lesson learned: national statistics aren't enough to cut through the haze of the race to college. Says Slavin, "It has to be *your* kids."

So when he set about helping Irvington High School in California to address its stress problem, Slavin started by conducting a survey. (If it's too tricky to get approvals to survey at school, try asking local health departments or pediatricians' offices to share data.) He wanted to ask students: "Just how much homework are you doing? How much sleep are you getting? How many of you feel excessively stressed, anxious, and depressed—and why? How many of you are cheating?" The results of the survey, completed in spring 2015, will help Slavin and Irvington Assistant Principal Jay Jackson design appropriate interventions and—they hope— convince students, parents, and teachers that change is needed.

- *Start with those who are ready.* Forcing change on people who don't believe in it tends not to be fruitful. So when Trigg County was just beginning its move toward project-based learning, High Tech High's Rosenstock advised the team to get the teachers who were open to innovation started, and to give them as much support as possible. That's what Trigg did, beginning its experiment with just a few teachers who really wanted to try something new. Once parents and fellow educators see the impact the new methods are having, the Trigg team wagers it'll be easier to bring them along.

- *Be for something, not against something.* This is the strategy employed by Torri Chappell, a teacher turned parent-activist in San Anselmo, California. When the going gets tricky, remember that our work always comes down to what's best for kids. Be for health, rich learning, and family time. Those are priorities everyone can get behind.

Epilogue

I N THE YEARS that I have been advocating for change, there have been times when I felt so frustrated that I nearly wanted to throw up my hands, discouraged by the incremental nature and the glacial pace of change. Even in the face of a need so urgent—our children sick, disengaged, unprepared, and grieving for their lost hours and thwarted selves—reforms still grind on maddeningly slowly.

In many communities I've visited, it takes months of task force meetings and private pleas and public forums to begin to address concerns as fundamental as health and learning. A single night off from homework, one out of 180 school days in a year, counts as a victory. Even Palo Alto, which suffered a teen suicide cluster while I was making my first film seven years ago, jumped into a flurry of discussion then but followed through on very few changes. "It was a fairly sad school for a number of years, in terms of being in crisis and then just simply marching in place," says the new Gunn High School principal, Denise Herrmann. As I was writing this book, three more Palo Alto teens took their lives. I'm convinced that Herrmann is serious about reform and optimistic about her chances—but even she must contend with the pace of bureaucracy. Before she starts a social and emotional learning program years in the making, for example, the idea will have to spend yet another year in planning.

Meanwhile, the Race to Nowhere remains as toxic as ever. I see it in news stories and statistics: cheating is rampant, childhood anxiety is epidemic, and elite colleges entice an ever more absurd number of applications, only to reject the vast majority of them. The annual survey of entering college

236

freshmen posted its worst mental health ratings ever in 2014—though who knows, this could be outdone in 2015. I also see it in communities and families I know (a friend called me recently looking for a therapist for her thirteen-year-old son, who was so overwhelmed with work that he didn't want to get out of bed).

And I still see it in my own home, where just the other day Zak put in eight hours at school, including a required math class that takes place *after* the last bell, and finished at four p.m. Then he had a doctor's appointment, and we dropped off dinner for a friend who'd just had surgery. Errands done, we arrived home at seven—at which point Zak, who thrives on physical activity, had been doing required tasks for eleven straight hours without a moment of exercise, and he still had homework to do. His life was not his own. When Zak went to bed at eleven, homework still not quite complete and no time outside, he told me he'd been having trouble falling asleep at night. Is it any wonder?

Our competitive, lockstep model of education continues to pain students in every part of the socioeconomic spectrum. Susan Engel, the Williams College psychologist and education expert, encapsulates the breadth of harm done in her new book, *The End of the Rainbow*:

> *By allowing the pursuit of money to guide our educational practices, we have miseducated everyone. We are so hell-bent on teaching disadvantaged children skills (both academic ones, such as reading, and social ones, such as obeying rules) that will lead to a job that we fail to teach them the pleasure of being part of a literate community, how to make their work meaningful, or how to draw strength from the group—skills that might offer them a satisfying life. Just as bad is that middle-class and privileged children are pushed to view every stage of their schooling as a platform for some future accomplishment ending in wealth. This deprives them of the chance to figure out what they really care about, how to think about complex topics with open minds, and how to find a sense of purpose in life.*

Blessedly, though, amid the great challenges of this work I have also found great reasons for hope. Some of the trailblazing schools featured here have progressed even further since my last visits. The Trigg County schools in Kentucky are now using performance assessments in their middle school, and this fall they plan to expand their project-based learning initiative, which didn't even exist two years ago, into eleven grades. Trigg County is also working with state officials to create a waiver allowing high school students who meet basic academic standards to craft their own, personalized graduation plan in place of the standard, one-size-fits-all exit exam.

Meanwhile, more than 550 New York State school principals signed a letter protesting state tests. The young and growing organization Student Voice, which aims to place young people's perspectives at the center of education debates, unveiled its Student Bill of Rights, including rights to wellness, personalized learning, fair assessment, and opportunities to participate in the world beyond the classroom. Plus, schools from all over the world continue to visit High Tech High, seeking to emulate its creative and captivating approach to learning.

Sometimes the bravery amazes me. At Monument Mountain Regional High School in Great Barrington, Massachusetts, whose innovations are featured in my new film, *Beyond Measure*, Principal Marianne Young had the courage to skip a grant opportunity worth tens of thousands of dollars. Why? Because it would have required her school to significantly shift its schedule and align its curriculum with the specifications of a private company, the College Board, so as to place a prescribed number of students in AP classes. Young's school, which just launched a student-directed civics course, and where students and teachers recently worked together to build a makerspace, had much better things to do.

In celebrating these successes, it's important to remember that, in education, every piece of progress is fragile. Every positive reform is only one new principal, one new superintendent, one school board election, or one new regulation away from reversal. In Gaithersburg, Maryland, for instance, the ouster of a supportive superintendent in spring 2014 makes the future of Principal Stephanie Brant's homework and teaching reforms uncertain. Brant said to me after she heard the news, "I'm scared." The teachers, students, and administrators who are brave enough to make change need our loud and unwavering support. Schools, likewise, need to see parents as true partners in transformation.

As I reflect upon my journey, starting from that useless student-stress forum at my children's school that sent me over the edge to make my first film, I see that our cause has come a long way. A decade ago, the race was a problem shrouded in silence. We feared that if we questioned the march to "success" we'd be left behind. We tried to keep up because everyone else appeared to be keeping up. Every child who felt crushed by the impossible standards around her and every parent who secretly thought this race seemed crazy suspected that they were the only ones.

Now we are talking about it openly—not only those of us who are living it but also school superintendents and politicians and TV pundits and columnists. We are publicly calling competitive childhood what it is: a perversion of values, a sickness, a poison. We have broken the barriers of awareness. There is still too much private suffering, denial, and shame. But now we know that we are not alone.

This is precisely the progression that Betty Friedan traced in her status-quo-shattering 1963 book, *The Feminine Mystique*. Friedan called out the toxic culture of a society that suffocated women with rigid expectations, and she explained how freedom required that we change not only institutions but also our own mindsets. We had to challenge flawed assumptions, to break the chains "of mistaken ideas and misinterpreted facts, of incomplete truths and unreal choices," she wrote. That is how I see our task for kids today: we, too, must come to see the purpose of school and the point of childhood in a whole new way. "You do have to say 'no' to the old way before you can begin to find the new 'yes' you need," wrote Friedan. "Giving a name to the problem that had no name was the necessary first step. But it wasn't enough." First: awareness. Next: revolution.

That is why we must continue trumpeting these stories of change, whether they're small or large. It's also what compelled me to make a second film spotlighting solutions. Each person, family, school, or community that dares to challenge convention shows others that it can be done. Sharing these real-life triumphs will help us bridge the second canyon, from awareness to action. Eventually, the stories will grow so ubiquitous that our movement will reach an inflection point. So many people will be calling for sanity in childhood and education that the defenders of the broken old culture will start to feel like the crazy ones. Then our children will be truly free to learn.

It is too late for my kids. It has been crushing for me at times to visit so many centers of educational innovation while my own children remained trapped in a traditional school experience. The best I could do was to make my home a completely different world for them—a place where they weren't constantly measured, where their individuality counted and their health came first.

All three of them will be okay, though they have lost much along the way. Shelby today is a much happier and healthier person, as a college junior, than she had the opportunity to be in middle school or high school. She works and pays all her own expenses except tuition, by choice, preferring to stand partly on her own. She's spending the summer working at a camp for children with serious illnesses. The old me might have worried about that, seeing all the fancy corporate internships the other kids were doing and fretting over her future. Now, I couldn't be happier. Who knows what a difference she might make to those children, or what interests of her own she might discover?

As Jamey completes her first year of college, finally empowered to choose her own classes and set her own schedule, I see her confidence blossoming. On her own volition, she applied for multiple jobs working with animals, secured a weekly internship with Colorado State University's veterinary school hospital, and figured out how to take a Zipcar to the site seventy miles away. I believe Jamey has been able to do this in large part because she arrived at college centered and balanced—much healthier than she would have been if Doug and I had pressured her to fit the mold throughout high school.

And Zak, a high school sophomore, has learned (in part due to our laying off him) to manage all his schoolwork on his own. He takes fewer academic classes than other kids, and I'm glad. He still has too much homework, but we support him in taking time each day to be outdoors, pursue hobbies, and get enough sleep. He understands the value of education but also feels confident advocating for himself and breaking away from others' expectations to chart his own path. The teamwork, sociability, and responsibility that he's learning through the pursuits he loves will serve him well in the long term, far more than bookwork alone could.

So, although my own kids are almost grown, I continue this work because I want other children to start life better. My heart is uplifted every time I hear about the success of young people who broke out of the straight and narrow race and instead took a winding path strewn with great mistakes. These are unsung heroes—living proof that there is more than one route to a meaningful life, that we can diverge from the norm and *not* be left behind. In my travels I have met and heard about many of them.

There is Claire Carroll, who grew up in a Detroit suburb and withstood odd looks and critical comments from her peers, all bound for faraway universities, when she decided to enroll in community college after high school. She wasn't sure what she wanted to do and needed time to explore. A trip to Nashville gave her a taste for the music business, so she started choosing classes that would prepare her for music public relations and took a minimum wage event-planning job with a Detroit radio station. Claire transferred into Michigan State University as a junior, joined the school's student-run public relations firm, became the president her senior year, and graduated with multiple job offers.

Jarreau, from working-class Rancho Cordova, California, believed as a kid that he wanted to be a doctor "because everybody else did." In college, he discovered that he hated studying biology but found a fascination with adolescent development. "Once I figured that out, I got to study a subject that I adored," he says. Jarreau became an alcohol abuse educator, as well as a spin instructor and life coach, and he loves it.

John Slater, another Michigander, skipped college altogether, except for a smattering of community college classes, and went to work in a lawn mower repair shop. What might have looked like a dead end was actually a beginning; he moved from there to a job as a mechanic at an auto dealership, then graduated to high-end cars, and finally went to work on Indy-style race cars. Along the way, he started his own design and fabrication business, taking custom orders. His mechanical expertise recently took him to a race in Monaco.

Finally, there is Nina Rubenstein, a onetime college dropout from rural Oregon with an irreverent wit and a taste for political debate. Nina is unabashedly honest about the ways she's stumbled. She recalls struggling to get through all the work in high school, although she found much of it useless, and spending "a lot of nights frustrated beyond function and probably crying." Her dad tried to reassure her: "This does not mean you're not smart, it means you're smart in a different way." After high school, she enrolled at Mills College in Oakland. Why did she go to college then? "Because that's what you did," she says. By her own admission, Nina wasn't ready. "I had no business being in college when I was eighteen," she says. "I was wasting time." (How many other teens who went to college on autopilot could say the same thing?)

After two years of halfhearted studying, Nina dropped out. She commenced a series of moves across the country, from city to city, working at Trader Joe's and wondering who she was. Unlike college, this was not wasted time. "I learned that work life is monotonous. I learned that school can be something you long for rather than resent," Nina remembers. Also, "I learned about being a grown-up and paying bills and being places on time."

The pivotal moment for Nina came in the unlikeliest of places. She had joined AmeriCorps and was working for the Washington Conservation Corps, where she earned so little that she qualified for food stamps, when she was invited to deploy to Alabama for a month of tornado-relief work. "I've always believed that every once in a while you should do something that scares you, and this was scary, so I did it," Nina says. Suddenly, she was dropped into the middle of devastation. She and her crewmates would arrive at a work site to find entire homes scattered across an open field, parts of them impaled on tree trunks broken off like toothpicks. They would labor all day clearing debris alongside the homeowners. Occasionally, they'd find an item intact—a daughter's favorite stuffed animal, pieces of a wedding album. The homeowners would cry, "and sometimes we would cry, too, and stop and hug, and then get back to the task of moving on," Nina recalls.

Later, she took on a role as a one-woman call center, handling calls to and from homeowners about the status of their work orders and developing relationships with them along the way. One day, a weary middle-aged man with leathered skin walked up to her in her parking-lot-turned-command-center. "Are you Nina?" he asked. "Oh my God, I recognized your voice, we've been talking on the phone for a week. Thank you *so much*." There, in the midst of so much loss and sadness and fear and uncertainty, Nina realized she had made an impact. And, she says, "It was like I got slapped in the face with my reasons for being."

Now show me where you'd find *that* in a traditional school curriculum.

Within weeks of returning home, Nina applied to complete her bachelor's degree in disaster management and homeland security studies at the Tulane University School of Continuing Studies. She moved to New Orleans and worked full-time as an office assistant while taking classes at night, made the Dean's List for consecutive semesters, and became president of Tulane's student chapter of the International Association of Emergency Managers. As this book went to press, Nina graduated with honors—a month shy of her twenty-ninth birthday—happy, highly employable, poised to use her talents for good, and finally believing that her dad was right.

———

I want so many more promising young people to make discoveries like Claire, Jarreau, John, and Nina did. I want to open up more winding pathways, more socially acceptable routes to a worthy life, and to ensure that kids won't feel dumb and defective if they choose to follow them. I want bright young minds, supported by healthy bodies, to spark with excitement about the worlds opened up to them by *learning*. Our children's future and our country's future depend on it.

We can do this. We can do this if parents organize together and simply say *no*. No, my child does not need more assignments on top of a thirty-five-hour workweek. No, you may not take up two weeks of my child's school year on state tests that kill children's curiosity and teach them nothing. No, a Harvard diploma is not the only possible evidence of my child's success. And the blowback be damned: "Maybe in the end I'll lose my job because test scores go down, who knows," said Amy Swann, then a Danville, Kentucky, principal who was daring to try creative and personal project-based lessons (and who did *not* lose her job, in the end). "But it's a battle that's worth taking. There are certain hills that are worth dying on, and I think kids are that."

We can only do this if parents join forces with educators who share our vision, and if we begin our work by listening to students, who already know what they need. All of our voices together are loud enough to rise above the madness and say: "No, it's not a race." The most important lessons and qualities cannot be measured. And insisting on measuring them will never lead our kids to thrive.

When I feel exasperated and worn down by the obstacles in our way, I remember a poem written by Colin, a high school sophomore in New Jersey. His mom, Jacqueline, found it in the trash and asked his permission to share it. The poem, titled "The Kids Aren't Alright," includes these lines:

> *There are so many things to speak about,*
> *The importance of not wasting time,*
> *So that you don't let it all tick down,*
> *And wake up when you're forty,*
> *Searching for the happiness,*
> *In the corporate grind,*
> *You were promised,*
> *By the greatest lie of all time,*
> *The American dream,*
> *Or the broken education system,*
> *Not enough for the poor kids,*
> *And all the wrong things for the rich kids,*
> *Screwing our generation over,*
> *Without ever admitting that,*
> *The kids aren't alright,*
> *But that's of no concern,*
> *Because the blame can be passed around,*
> *Make us somebody else's problem,*
> *Parents blame the school,*
> *The school blames the teachers,*
> *The teachers blame the students,*
> *And the students blame the parents,*
> *Because they haven't learned a thing,*
> *Or the experience is stressing them out beyond belief,*
> *And as the numbers of use and abuse rise,*
> *The blame keeps getting passed along,*
> *Because we're the future's problem now . . .*

After finding the poem, Jacqueline wrote her son a three-page letter spelling out in thoughtful detail the changes that our schools and our society need. The letter began with the words, *I am sorry for letting you down*, and ended with a promise: *I will work to enact change to make this happen for you.*

In that spirit, I write the following to Shelby, Zak, and Jamey:

In your honor, I will work fearlessly to undo the cultural tangle that tells you your only value lies in grades, admissions, scores, and fortune. I will insist upon an education system that cherishes individual minds, nurtures healthy bodies, and opens myriad doors to students instead of shutting all but one. I will collaborate, with perseverance and integrity, with everyone who shares this goal.

You survived this trial, to your credit, with your *selves* intact. But we, the adults in society, owe you something better than that. And if we want our society to thrive when you inherit it, we must deliver. I commit my own time, strength, and energy to creating a world in which each child, fragile and hopeful as each is born, can sustain the curiosity and possibility that I saw fade from your eyes and only recently return. Childhood is no time for constant panic or pervasive self-doubt. Childhood is the *very* time for curiosity, for possibility, and for discovering who you really are in a setting that's supportive and safe.

I take up this quest so that the children who follow you will have that chance. And so that you know, beyond any doubt, what matters most to me.

Acknowledgments

Since my first days shooting *Race to Nowhere*, my work has always been an act of collaboration. This book is no exception. A chorus of voices inspired, supported, and shaped it from first concept to final copy. That chorus—loud and growing louder—is made up of the thousands of students, parents, teachers, principals, pediatricians, professors, researchers, counselors, and coaches who believe in a better way to raise and educate our children. Their letters, phone calls, and conversations have forged my thinking about the past and future of American education. Moreover, they have become the fabric of this book: the insights and examples that reflect an exciting and growing movement to revolutionize learning in the classroom and beyond. Jacqueline Rush, a student who passed away in 2014, deserves special recognition for the joy and generosity with which she lived and the determination with which she continued to participate in our work even as she battled cancer. To each of you in this movement, I offer my respect and gratitude.

Thank you, in particular, to the people whose personal and professional stories appear in these pages, and to the many more who have welcomed me into your living rooms, classrooms, and offices over the years, unafraid to stand up to the status quo and to reveal your struggles along the way. Your courage to share your lives, work toward change, and translate your concern into action is the reason I wrote this book.

I owe special thanks to my writing team, especially the formidable and speedy Grace Rubenstein, my cowriter and collaborator for the past year, whose powers of synthesis and storytelling, and whose reportorial eye, have helped mold into book form my eight-year journey through the American education landscape. Caitlin Boyle deserves huge appreciation as a thought partner and wordsmith who helped hone and polish every paragraph, from the first outline through the final draft. Thanks, too, to Sara Bernard, for stalwart research; to Mitzi Mock, for invaluable first-read feedback and fact-checking; to Sara Godley, for detailed management of our releases and critical support on deadline; to Chelsea May Bedard, for nurturing our relationships with the international Race to Nowhere community and meticulously documenting community members' trials and successes; and to Sara Truebridge, for her expertise, friendship, reading of drafts, and engagement in an ongoing dialogue about these issues. Sincere thanks, as well, go to Jess Deutsch and Donna Jackson Nakazawa for their early contributions; to Sharon Wood, Mary Ellen Hannibal, Jason Friedman, Michelle Ferber, and Sara Bennett, for the time and thoughtful feedback they offered as early readers of the manuscript; to Elizabeth Kaplan, the literary agent who believed in this story and helped shepherd it to Simon & Schuster; and to Millicent Bennett, my editor, whose careful eye and keen sense of structure guided us to a stronger book. Constructive feedback is an essential ingredient in my work, and I am grateful to everyone who has provided it.

My friends and family also played essential roles in this book's realization. My parents, sisters, and brother have been and continue to be an invaluable source of love and support. Doug encouraged me to take on this ambitious quest for change and, despite its demands, to see it through. Aunt Jackie, an author in her own right, urged me to write and provided helpful input. My mother, in particular, instilled in me a passion for learning and a respect for the power of education, while prioritizing effort over achievement. She was ahead of her time.

Finally, my deepest appreciation goes to my children, whose company, love, and spirit have made my life richer from the moment they were born. Shelby, thank you for challenging me, reading drafts, offering constructive feedback, and sharing your school memories. Jamey, thank you for allowing me to tell your stories and contributing your own wisdom and reflections about your educational path. And Zak, thank you for seeing humor in your experiences even as they shape you, cooking gourmet meals and snacks for a mother hard at work, and pulling me away from the computer to spend time outside with you. Without each of you, this book would not exist.

—Vicki Abeles

My appreciation goes to Kathleen Foote, for reading me the storybooks that inspired me to write. Donald Rubenstein, for urging me to grab life's lapels and never doubting that I could. Both parents, for never expecting any more than that I be honest, responsible, kind, and true to myself—thus sparing me from the extremes of the Race to Nowhere. Jim Daly, for the patience, advice, and entertainment during my long months on book deadline. And the San Francisco Writers Grotto, for supporting me every step of the way.

—Grace Rubenstein

Notes

Prologue: Out of Nowhere

7 *It is, against all odds*: "Fast Facts: Back to school statistics [2014]," National Center for Education Statistics, accessed May 8, 2015, http://nces.ed.gov/fastfacts/display .asp?id=372.

1. Sicker, Not Smarter

19 *On the American Psychological Association's*: American Psychological Association, *Stress in America: Are Teens Adopting Adults' Stress Habits?* (Washington, DC: February 11, 2014).

19 *Meanwhile, 30 percent of high schoolers*: "1991–2013 High School Youth Risk Behavior Survey Data," Centers for Disease Control and Prevention, accessed June 2, 2015, http://nccd.cdc.gov/youthonline.

19 *By her calculations*: Jean M. Twenge et al., "Birth cohort increases in psychopathology among young Americans, 1938–2007: A cross-temporal meta-analysis of the MMPI," *Clinical Psychology Review* 30 (2010), 145–54.

19 *This doesn't bode well*: National Institute of Mental Health, "Depression in Children and Adolescents (Fact Sheet)," accessed online June 15, 2015, http://www.nimh.nih.gov /health/publications/depression-in-children-and-adolescents/index.shtml.

Stephanie L. Burcusa and William G. Iacono, "Risk for Recurrence in Depression," *Clinical Psychology Review* 27, no. 8 (December 2007), 959–85.

19 *Federal data also show*: "Death rates for suicide, by sex, race, Hispanic origin, and age: United States, selected years 1950–2010," Centers for Disease Control and Prevention, accessed June 2, 2015, http://www.cdc.gov/nchs/data/hus/2011/039.pdf.

19 *What's less well known*: "Suicide Prevention: Youth Suicide," Centers for Disease Control and Prevention, last modified March 10, 2015, http://www.cdc.gov/violence prevention/pub/youth_suicide.html.

21 *Wehmhoefer observed extreme anxiety*: Jan Hoffman, "Anxious Students Strain College Mental Health Centers," *New York Times*, May 27, 2015, accessed online.

21 *In the latest National Survey*: Robert P. Gallagher, *National Survey of College Counseling*

Centers 2014, monograph series no. 9V (Alexandria, VA: International Association of Counseling Services Inc., 2014), http://www.collegecounseling.org/wp-content/up loads/NCCCS2014_v2.pdf.

21   *Indeed, more than half*: American College Health Association, "American College Health Association–National College Health Assessment II: Reference Group Executive Summary Spring 2014" (Hanover, MD: American College Health Association, 2014), p. 15.

21   *One in three*: Ibid., p. 14.

21   *Tulane University, particularly hard hit*: Liz Goodwin, "Tulane's mental health meltdown," *Yahoo News*, April 5, 2015, http://news.yahoo.com/tulane-s-mental-health -meltdown-144028239.html.

21   *"The increased need for mental health services"*: April Dembosky, "Students Struggle to Access Mental Health Services on UC Campuses," KQED News, September 19, 2014, http://ww2.kqed.org/stateofhealth/2014/09/19/students-struggle-to-access-mental -health-services-on-uc-campuses/.

21   *In 2014, these students' ratings*: Cooperative Institutional Research Program, *The American Freshman: National Norms Fall 2014* (Higher Education Research Institute at University of California, Los Angeles, February 2015), http://www.heri.ucla.edu/briefs /TheAmericanFreshman2014-Brief.pdf.

22   *This rare disease*: R. L. Richards, "The Term 'Causalgia,'" *Medical History* 11, no. 1 (January 1967), 97–99.

         "Complex Regional Pain Syndrome Fact Sheet," National Institute of Neurological Disorders and Stroke, last modified February 23, 2015, http://www.ninds.nih.gov /disorders/reflex_sympathetic_dystrophy/detail_reflex_sympathetic_dystrophy.htm.

         Edin Randall, personal communication, December 3, 2014.

24   *Researchers from the CDC*: Danice K. Eaton et al., "Prevalence of Insufficient, Borderline, and Optimal Hours of Sleep Among High School Students—United States, 2007," *Journal of Adolescent Health* 46, no. 4 (April 2010), 399–401.

24   *The rise of sleeplessness*: Jennifer Moses, "Waking Up to Young Kids' Sleep Troubles," *Wall Street Journal*, November 5, 2011, http://www.wsj.com/articles/SB10001424052 9702045282045770120232998869S2.

24   *As Cornell University sleep expert*: James Mass and Rebecca Robbins, *Sleep for Success* (Bloomington, IN: Authorhouse, 2011).

24   *In a National Sleep Foundation poll*: National Sleep Foundation, *2014 Sleep in America Poll: Sleep in the Modern Family* (Arlington, VA: March 2014), http://sleepfoundation .org/sleep-polls-data/sleep-in-america-poll/2014-sleep-in-the-modern-family/.

24   *A 2014 report on teen sleep*: Adolescent Sleep Working Group, Committee on Adolescence and Council on School Health, "Policy Statement: School Start Times for Adolescents" *Pediatrics* 134, no. 3 (September 2014), 1697.

24   *Sleep plays a key role*: "Why Sleep Matters: Sleep, Learning, and Memory," Harvard Medical School, last modified December 18, 2007, http://healthysleep.med.harvard .edu/healthy/matters/benefits-of-sleep/learning-memory.

24   *Just how foggy*: Po Bronson, "Snooze or Lose," *New York*, October 7, 2007, http://nymag .com/news/features/38951/.

25   *Insufficient sleep is known*: Eaton et al., "Prevalence of Insufficient, Borderline, and Optimal Hours."

27   *For his 2012 story*: Alan Schwarz, "Risky Rise of the Good-Grade Pill," *New York Times*, June 9, 2012, http://www.nytimes.com/2012/06/10/education/seeking-academic -edge-teenagers-abuse-stimulants.html.

27   *The availability of prescription*: Nora D. Volkow, testimony to US Congress (September 22, 2010), http://www.drugabuse.gov/about-nida/legislative-activities/testimony -to-congress/2010/09/prescription-drug-abuse.

27   *Prescription rates for teens*: Samuel H. Zuvekas and Benedetto Vitiello, "Stimulant Medication Use among U.S. Children: A Twelve-Year Perspective," *American Journal of Psychiatry* 169, no. 2 (2012), 160–66.

28   *In the national 2013 Monitoring the Future*: "DrugFacts: High School and Youth Trends," National Institute on Drug Abuse, last modified December 2014, http://www.drugabuse.gov/publications/drugfacts/high-school-youth-trends.

29   *In the radio report*: Dembosky, "Students Struggle to Access Mental Health Services."

29   *This work, originating*: American Academy of Pediatrics, "The Lifelong Effects of Early Childhood Adversity and Toxic Stress," *Pediatrics* 129, no. 1 (January 1, 2012), 232–46.

Candice L. Odgers and Sara R. Jaffee, "Routine Versus Catastrophic Influences on the Developing Child," *Annual Review of Public Health* 34 (2013), 29–48.

30   *Stress begins its spread*: American Academy of Pediatrics, "The Lifelong Effects."

31   *In fact, a survey*: Odgers and Jaffee, "Routine Versus Catastrophic Influences."

32   *A psychology professor at Arizona State University*: Suniya S. Luthar, Samuel H. Barkin, and Elizabeth J. Crossman, " 'I can, therefore I must': Fragility in the upper-middle classes," *Developmental Psychopathology* 25, no. 4, pt. 2 (November 2013), 1529–49.

33   *School counselors widely report*: Sharon Noguchi, "Teen Health: Depression, Anxiety, and Social Phobias Rising in Kids, Educators Say," *San Jose Mercury-News*, February 5, 2014, accessed online, http://www.mercurynews.com/health/ci_25074044/teen -health-depression-anxiety-and-social-phobias-rising.

34   *All together, the glittering images*: Jean M. Twenge and Tim Kasser, "Generational Changes in Materialism and Work Centrality, 1976–2007," *Personality and Social Psychology Bulletin*, 39, no. 7 (May 2013), 883–97.

36   *Research has linked chronic stress*: American Academy of Pediatrics, "The Lifelong Effects of Early Childhood Adversity and Toxic Stress."

36   *Loss also occurs*: Ibid.

36   *"[T]he brain's malleability"*: Laurence Steinberg, *Age of Opportunity: Lessons from the New Science of Adolescence* (Boston: Eamon Dolan/Houghton Mifflin Harcourt, 2014), p. 9.

37   *America's high school and college graduation rates*: Henry M. Levin and Cecilia E. Rouse, "The True Cost of High School Dropouts," *New York Times*, January 25, 2012, accessed online.

OECD, "Education at a Glance 2013: OECD Indicators," OECD Publishing (2013), http://dx.doi.org/10.1787/eag-2013-en.

37   *And while the high school graduation rate*: Janie Boschma, "A Surge in U.S. High School

Graduation Rates," *The Atlantic*, November 7, 2014, http://www.theatlantic.com/edu
cation/archive/2014/11/high-school-graduation-rates-at-an-all-time-high/382494/.

US Department of Education, "Profile of Undergraduate Students, 2011–2012,"
NCES Web Table 2015-167, October 2014.

37 *This is one of the reasons*: US Department of Education, National Center for Education
Statistics, "The Condition of Education 2014: Institutional Retention and Graduation
Rates for Undergraduate Students," NCES 2014-083 (2014).

38 *College professors increasingly*: William Deresiewicz, *Excellent Sheep: The Miseducation of
the American Elite and the Way to a Meaningful Life* (New York: Free Press, 2014).

Abigail Baird, personal communication. Alison Gopnik, personal communication.

38 *But more and more*: Chegg Inc., *Bridge That Gap: Analyzing the Student Skills Index* (Fall
2013), https://www.insidehighered.com/sites/default/server_files/files/Bridge%20
That%20Gap-v8.pdf.

Center for Professional Excellence, *2014 National Professionalism Survey: Career Development Report* (York College of Pennsylvania, 2014), http://www.ycp.edu/media/york
-website/cpe/2014-National-Professionalism-Survey—-Career-Development-Report.pdf.

Millennial Branding and American Express, *The Gen Y Workplace Expectations Study*
(Boston: September 3, 2013), http://millennialbranding.com/2013/gen-workplace
-expectations-study/.

38 *Analyzing thirty-five years of data*: James J. Heckman, Jora Stixrud, and Sergio Urzua,
"The Effects of Cognitive and Noncognitive Abilities on Labor Market Outcomes
and Social Behavior" (paper presented at the American Economic Association annual
meeting, Boston, January 2006, and six other locations).

38 *A 2011 analysis at the University of Michigan*: University of Michigan, "Empathy: College students don't have as much as they used to," news release, May 27, 2010, http://
ns.umich.edu/new/releases/7724-empathy-college-students-don-t-have-as-much-as
-they-used-to.

39 *A Harvard Graduate School of Education survey*: Rick Weissbourd et al., *The Children We
Mean to Raise: The Real Messages Adults Are Sending About Values* (Cambridge, MA:
Making Caring Common Project, Harvard Graduate School of Education, 2014),
http://sites.gse.harvard.edu/sites/default/files/making-caring-common/files/mcc_the
_children_we_mean_to_raise_0.pdf.

39 *Evidence from the Josephson*: Josephson Institute of Ethics, *2012 Report Card on the
Ethics of American Youth* (Los Angeles: 2012), http://charactercounts.org/pdf/report
card/2012/ReportCard-2012-DataTables.pdf.

39 *Daniel Kahneman and his colleagues*: Daniel Kahneman et al., "Would You Be Happier If
You Were Richer? A Focusing Illusion," *Science* 312 (2006), 1908–10.

Daniel Kahneman and Angus Deaton, "High Income Improves Evaluation of Life
But Not Emotional Well-Being," *Proceedings of the National Academy of Sciences*, 107,
38 (2010), 16489–93.

40 *The dean and director*: William Fitzsimmons, Marlyn E. McGrath, and Charles Ducey,
"Time Out or Burn Out for the Next Generation," Harvard College, 2000 (revised
2011), https://college.harvard.edu/admissions/preparing-college/should-i-take-time.

2. It's About Time

43 *"This disease of being 'busy'"*: Omid Safi, "The Disease of Being Busy," *On Being With Krista Tippett*, November 6, 2014, http://onbeing.org/blog/the-disease-of-being-busy /7023.

44 *Let's start by turning the lens*: Tira Okamoto, personal communication.

46 *Seduced by society*: Brigid Schulte, personal communication.

46 *"As parents, we want"*: Ron J. Turker, "All Played Out," *New York Times*, July 27, 2014, accessed online.

47 *A team at the University of Michigan*: F. Thomas Juster, Hiromi Ono, and Frank P. Stafford, *Changing Times of American Youth: 1981–2003* (Ann Arbor, MI: Institute for Social Research, University of Michigan, 2004).

47 *University of Washington researchers*: Pooja S. Tandon, Brian E. Saelens, and Dimitri A. Christakis, "Active Play Opportunities at Child Care," *Pediatrics* 135, no. 6 (June 2015), 1425–31.

47 *Boston College psychologist*: Peter Gray, "The Decline of Play and the Rise of Psychopathology in Children and Adolescents," *American Journal of Play* 3, no. 4 (2011), 443–63.

48 *An explanation of what makes downtime*: Mary Helen Immordino-Yang, Joanna A. Christodoulou, and Vanessa Singh, "Rest Is Not Idleness: Implications of the Brain's Default Mode for Human Development and Education," *Perspectives on Psychological Science* 7, no. 4 (July 2012), 352–64.

48 *The author Tim Kreider*: Tim Kreider, "The 'Busy' Trap," *New York Times* Opinionator, June 30, 2012, http://opinionator.blogs.nytimes.com/2012/06/30/the-busy-trap/.

49 *She examined the scores*: Kyung-Hee Kim, "The Creativity Crisis: The Decrease in Creative Thinking Scores on the Torrance Tests of Creative Thinking," *Creativity Research Journal* 23, no. 4 (2011), 285–95.

49 *One MIT undergraduate dean*: Annie Murphy Paul, "In Praise of Tinkering," TIME.com, October 19, 2011, http://ideas.time.com/2011/10/19/in-praise-of-tinkering-2/.

49 *"When you're playing with other kids"*: Annie Murphy Paul, personal communication.

50 *Indeed, a 2014 study*: Jane E. Barker, "Less-structured time in children's daily lives predicts self-directed executive functioning," *Frontiers in Psychology* 5 (June 17, 2014), 593.

51 *The consequences, besides lost time*: John P. DiFiori et al., "Overuse injuries and burnout in youth sports: A position statement from the American Medical Society for Sports Medicine," *British Journal of Sports Medicine* 48 (2014), 287–88.

University of Florida Sport Policy & Research Collaborative, "Research brief: What does the science say about athletic development in children?" prepared for the Aspen Institute Sports & Society Program's Project Play (September 13, 2013).

51 *"Many parents have come to believe"*: Brooke De Lench, "Early Specialization: Nine Reasons Why It Is a Bad Idea," MomsTeam.com, accessed June 2, 2015, http://www .momsteam.com/successful-parenting/early-specialization-in-youth-sports-supported -by-myths-and-competitive-culture-not-facts.

53 *The expectations have grown*: Michael Lingberg, "New CIF rule limits high school sports to 18 hours of practice per week," *Porterville Recorder*, May 14, 2014.

53 *One study of hers*: Edin T. Randall and Amy M. Bohnert, "Understanding threshold effects of organized activity involvement in adolescents: Sex and family income as moderators," *Journal of Adolescence* 35 (2012), 107–88.

55 *Its official recommendation*: Adolescent Sleep Working Group, "Policy Statement: School Start Times for Adolescents."

55 *One alarming study*: Robert Daniel Vorona et al., "Dissimilar Teen Crash Rates in Two Neighboring Southeastern Virginia Cities with Different High School Start Times," *Journal of Clinical Sleep Medicine* 7, no. 2 (2011), 145–51.

55 *Rock Bridge High School*: Jan Hoffman, "To Keep Teenagers Alert, Schools Let Them Sleep In," *New York Times*, March 13, 2014, http://well.blogs.nytimes.com/2014/03 /13/to-keep-teenagers-alert-schools-let-them-sleep-in/.

57 *In 2001, Michael Rettig*: Michael D. Rettig and Robert Lynn Canady, "Block Scheduling: More Benefits than Challenges," *National Association of Secondary School Principals Bulletin* 85 (2001), 78–86, http://csapstaff.ednet.ns.ca/htony/cyberquete/bloc%20 scheduling.pdf.

60 *This strategy has parallels*: "How to Stop Sleeping With Your Smartphone," *Bloomberg Business*, May 29, 2012, http://www.bloomberg.com/news/articles/2012-05-29/how -to-stop-sleeping-with-your-smartphone.

62 *American workers clock*: Claire Cain Miller, "The 24/7 Work Culture's Toll on Families and Gender Equality," *New York Times*, TheUpshot, May 28, 2015, http://www.nytimes.com /2015/05/31/upshot/the-24-7-work-cultures-toll-on-families-and-gender-equality.html.

62 *And stubborn gender norms*: Brigid Schulte, *Overwhelmed: Work, Love, and Play When No One Has the Time* (New York: Sarah Crichton Books, 2014).

64 *Past PTSA president*: Brigid Schulte, "In McLean, a crusade to get people to back off in the parenting arms race," *Washington Post*, March 23, 2014, http://www.washington post.com/lifestyle/style/in-mclean-a-crusade-to-get-people-to-back-off-in-the-parenting -arms-race/2014/03/23/9259c6a2-a552-11e3-a5fa-55f0c77bf39c_story.html.
    Wilma Bowers, personal communication.
    Brigid Schulte, "Health experts have figured out how much time you should sit each day," *Washington Post*, June 2, 2015, http://www.washingtonpost.com/blogs/wonk blog/wp/2015/06/02/medical-researchers-have-figured-out-how-much-time-is-okay -to-spend-sitting-each-day/.

64 *Not what columnist*: David Brooks, "The Moral Bucket List," *New York Times*, April 11, 2015, http://www.nytimes.com/2015/04/12/opinion/sunday/david-brooks-the-moral -bucket-list.html.

3. Homework: Take Back Our Nights

69 *The superintendent of schools in Swampscott*: Donna Krache, "Homework: How much, how often?" CNN Schools of Thought blog, December 9, 2011, http://schoolsof thought.blogs.cnn.com/2011/12/09/homework-how-much-how-often/.

69 *Galloway, New Jersey*: Associated Press, "Galloway schools won't give homework on

weekend to K-6 students," NJ.com, August 19, 2011, http://www.nj.com/news/index
.ssf/2011/08/galloway_schools_wont_give_hom.html.

69   *Mango Elementary School in Fontana*: Winnie Hu, "New Recruit in Homework Revolt:
The Principal," *New York Times*, June 15, 2011, http://www.nytimes.com/2011/06/16
/education/16homework.html.

69   *It was standard issue*: William J. Reese, *The Origins of the American High School* (New
Haven, CT: Yale University Press, 1999), 201.

69   *Complaints cropped up*: Ibid.

70   *Assignments of that era*: Brian Gill and Steven Schlossman, " 'A Sin Against Childhood':
Progressive Education and the Crusade to Abolish Homework, 1897–1491," *American
Journal of Education* 105, no. 1 (November 1996), 27–66.

Karen Bates, "The Futility of the Spelling Grind Revisited," *History of Reading
News* 26, no. 2 (Spring 2003), http://www.historyliteracy.org/scripts/search_display
.php?Article_ID=244.

70   *In 1900, Ladies' Home Journal*: Cathy Vatterott, *Rethinking Homework: Best Practices
That Support Diverse Needs* (Alexandria, VA: Association for Supervision and Curriculum Development, 2009), 1–25.

70   *The campaign fueled the rise*: Gill and Schlossman, " 'A Sin Against Childhood.' "

70   *In the competitive frenzy*: Vatterott, *Rethinking Homework*.

70   *The freer-thinking 1970s*: Ibid.

70   *As a result, the commission*: David P. Gardner et al., *A Nation at Risk: The Imperative for
Educational Reform* (Washington, DC: National Commission on Excellence in Education, April 1983), 29, http://files.eric.ed.gov/fulltext/ED226006.pdf.

70   *A University of Michigan study*: Sandra L. Hofferth and John F. Sandberg, "Changes in
American Children's Time, 1981–1997," University of Michigan, Population Studies
Center Research Reports No. 00-456, September 11, 2000.

70   *A later Michigan study*: Juster, Ono, and Stafford, *Changing Times of American Youth*.

71   *By 2005, parents*: "Stress Levels High for Bay Area Kids, Parents Say," Lucile Packard
Foundation for Children's Health, October 27, 2005, http://www.lpfch.org/newsroom
/releases/parentpoll10_27_05.html.

71   *Some news stories have proclaimed*: Allie Bidwell, "Homework Loads Haven't Changed
Much in 30 Years," *U.S. News & World Report*, March 18, 2014, http://www.usnews
.com/news/articles/2014/03/18/report-students-today-have-no-more-homework-than
-30-years-ago.

74   *In 2006, Duke University's Harris Cooper*: Harris Cooper et al., "Does homework improve academic achievement: A synthesis of research, 1987–2003," *Review of Educational Research* 76, no. 1 (2006), 1–62.

74   *Another study in 2011*: Ozkan Eren and Daniel Henderson, "Are we wasting our children's time by giving them more homework?" *Economics of Education Review* 30, no. 5
(2011), 950–61

75   *There's an even more pernicious problem*: Organization for Economic Cooperation and
Development (OECD), "Does homework perpetuate inequities in education?" *PISA
in Focus*, December 2014.

75 *These same inequalities*: Valerie Strauss, "French president pushing homework ban as part of ed reforms," *Washington Post*, October 15, 2012, http://www.washingtonpost .com/blogs/answer-sheet/wp/2012/10/15/french-president-pushing-homework-ban -as-part-of-ed-reforms/.

76 *Many of the countries*: OECD, "Does homework perpetuate inequities in education?"

76 *One of the consistent superstars*: Ibid.

76 *OECD researchers put*: Ibid.

76 *Depending on whom*: National Center for Education Statistics, "Youth Indicators 2011: America's Youth: Transitions to Adulthood," US Department of Education Institute of Education Sciences, Table 35, accessed June 15, 2015, https://nces.ed.gov /pubs2012/2012026/tables/table_35.asp.
    University of Phoenix College of Education, "Homework anxiety: Survey reveals how much homework K-12 students are assigned and why teachers deem it beneficial," press release, February 24, 2014, http://www.phoenix.edu/news/releases/2014/02 /survey-reveals-how-much-homework-k-12-students-are-assigned-why-teachers-deem -it-beneficial.html.

76 *When OECD researchers looked*: OECD, "Does homework perpetuate inequities in education?"

77 *The writer Karl Taro Greenfeld*: Karl Taro Greenfeld, "My Daughter's Homework Is Killing Me," *The Atlantic*, October 2013.

77 *Yet here there is even* less *evidence*: Etta Kralovec, personal communication.

78 *In a seminal 1993 study*: K. Anders Ericsson, Ralf Th. Krampe, and Clemens Tesch-Romer, "The Role of Deliberate Practice in the Acquisition of Expert Performance," *Psychological Review* 100, no. 3 (1993), 363–406.

79 *In a National Sleep Foundation poll*: National Sleep Foundation, *2014 Sleep in America Poll*.

79 *And researchers at Northwestern University*: Emma K. Adam, Emily K. Snell, and Patricia Pendry, "Sleep Timing and Quantity in Ecological and Family Context: A Nationally Representative Time-Diary Study," *Journal of Family Psychology* 21, no. 1 (2007), 4–19.

79 *Exercise, too, is so often*: Sara Bennett and Nancy Kalish, *The Case Against Homework: How Homework Is Hurting Children and What Parents Can Do About It* (New York: Harmony, 2007), 81–100.

79 *Time outdoors also has dwindled*: Richard Louv, *Last Child in the Woods: Saving Our Children from Nature-Deficit Disorder* (Chapel Hill, NC: Algonquin, 2008).

79 *A 2006 Scholastic study*: Scholastic and Yankelovich, *Kids & Family Reading Report* (2006), http://www.scholastic.com/aboutscholastic/news/KFRR_0207.pdf.

81 *"The biggest problem growing up today"*: Terri Lobdell, "Getting Off the Treadmill," *Palo Alto Weekly*, November 18, 2011, 33–38.

81 *Damon's research has demonstrated*: William Damon, Jenni Menon, and Kendall Cotton Bronk, "The Development of Purpose During Adolescence," *Applied Developmental Science* 7, no. 3 (2003), 119–28.

81 *His studies show that*: Lobdell, "Getting Off the Treadmill."

81 *As Damon explains*: William Damon, "How Can We Encourage a Sense of Purpose

and Meaning Early in Life?" *Big Questions Online*, December 9, 2014, https://www.big
questionsonline.com/content/how-can-we-encourage-sense-purpose-and-meaning
-early-life.

81   *In that context*: Lobdell, "Getting Off the Treadmill."

82   *The United Nations Convention*: United Nations, "United Nations Convention on the
Rights of the Child, Fact Sheet No. 10, Rev. 1," November 20, 1989, http://www.ohchr
.org/Documents/Publications/FactSheet10rev.1en.pdf.

82   *Yet in 2014, UCLA's annual survey*: Cooperative Institutional Research Program, *The
American Freshman*.

86   *When Manhattan's P.S. 116*: "Parents outraged after elementary school abolished home
work," AOL News, March 6, 2015, http://www.aol.com/article/2015/03/06/parents
-outraged-after-elementary-school-abolished-homework/21150479/.

86   *So Ackerman penned*: David Ackerman, letter published in *The Almanac*, March 5, 2007,
http://www.almanacnews.com/news/2007/03/05/oak-knoll-principals-letter-on-home
work-policy-.

4. Testing: Learning Beyond the Bubble

98   *Combine those with the extra deluge*: Melissa Lazarín, *Testing Overload in America's
Schools* (Washington, DC: Center for American Progress, October 2014), https://cdn
.americanprogress.org/wp-content/uploads/2014/10/LazarinOvertestingReport.pdf.

98   *At Castle Bridge elementary school*: Dao X. Tran, "Forget Teaching to the Test—Castle
Bridge Boycotts It!" in *The New Uprising Against High-Stakes Testing*, ed. Jesse Hagopian
(Chicago: Haymarket, 2014), 211–18.

98   *In Providence, a crowd*: Cauldierre McKay, Aaron Regunberg, and Tim Shea, "Testing
Assumptions: Zombies, Flunkies, and the Providence Student Union," in *The New
Uprising Against High-Stakes Testing*, ed. Jesse Hagopian (Chicago: Haymarket, 2014),
135–40.

99   *The protests reached*: Valerie Strauss, "Report: 175,000-plus N.Y. students opt out of
Common Core test, more expected," *Washington Post*, April 18, 2015, http://www
.washingtonpost.com/blogs/answer-sheet/wp/2015/04/18/report-175000-plus-n-y
-students-opt-out-of-common-core-test-more-expected/.

99   *Opt-out groups*: Kimberly Wiggins, "'Opting out' becoming more popular option for
Central Florida families," Fox 35 Orlando, November 14, 2014, http://www.myfox
orlando.com/story/27387181/opting-out-becoming-more-popular-option-for-central
-florida-families.

        Amy Moore, "Parents need authority to opt-out of testing," *Des Moines Register*,
November 13, 2014, http://www.desmoinesregister.com/story/opinion/abetteriowa
/2014/11/13/amy-moore-school-testing-opt-out/18969065/.

99   *The previous fall*: Daniel Wallis, "Thousands of high school students skip Colorado state
tests," Reuters, November 14, 2014, http://www.reuters.com/article/2014/11/14/us
-usa-colorado-education-idUSKCN0IY2HO20141114.

99   *According to the national organization*: Monty Neill, executive director of FairTest, personal communication.

99   *Meanwhile, signatures on*: "The State of National Rebellion Against High-Stakes Testing," *FairTest Examiner*, October 2012, http://fairtest.org/state-national-rebellion-against-highstakes-testing.

Cindy Long and Sara Robertson, "NEA Launches Campaign to End 'Toxic Testing,'" National Education Association, accessed June 2, 2015, http://www.nea.org/home/59747.htm.

101   *The nonpartisan Center on Education Policy*: Jennifer McMurrer, "NCLB Year 5: Choices, Changes, and Challenges: Curriculum and Instruction in the NCLB Era," Center on Education Policy, July 24, 2007, http://www.cep-dc.org/displayDocument.cfm?DocumentID=312.

101   *And the trend has continued*: Tim Walker, "The Testing Obsession and the Disappearing Curriculum," *NEA Today*, September 2, 2014, http://neatoday.org/2014/09/02/the-testing-obsession-and-the-disappearing-curriculum-2/.

102   *Researchers at the RAND Corporation*: Kun Yuan and Vi-Nhuan Le, *Estimating the Percentage of Students Who Were Exposed to Deeper Learning on the State Achievement Tests* (RAND Education, February 2012), http://www.hewlett.org/uploads/documents/Estimating_Percentage_Students_Tested_on_Cognitively_Demanding_Items_Through_the_State_Achievement_Tests_RAND_3_2012.pdf.

104   *In one study, Clark University*: Wendy Grolnick, personal communication.

105   *A University of Virginia study*: Daphna Bassok, Scott Latham, and Anna Rorem, "Is Kindergarten the New First Grade?" EdPolicyWorks Working Paper Series, no. 20, http://curry.virginia.edu/uploads/resourceLibrary/20_Bassok_Is_Kindergarten_The_New_First_Grade.pdf.

105   *Schools now routinely*: Valerie Strauss, "Report: Requiring kindergarteners to read—as Common Core does—may harm some," *Washington Post*, January 13, 2015, http://www.washingtonpost.com/blogs/answer-sheet/wp/2015/01/13/report-requiring-kindergartners-to-read-as-common-core-does-may-harm-some/.

106   *In fact, evidence suggests*: David Kohn, "Let the Kids Learn Through Play," *New York Times*, May 16, 2015, http://www.nytimes.com/2015/05/17/opinion/sunday/let-the-kids-learn-through-play.html.

106   *To illuminate the link*: Brent D. Fulton, Richard M. Scheffler, and Stephen P. Hinshaw, "State Variation in Increased ADHD Prevalence: Links to NCLB School Accountability and State Medication Laws," *Psychiatric Services* (2015), provided in advance of publication.

107   *A case on Long Island*: Jenny Anderson and Winnie Hu, "20 Students Now Accused in L.I. on Cheating," *New York Times*, November 22, 2011, http://www.nytimes.com/2011/11/23/education/more-students-charged-in-long-island-sat-cheating-case.html.

107   *At Middleton High School*: Elena Kadvany and Chris Kenrick, "Wisconsin Principal Named to Head Gunn High School," *Palo Alto Weekly*, May 19, 2014, http://www.paloaltoonline.com/news/2014/05/16/wisconsin-principal-named-to-head-gunn-high-school.

Denise Herrmann and Lisa Jondle, "Letter to Middleton HS Parents," Madison.com,

December 20, 2013, http://host.madison.com/letter-to-middleton-hs-parents/pdf_bd 7e8103-3f30-5034-899d-78cf18831471.html.

108   *Susan Engel, an education psychologist*: Susan Engel, "7 things every kid should master," *Boston Globe Magazine*, February 26, 2015, http://www.bostonglobe.com/magazine /2015/02/26/things-every-kid-should-master/uM72LGr63zeaStOp9zGyrJ/story .html.

108   *Daniel Koretz, a Harvard psychometrician*: Daniel Koretz, *Measuring Up: What Educational Testing Really Tells Us* (Cambridge, MA: Harvard University Press, 2009), 10.

108   *That's because, scientifically speaking*: Grace Rubenstein, "Reinventing the Big Test: The Challenge of Authentic Assessment," *Edutopia*, March 18, 2008, http://www.edutopia .org/testing-authentic-assessment-reform.

109   *And experiments such as those*: Heckman, Stixrud, and Urzua, "The Effects of Cognitive and Noncognitive Abilities."

109   *"Innovation comes from"*: Yong Zhao, *Catching Up or Leading the Way: American Education in the Age of Globalization* (Alexandria, VA: ASCD, 2009), 68.

109   *China's historical devotion*: Ibid., 81.

110   *The flourishing of*: Ibid., 95–96.

110   *By contrast, Finnish children*: Anu Partanen, "What We're Ignoring About Finnish Schools' Success," *The Atlantic*, December 29, 2011, http://www.theatlantic.com/na tional/archive/2011/12/what-americans-keep-ignoring-about-finlands-school-success /250564/.

   Pasi Sahlberg, "Teach for Finland? Why It Won't Happen," *Washington Post*, February 12, 2015, http://www.washingtonpost.com/blogs/answer-sheet/wp/2015/02/12 /teach-for-finland-why-it-wont-happen/.

110   *Plus, young children*: Partanen, "What We're Ignoring."

113   *Students in the consortium*: Performance Standards Consortium, *Educating for the 21st Century: Data Report on the New York Performance Standards Consortium*, http://www .nyclu.org/files/releases/testing_consortium_report.pdf.

113   *Of those who enter*: Ibid.

   "Retention Rates—First-Time College Freshmen Returning Their Second Year" (2008), NCHEMS Information Center, accessed June 5, 2015, http://www.higher edinfo.org/dbrowser/?year=2008&level=nation&mode=map&state=0&submeasure =223.

116   *In 2011, under the leadership*: Carmen Coleman, personal communication.

116   *Within a couple of years*: Anya Kamenetz, "In Kentucky, Moving Beyond Dependence on Tests," National Public Radio, June 1, 2014, http://www.npr.org/sections/ed/2014 /06/01/317433695/in-kentucky-students-succeed-without-tests.

117   *After Danville initiated*: Amy Swann, personal communication.

120   *FairTest reports that by fall*: Monty Neill, personal communication.

120   *That same fall*: Patrick O'Donnell, "Is student testing excessive? Is it working? National educators raise those questions today," *Cleveland Plain Dealer*, October 15, 2014, http://www.cleveland.com/metro/index.ssf/2014/10/is_student_testing_excessive _is_it_working_national_educators_raise_those_questions_today.html.

120   *On a smaller scale*: Peter Marteka, "Glastonbury Principal May Gauge Support for Pub-
         lishing Honor Rolls," *The Hartford Courant,* September 12, 2011.
                Margaret Smith, "Acton-Boxborough Schools Will Not Publish Honor Rolls,"
         WickedLocal.com, December 16, 2011.

120   *the whole district of Windsor Locks*: David Desroches, "Goodbye to Grades: Windsor
         Locks Schools Pioneer a New Way to Assess Students," WNPR, June 8, 2015, http://
         wnpr.org/post/goodbye-grades-windsor-locks-schools-pioneer-new-way-assess-stu
         dents.

120   *"The Common Core, however dressed"*: Yong Zhao, "Common Sense Vs. Common Core:
         How to Minimize the Damages of the Common Core," Zhao Learning blog, June 17,
         2012, http://zhaolearning.com/2012/06/17/common-sense-vs-common-core-how
         -to-minimize-the-damages-of-the-common-core/.

121   *We can begin, of course*: Lazarín, *Testing Overload in America's Schools.*

122   *Test scores are well known*: Sean F. Reardon, "No Rich Child Left Behind," *New York
         Times,* April 27, 2013, http://opinionator.blogs.nytimes.com/2013/04/27/no-rich
         -child-left-behind/.

122   *Dozens of high schools*: Jay Mathews, "A Rankings Boycott, of Sorts, Leads to an Invigo-
         rating Exchange," *Washington Post,* April 14, 2008, http://www.washingtonpost.com
         /wp-dyn/content/article/2008/04/13/AR2008041302372.html.

5. College Admissions: Break Free from The Frenzy

128   *For the class of 2018*: Nick Anderson, "College admission rates for Class of 2018: an
         imperfect but closely watched metric," *Washington Post,* April 3, 2014, http://www
         .washingtonpost.com/local/education/college-admission-rates-for-class-of-2018-an
         -imperfect-but-closely-watched-metric/2014/04/03/820ff578-b6af-11e3-8cc3-d4bf5
         6577eb_story.html.

128   *Those odds may not*: Kevin Carey, "For Accomplished Students, Reaching a Good Col-
         lege Isn't as Hard as It Seems," *New York Times,* TheUpshot, November 29, 2014, http://
         www.nytimes.com/2014/11/30/upshot/for-accomplished-students-reaching-a-top
         -college-isnt-actually-that-hard.html.

129   *Dodds's charges are suffering*: Jeff Mitchell, "Harvard-or-Walmart Syndrome," essay
         published online, accessed June 19, 2015, http://jeffmitchellassociates.com/Jeff/har
         vardorwalmart3.pdf.

129   *The* New York Times*'s Frank Bruni*: Frank Bruni, "How to Survive the College Admis-
         sions Madness," *New York Times,* March 13, 2015, http://www.nytimes.com/2015/03
         /15/opinion/sunday/frank-bruni-how-to-survive-the-college-admissions-madness.html.

130   *The craziest extreme*: Peter Waldman, "How to Get Into an Ivy League College—
         Guaranteed," *Bloomberg Businessweek,* September 4, 2014, http://www.bloomberg
         .com/news/articles/2014-09-04/how-to-get-into-an-ivy-league-college-guaranteed.

131   *As Deresiewicz tells it*: Deresiewicz, *Excellent Sheep,* 27–40.

131   *Between 1970 and 2010*: "Number Enrolled in College by Type of School and Enroll-

ment Status, 1970 to 2013," US Census Bureau, accessed June 5, 2015, http://www
.census.gov/hhes/school/data/cps/historical/FigureA-7_2013.pdf.

132 *In fact, over the past forty-five years*: Kevin Eagan et al., "The American Freshman: Na-
tional Norms Fall 2014," Cooperative Institutional Research Program at the Higher
Education Research Institute at UCLA, p. 44, http://www.heri.ucla.edu/monographs
/TheAmericanFreshman2014.pdf.

   Robert J. Panos, Alexander W. Astin, and John A. Creager, "National Norms for
Entering College Freshmen—Fall 1967," Office of Research, American Council
on Education, 34, http://www.heri.ucla.edu/monographs/TheAmericanFreshman
2014.pdf.

132 *The annual lineup purports*: "How U.S. News Calculated the 2015 Best Colleges Rankings," *U.S. News & World Report*, September 8, 2014, http://www.usnews.com/educa
tion/best-colleges/articles/2014/09/08/how-us-news-calculated-the-2015-best-col
leges-rankings.

132 Washington Monthly *deserves*: "2014 National Universities Rankings," *Washington
Monthly*, accessed June 19, 2015, http://www.washingtonmonthly.com/college_guide
/rankings-2014/national-universities-rank.php.

133 *Arizona State University psychologist*: Suniya Luthar et al., " 'I can, therefore I must': Fragility in the upper-middle classes."

133 *Reed argued that*: "Reed and the Rankings Game," Reed College, last modified September 9, 2014, http://www.reed.edu/apply/college-rankings.html.

133 *The college paid a price*: Ibid.

133 *I was shocked to learn*: Daniel Golden, "Glass Floor: Colleges Reject Top Applicants,
Accepting Only the Students Likely to Enroll," *Wall Street Journal*, May 29, 2001,
http://www.wsj.com/articles/SB991083160294634500.

133 *A school's ranking*: "How U.S. News Calculated the 2015 Best Colleges Rankings."

133 *In part for these reasons*. Stephen Burd and Rachel Fishman, "Ten Ways Colleges Work
You Over," *Washington Monthly*, September/October 2014, http://www.washington
monthly.com/magazine/septemberoctober_2014/features/ten_ways_colleges_work
_you_ove051760.php?page=all. Lloyd Thacker, executive director of the Education
Conservancy, personal communication.

134 *The National Association for College Admission Counseling*: Melissa E. Clinedinst, Sarah
F. Hurley, and David A. Hawkins, "State of College Admission 2013," National Association for College Admission Counseling, 2014.

134 *College professors widely*: Deresiewicz, *Excellent Sheep*.

   Abigail Baird, personal communication. Alison Gopnik, personal communication.

136 Politico *reports that*: Stephanie Simon, "Advanced Placement classes failing students,"
Politico, August 21, 2013, http://www.politico.com/story/2013/08/education-ad
vanced-placement-classes-tests-95723.html.

136 *At the same time*: Janet Lorin and Lisa Wolfson, "Not-for-Profit College Board Getting Rich as Fees Hit Students," *Bloomberg Businessweek*, August 17, 2011, http://www
.bloomberg.com/news/articles/2011-08-18/not-for-profit-college-board-getting-rich
-as-fees-hit-students.

Rick Cohen, "Is the College Board a NINO (Nonprofit in Name Only)?" *Nonprofit Quarterly*, October 16, 2012, https://nonprofitquarterly.org/policysocial-context/21 184-is-the-college-board-a-nino-nonprofit-in-name-only.html.

136 *Yet in 2012*: Simon, "Advanced Placement classes failing students."

136 *The passing rates*: Ibid.

137 *A Harvard and University of Virginia survey*: Steve Bradt, "High school AP courses do not predict college success in science," *Harvard Gazette*, 2007, http://news.harvard.edu /gazette/2006/02.23/05-ap.html.

137 *And a study of more than*: Saul Gesier and Veronica Santelices, "The Role of Advanced Placement and Honors Classes in College Admissions," University of California, Berkeley, Center for Studies on Higher Education, Research and Occasional Paper Series, CSHE.4.04 (2004).

137 *Middlebury College math professor*: Priscilla Bremser, letter to the editor, *New York Times*, January 11, 2011, http://www.nytimes.com/2011/01/17/opinion/lweb17math.html.

137 *Besides, some private colleges*: Tamar Lewin, "Dartmouth Stops Credits for Excelling on A.P. Test," *New York Times*, January 17, 2013, http://www.nytimes.com/2013/01/18 /education/dartmouth-stops-credits-for-excelling-on-ap-test.html.

138 *The U.S. News & World Report "Best High Schools"*: Robert Morse, "How U.S. News Calculated the 2015 Best High Schools Rankings," *U.S. News & World Report*, May 11, 2015, http://www.usnews.com/education/best-high-schools/articles/how-us-news -calculated-the-rankings.

138 *And schools whose students*: Jay Mathews, "Jay Mathews's method of selecting America's Most Challenging High Schools," *Washington Post*, April 4, 2014, http://www.washing tonpost.com/local/education/abcs-of-americas-most-challenging-high-schools/2014 /04/02/bf19b1c2-b8f1-11e3-899e-bb708e3539dd_story.html.

142 *To restrain runaway competition*: Barry Schwartz, "Top Colleges Should Select Randomly From a Pool of 'Good Enough,'" *Chronicle of Higher Education*, February 25, 2005.

143 *Indeed, SAT scores parallel*: Josh Zumbrun, "SAT Scores and Income Inequality: How Wealthier Kids Rank Higher," *Wall Street Journal*, October 7, 2014, http://blogs.wsj .com/economics/2014/10/07/sat-scores-and-income-inequality-how-wealthier-kids -rank-higher/.

143 *Even the National Association*: National Association for College Admission Counseling, *Report of the Commission on the Use of Standardized Tests in Undergraduate Admission* (Arlington, VA: September 2008), http://www.nacacnet.org/research/Publications Resources/Marketplace/Documents/TestingComission_FinalReport.pdf.

144 *FairTest, a Boston-based organization*: "Colleges and Universities That Do Not Use SAT/ACT Scores for Admitting Substantial Numbers of Students Into Bachelor Degree Programs," FairTest, last modified summer 2015, http://fairtest.org/university /optional.

144 *A 2014 study backed by NACAC*: William C. Hiss and Valerie W. Franks, *Defining Promise: Optional Standardized Testing in American College and University Admissions* (National Association for College Admission Counseling, February 5, 2014), http://www.nacacnet .org/research/research-data/nacac-research/Documents/DefiningPromise.pdf.

145   *This "dimensional" application*: Scott Jaschik, " 'Dimensional' Admissions," *Insider Higher Ed*, September 25, 2014, https://www.insidehighered.com/news/2014/09/25/ben nington-introduces-new-option-applicants.

145   *Bard president Leon Botstein*: Ariel Kaminer, "Didn't Ace SAT? Just Design Microbe Transplant Research," *New York Times*, September 28, 2013, http://www.nytimes.com /2013/09/29/nyregion/didnt-ace-sat-just-design-microbe-transplant-research.html.

146   *It turns out that a college's admission rate*: "How U.S. News Calculated the 2015 Best Colleges Rankings."

147   *The 2013 Chegg Student Skill Index*: Chegg Inc., *Bridge That Gap*.

148   *Limit the number of times*: Wake Forest University, " 'Conscientious Objector' Opts Out of SAT," *Rethinking Admissions* blog, October 29, 2010, http://blog.rethinkingadmis sions.wfu.edu/2010/10/%E2%80%9Cconscientious-objector%E2%80%9D-opts-out -of-sat/.

150   *And individual educators*: Esther Wojcicki, "College Applications: Why Many Students Should Pass on Ivy League Schools," *Edutopia*, March 12, 2010, http://www.edutopia .org/college-admissions-school-choice.

6. Teaching and Learning: This Way Up

156   *"What was considered"*: National Education Association, *An Educator's Guide to the "4 Cs,"* http://www.nea.org/assets/docs/A-Guide-to-Four-Cs.pdf.

156   *A group of leaders*: "Framework for 21st Century Learning," Partnership for 21st Century Learning, accessed June 19, 2015, http://www.p21.org/about-us/p21-framework.

157   *Tony Wagner, an educator*: Tony Wagner, *The Global Achievement Gap: Why Even Our Best Schools Don't Teach the New Survival Skills Our Children Need—and What We Can Do About It* (New York: Basic Books, 2010).

157   *Yet when the*: American Management Association, *AMA 2012: Critical Skills Survey* (March 2013), http://playbook.amanet.org/wp-content/uploads/2013/03/2012 -Critical-Skills-Survey-pdf.pdf.

158   *One study published*: Robert C. Pianta et al., "Opportunities to Learn in America's Elementary Classrooms," *Science* 315, no. 5820 (March 30, 2007), 1795–96.

158   *Teachers of English*: Wagner, *The Global Achievement Gap*, 36.

159   *A 2014 study at the Universities of Washington*: Scott Freeman et al., "Active Learning Increases Student Performance in Science, Engineering, and Mathematics," *Proceedings of the National Academy of Sciences* 111, no. 23 (June 10, 2014), 8410–15.

163   *The outcome: 98 percent*: "Results," High Tech High, accessed June 5, 2015, http://www .hightechhigh.org/about/results.php.

        "Fast Facts: Graduation Rates," National Center for Education Statistics, accessed June 5, 2015, http://nces.ed.gov/fastfacts/display.asp?id=40.

164   *On the whole, though*: Brigid Barron and Linda Darling-Hammond, *Teaching for Meaningful Learning: A Review of Research on Inquiry-Based and Cooperative Learning*

(Edutopia, 2008), http://www.edutopia.org/pdfs/edutopia-teaching-for-meaningful-learning.pdf.

Neal Finkelstein et al., *Effects of Problem Based Economics on high school economics instruction* (Washington, DC: Institute of Education Sciences, US Department of Education, July 2010), http://ies.ed.gov/ncee/edlabs/regions/west/pdf/REL_20104012.pdf.

Nate K. Hixson, Jason Ravitz, and Andy Whisman, *Extended Professional Development in Project-Based Learning: Impacts on 21st Century Skills Teaching and Student Achievement* (Charleston, WV: Office of Research, West Virginia Department of Education, September 2012), http://wvde.state.wv.us/research/reports2012/PBLEvaluation_092012.pdf.

164 *Students learning this way*: Andrew Walker and Heather Leary, "A Problem Based Learning Meta Analysis: Differences Across Problem Types, Implementation Types, Disciplines, and Assessment Levels," *Interdisciplinary Journal of Problem-Based Learning* 3, no. 1 (2009).

Finkelstein et al., *Effects of Problem Based Economics*.

164 *And studies show that*: Walker and Leary, "A Problem Based Learning Meta Analysis."

164 *One study of five thousand*: Robert Geier et al., "Standardized test outcomes for students engaged in inquiry-based science curricula in the context of urban reform," *Journal of Research in Science Teaching* 45, no. 8 (August 29, 2008), 922–39.

164 *A US Department of Education*: Finkelstein et al., *Effects of Problem Based Economics*.

175 *And the state, like many others*: Taylor White, "Giving Credit Where Credit's Due: A 50-State Scan of Course Credit Policies," Carnegie Foundation for the Advancement of Teaching, August 5, 2013, http://www.carnegiefoundation.org/blog/giving-credit-where-credits-due-a-50-state-scan-of-course-credit-policies/.

175 *Trigg could choose to switch*: Shannon Burcham, personal communication.

178 *High Tech High also gets away*: School Report [High Tech High], 2012–13 Accountability Progress Reporting, California Department of Education, http://dq.cde.ca.gov/dataquest/Acnt2013/2013GrowthSch.aspx?allcds=37683383731247.

7. First, Be Well

183 *In a positive state of mind*: Carlos A. Estrada, Alice M. Isen, and Mark J. Young, "Positive Affect Facilitates Integration of Information and Decreases Anchoring in Reasoning among Physicians," *Organizational Behavior and Human Decision Processes* 72, no. 1 (1997), 117–35.

183 *Happy job candidates*: Jerry M. Burger and David F. Caldwell, "Personality, Social Activities, Job-Search Behavior and Interview Success: Distinguishing Between PANAS Trait Positive Affect and NEO Extraversion," *Motivation and Emotion* 24, no. 1 (2000), 51–62.

183 *Optimistic businesspeople*: MetLife case study, described in Shawn Achor, *The Happiness*

Advantage: The Seven Principles of Positive Psychology That Fuel Success and Performance at Work (New York: Crown Business, 2010).

183 *And students who were*: T. Bryan and J. Bryan, "Positive mood and math performance," *Journal of Learning Disabilities* 24, no. 8 (October 1991), 490–94.

183 *One study, published in*: Sonja Lyubomirsky, Laura King, and Ed Diener, "The Benefits of Frequent Positive Affect: Does Happiness Lead to Success?" *Psychological Bulletin* 131, no. 6 (November 2005), 803–55.

183 *International business leader*: Heffernan, Margaret, "Why it's time to forget the pecking order at work," TED Talk, Monterey, California, May 2015, http://www.ted.com /talks/margaret_heffernan_why_it_s_time_to_forget_the_pecking_order_at_work.

Juliet Blake and Kate Torgovnick May, "Career advice for millennials (and really, anyone) from Margaret Heffernan," TED Blog, July 3, 2015, http://blog.ted.com /career-advice-for-millennials-and-really-anyone-from-margaret-heffernan/.

184 *UNICEF, in a 2013 report*: Peter Adamson, *Child well-being in rich countries: A comparative overview* (Florence: UNICEF Office of Research, 2013).

184 *Researchers have found that, even in the most terrible circumstances*: Sara Truebridge and Bonnie Benard, "Reflections on Resilience," *Educational Leadership* 71, no. 1 (September 2013), 66–67.

184 *Children with the capacity*: Staci M. Zolkoski and Lyndal M. Bullock, "Resilience in children and youth: A review," *Children and Youth Services Review* 34 (2012), 2295–303.

Edward M. Hallowell, *The Childhood Roots of Adult Happiness: Five Steps to Help Kids Create and Sustain Lifelong Joy* (New York: Ballantine, 2002), 21.

185 *Ed Hallowell, psychiatrist*: Ibid., 33.

185 *Depression rates among first-year medical students*: Stuart J. Slavin, Debra L. Schindler, and John T. Chibnall, "Medical Student Mental Health 3.0: Improving Student Wellness Through Curricular Changes," *Academic Medicine* 89, no. 4 (April 2014), 573–77. Current data provided by Stuart Slavin via personal communication.

188 *This was an improvement*: National Association for College Admission Counseling, "Effective Counseling in Schools Increases College Access," *NACAC Research to Practice Brief* 1 (2006), 3.

188 *A high school in Naperville*: Mona Iskander, "A physical education in Naperville," PBS *Need to Know*, February 8, 2011, http://www.pbs.org/wnet/need-to-know/video/a -physical-education-in-naperville-ill/7134/.

189 *Research demonstrates that connections*: Hallowell, *The Childhood Roots of Adult Happiness*, 81–82.

Truebridge and Benard, "Reflections on Resilience."

Bonnie Benard, *Resiliency: What We Have Learned* (San Francisco: WestEd, 2004), 43.

189 *One study in New Zealand*: Craig A. Olsson, "A 32-Year Longitudinal Study of Child and Adolescent Pathways to Well-Being in Adulthood," *Journal of Happiness Studies* 14, no. 3 (July 25, 2012), 1069–83.

190 *"What resilience research"*: Benard, *Resiliency*, 66.

191 *A Palo Alto High School junior*: Carolyn Walworth, "Paly student tells of school

stress: 'Students are gasping for air,'" *The Almanac*, March 26, 2015, http://www
.almanacnews.com/news/2015/03/26/guest-opinion-on-school-stress-students-are
-gasping-for-air.

192   *He lost his first bid*: "Editorial: Catherine Crystal Foster and Ken Dauber for Palo Alto
School Board," *Palo Alto Daily News*, November 1, 2014, http://www.mercurynews
.com/peninsula/ci_26796880/catherine-crystal-foster-and-ken-dauber-palo-alto.

193   *In the 2012 survey*: Palo Alto Union High School District data compiled and published
by We Can Do Better Palo Alto: https://docs.google.com/spreadsheets/d/1sYGu2
-HNWsboTOOI3pCTrp61ara73SuOW0nxWZXEtkE/edit#gid=0.

195   *At the WINGS*: Grace Rubenstein, "The WINGS Story: An After-School Program
Helps Students Beat the Odds," *Edutopia*, October 11, 2010, http://www.edutopia.org
/stw-social-emotional-learning-after-school-wings-story.

196   *The earliest SEL programs*: "Social and Emotional Learning: A Short History," *Edutopia*,
October 6, 2011, http://www.edutopia.org/social-emotional-learning-history.

196   *Now SEL is practiced*: Joseph A. Durlak et al., eds., *Handbook of Social and Emotional
Learning: Research and Practice* (New York: Guilford, 2015), 3.

196   *Some entire city districts*: Lija Farnham et al., "Rethinking How Students Succeed," *Stanford Social Innovation Review*, February 17, 2015, http://www.ssireview.org/up_for_de
bate/article/rethinking_how_students_succeed.

196   *A landmark 2011 study*: Joseph A. Durlak et al., "The Impact of Enhancing Students'
Social and Emotional Learning: A Meta-Analysis of School-Based Universal Interventions," *Child Development* 82, no. 1 (January/February 2011), 474–501.

196   *Another study looking at*: Joseph A. Durlak and Roger P. Weissberg, *The Impact of After-
School Programs That Promote Personal and Social Skills* (Chicago: Collaborative for
Academic, Social, and Emotional Learning, 2007), http://www.lions-quest.org/pdfs
/AfterSchoolProgramsStudy2007.pdf.

197   *Psychology "has been sidetracked"*: C. R. Snyder, Shane J. Lopez, and Jennifer Teramoto
Pedrotti, *Positive Psychology: The Scientific and Practical Explorations of Human Strengths*
(Los Angeles: Sage, 2010), 4.

197   *The ensuing research*: Martin Seligman et al., "Positive education: positive psychology
and classroom interventions," *Oxford Review of Education* 35, no. 3 (June 2009), 293–
311.

197   *They use stories*: "The Penn Resiliency Project," Positive Psychology Center, accessed
June 19, 2015, http://www.ppc.sas.upenn.edu/prpsum.htm.

197   *The results so far*: Ibid.

197   *The skills for happiness*: University of Pennsylvania, "Positive Health," website of the Authentic Happiness program, accessed June 19, 2015, https://www.authentichappiness
.sas.upenn.edu/learn/positivehealth.

199   *A UC Davis study*: Amy Smith et al., *Mindful Schools Program Evaluation* (UC Davis
School of Education, June 2012), http://education.ucdavis.edu/sites/main/files/file
-attachments/mindful_schools_final_report.081512.pdf.

199   *Studies of other mindfulness programs*: Kimberly A. Schonert-Reichl et al., "Enhancing Cognitive and Social–Emotional Development Through a Simple-to-Administer

Mindfulness-Based School Program for Elementary School Children: A Randomized Controlled Trial," *Developmental Psychology* 51, no. 1 (2015), 52–66.

Sanford Nidich et al., "Academic Achievement and Transcendental Meditation: A Study with At-Risk Urban Middle School Students," *Education* 131, no. 3 (Spring 2011), 556–64.

199   *My favorite stat*: David L. Kirp, "Meditation transforms roughest San Francisco schools," *San Francisco Chronicle*, January 12, 2014, http://m.sfgate.com/opinion/openforum /article/Meditation-transforms-roughest-San-Francisco-5136942.php.

200   *In an interview*: "Segment: Sherry Turkle on Being Alone Together," Moyers & Company, October 18, 2013, http://billmoyers.com/segment/sherry-turkle-on-being-alone -together/.

202   *As to the confounding question*: "Media and Children," American Academy of Pediatrics, accessed June 19, 2015, https://www.aap.org/en-us/advocacy-and-policy/aap-health -initiatives/Pages/Media-and-Children.aspx.

202   *I take comfort*: "How much screen time is OK for my kid(s)?" Common Sense Media, accessed June 19, 2015, https://www.commonsensemedia.org/screen-time/how-much -screen-time-is-ok-for-my-kids.

204   *It also does not put the idea*: Adam Strassberg, "Guest Opinion: Keep Calm and Parent On," *Palo Alto Weekly*, March 16, 2015, http://www.paloaltoonline.com/news/2015 /03/16/guest-opinion-keep-calm-and-parent-on.

8. Action: How You Can Replace the Race to Nowhere

211   *Children should be going to bed*: "Sleep Duration Recommendations," National Sleep Foundation, accessed June 5, 2015, http://sleepfoundation.org/sites/default/files /STREPchanges_1.png.

215   *Parents have done this effectively*: Monty Neill, personal communication.

Epilogue

236   *The annual survey of entering college freshmen*: Cooperative Institutional Research Program, *The American Freshman*.

237   *Susan Engel, the Williams College psychologist*: Susan Engel, *The End of the Rainbow: How Educating for Happiness (Not Money) Would Transform Our Schools* (New York: New Press, 2015).

238   *Meanwhile, more than 550*: Lazarín, *Testing Overload in America's Schools*.

238   *The young and growing*: "The Student Bill of Rights," Student Voice, accessed June 19, 2015, http://www.sturights.org/.

239   *"You do have to say 'no'"*: Betty Friedan, *The Feminine Mystique* (New York: W.W. Norton & Co., 1963).

Selected Bibliography

THE FOLLOWING RESOURCES were influential in shaping the thinking that went into this book and honing my ideas about the culture of school and childhood. While far from exhaustive, this list includes a range of materials that offer diverse insights and information that might be helpful for those delving deeper into the issues I've explored. To avoid duplication (and save paper), I've left out most of the citations that appear in the notes, except a select few that I consider essential reading. However, there are many valuable resources in the notes, as well.

In addition to the published works listed here, countless people and school communities have helped to hone my perspective on childhood and education over the last eight years. Together with my colleagues, I have observed practices firsthand in hundreds of schools, filmed at dozens of them, and interviewed hundreds of experts, educators, and activists. The following organizations also supported some of the research in this book and are valuable resources in their own right:

- The National Center for Fair and Open Testing, at fairtest.org

- The Buck Institute for Education, at bie.org

- *Edutopia,* a publication of the George Lucas Educational Foundation, at edutopia.org

- The Education Conservancy, at educationconservancy.org

- Colleges That Change Lives, at ctcl.org

- The Collaborative for Academic, Social, and Emotional Learning, at casel.org

New conversations, articles, blog posts, testimonials, TED Talks, and other inputs continue to mold my thinking every day. For up-to-date resources, visit the Race to Nowhere website at reellinkfilms.com.

Books

Baker, David P., and Gerald K. LeTendre. *National Differences, Global Similarities: World Culture and the Future of Schooling.* Redwood City, CA: Stanford University Press, 2005.

Benard, Bonnie. *Resiliency: What We Have Learned.* San Francisco: WestEd, 2004.

Bennett, Sara, and Nancy Kalish. *The Case Against Homework: How Homework Is Hurting Children and What Parents Can Do About It,* reprint edition. New York: Harmony, 2007.

Berger, Ron. *An Ethic of Excellence: Building a Culture of Craftsmanship with Students.* Portsmouth, NH: Heinemann, 2003.

Boaler, Jo. *Mathematical Mindsets: Unleashing Students' Potential through Creative Math, Inspiring Messages and Innovative Teaching.* Hoboken, NJ: Jossey-Bass, 2015.

———. *What's Math Got to Do with It?: How Teachers and Parents Can Transform Mathematics Learning and Inspire Success,* revised edition. New York: Penguin Books, 2015.

Bronson, Po, and Ashley Merryman. *NurtureShock: New Thinking About Children,* reprint edition. New York: Twelve, 2011.

Califano, Joseph A., Jr. *How to Raise a Drug-Free Kid: The Straight Dope for Parents,* revised edition. New York: Touchstone, 2014.

Carter, Christine. *Raising Happiness: 10 Simple Steps for More Joyful Kids and Happier Parents,* reprint edition. New York: Ballantine Books, 2011.

Damon, William. *The Path to Purpose: How Young People Find Their Calling in Life.* New York: Free Press, 2009.

Deresiewicz, William. *Excellent Sheep: The Miseducation of the American Elite and the Way to a Meaningful Life,* reprint edition. New York: Free Press, 2014.

Dweck, Carol. *Mindset: The New Psychology of Success,* reprint edition. New York: Ballantine Books, 2007.

Elkind, David. *The Hurried Child,* 25th anniversary edition. Boston: Da Capo Press, 2006.

Engel, Angela. *Seeds of Tomorrow: Solutions for Improving Our Children's Education.* Boulder, CO: Paradigm Publishers, 2010.

Engel, Susan. *The End of the Rainbow: How Educating for Happiness (Not Money) Would Transform Our Schools.* New York: New Press, 2015.

Frankenstein, Diane W. *Reading Together: Everything You Need to Know to Raise a Child Who Loves to Read.* New York: Perigee Books, 2009.

Frost, Maya. *The New Global Student: Skip the SAT, Save Thousands on Tuition, and Get a Truly International Education.* New York: Harmony, 2009.

Gardner, Howard. *Five Minds for the Future.* Boston: Harvard Business Review Press, 2009.

Green, Elizabeth. *Building a Better Teacher.* New York: W. W. Norton & Co., 2014.

Grolnick, Wendy S., and Kathy Seal. *Pressured Parents, Stressed-out Kids: Dealing with Competition While Raising a Successful Child.* Amherst, MA: Prometheus Books, 2008.

Guinier, Lani. *The Tyranny of the Meritocracy: Democratizing Higher Education in America.* Boston: Beacon Press, 2015.

Hagopian, Jesse, ed. *More Than a Score: The New Uprising Against High-Stakes Testing.* Chicago: Haymarket Books, 2014.

Hallowell, Edward M. *The Childhood Roots of Adult Happiness: Five Steps to Help Kids Create and Sustain Lifelong Joy.* New York: Ballantine Books, 2003.

Harris, Phillip, Bruce M. Smith, and Joan Harris. *The Myths of Standardized Tests: Why They Don't Tell You What You Think They Do.* Washington, DC: Rowman & Littlefield Publishers, 2011.

Hinshaw, Stephen, and Rachel Kranz. *The Triple Bind: Saving Our Teenage Girls from Today's Pressures.* New York: Ballantine Books, 2009.

Kohn, Alfie. *The Homework Myth: Why Our Kids Get Too Much of a Bad Thing,* reprint edition. Boston: Da Capo Press, 2007.

———. *The Myth of the Spoiled Child: Challenging the Conventional Wisdom About Children and Parenting.* Boston: Da Capo Lifelong Books, 2014.

———. *Punished by Rewards: The Trouble with Gold Stars, Incentive Plans, A's, Praise, and Other Bribes,* 2nd edition. New York: Mariner Books, 1999.

Koretz, Daniel. *Measuring Up: What Educational Testing Really Tells Us.* Cambridge, MA: Harvard University Press, 2009.

Kralovec, Etta, and James Buell. *The End of Homework: How Homework Disrupts Families, Overburdens Children, and Limits Learning.* Boston: Beacon Press, 2001.

Levine, Madeline. *The Price of Privilege: How Parental Pressure and Material Advantage Are Creating a Generation of Disconnected and Unhappy Kids,* reprint edition. New York: Harper Perennial, 2008.

Levitt, Steven D., and Stephen J. Dubner. *Freakonomics: A Rogue Economist Explores the Hidden Side of Everything.* New York: William Morrow Paperbacks, 2009.

Louv, Richard. *Last Child in the Woods: Saving Our Children from Nature-Deficit Disorder.* Chapel Hill, NC: Algonquin Books, 2008.

Medina, John. *Brain Rules: 12 Principles for Surviving and Thriving at Work, Home, and School,* 2nd edition. Edmonds, WA: Pear Press, 2014.

Mogel, Wendy. *The Blessing of a B Minus: Using Jewish Teachings to Raise Resilient Teenagers,* reprint edition. New York: Scribner, 2011.

Nakazawa, Donna Jackson. *The Last Best Cure: My Quest to Awaken the Healing Parts of My Brain and Get Back My Body, My Joy, and My Life.* New York: Hudson Street Press, 2013.

Payne, Kim John, and Lisa M. Ross. *Simplicity Parenting: Using the Extraordinary Power of Less to Raise Calmer, Happier, and More Secure Kids.* New York: Ballantine Books, 2010.

Pink, Daniel H. *Drive: The Surprising Truth About What Motivates Us.* New York: Riverhead Books, 2011.

———. *A Whole New Mind: Why Right-Brainers Will Rule the Future.* New York: Riverhead Books, 2006.

Pope, Loren. *Colleges That Change Lives: 40 Schools That Will Change the Way You Think About Colleges,* 4th revised edition. Revised by Hilary Masell Oswald. New York: Penguin Books, 2012.

Ravitch, Diane. *The Death and Life of the Great American School System: How Testing and Choice Are Undermining Education,* revised and expanded edition. New York: Basic Books, 2011.

———. *Reign of Error: The Hoax of the Privatization Movement and the Danger to America's Public Schools,* reprint edition. New York: Vintage, 2014.

Ripley, Amanda. *The Smartest Kids in the World: And How They Got That Way,* reprint edition. New York: Simon & Schuster, 2014.

Robinson, Ken. *Out of Our Minds: Learning to Be Creative,* 2nd edition. North Mankato, MN: Capstone, 2011.

Robinson, Ken, and Lou Aronica. *Creative Schools: The Grassroots Revolution That's Transforming Education.* New York: Viking, 2015.

———. *The Element: How Finding Your Passion Changes Everything,* reprint edition. New York: Penguin Books, 2009.

Rubin, Gretchen. *The Happiness Project: Or, Why I Spent a Year Trying to Sing in the Morning, Clean My Closets, Fight Right, Read Aristotle, and Generally Have More Fun,* reprint edition. New York: Harper Paperbacks, 2011.

Sahlberg, Pasi. *Finnish Lessons 2.0: What Can the World Learn from Educational Change in Finland?,* 2nd edition. New York: Teachers College Press, 2014.

Schulte, Brigid. *Overwhelmed: How to Work, Love, and Play When No One Has the Time,* reprint edition. New York: Picador, 2015.

Schwartz, Barry. *The Paradox of Choice: Why More Is Less.* New York: Harper Perennial, 2005.

Seligman, Martin E. P. *Authentic Happiness: Using the New Positive Psychology to Realize Your Potential for Lasting Fulfillment.* New York: Atria Books, 2004.

Selingo, Jeffrey J. *College (Un)bound: The Future of Higher Education and What It Means for Students,* reprint edition. Seattle: Amazon Publishing, 2015.

Senior, Jennifer. *All Joy and No Fun: The Paradox of Modern Parenthood,* reprint edition. New York: Ecco, 2015.

Siegel, Daniel J., and Tina Payne Bryson. *The Whole-Brain Child: 12 Revolutionary Strategies to Nurture Your Child's Developing Mind.* New York: Bantam, 2012.

Steinberg, Laurence. *Age of Opportunity: Lessons from the New Science of Adolescence.* New York: Eamon Dolan/Houghton Mifflin Harcourt, 2014.

Strauch, Barbara. *The Primal Teen: What the New Discoveries about the Teenage Brain Tell Us about Our Kids,* reprint edition. New York: Anchor, 2004.

Thacker, Lloyd, ed. *College Unranked: Ending the College Admissions Frenzy.* Cambridge, MA: Harvard University Press, 2005.

Thomas, Douglas, and John Seely Brown. *A New Culture of Learning: Cultivating the Imagination for a World of Constant Change.* Seattle: CreateSpace Independent Publishing Platform, 2011.

Tough, Paul. *How Children Succeed: Grit, Curiosity, and the Hidden Power of Character,* reprint edition. New York: Mariner Books, 2013.

Truebridge, Sara. *Resilience Begins with Beliefs: Building on Student Strengths for Success in School.* New York: Teachers College Press, 2013.

Turkle, Sherry. *Alone Together: Why We Expect More from Technology and Less from Each Other.* New York: Basic Books, 2012.

Twenge, Jean. *Generation Me: Why Today's Young Americans Are More Confident, Assertive, Entitled—and More Miserable Than Ever Before.* New York: Atria Books, 2007.

Wagner, Tony. *Creating Innovators: The Making of Young People Who Will Change the World,* reprint edition. New York: Scribner, 2015.

———. *The Global Achievement Gap: Why Even Our Best Schools Don't Teach the New Survival Skills Our Children Need—and What We Can Do About It,* revised and updated edition. New York: Basic Books, 2014.

Zhao, Yong. *Catching Up or Leading the Way: American Education in the Age of Globalization.* Alexandria, VA: Association for Supervision & Curriculum Development, 2009.

———. *World Class Learners: Educating Creative and Entrepreneurial Students.* Newbury Park, CA: Corwin, 2012.

Articles

Adolescent Sleep Working Group, Committee on Adolescence, and Council on School Health. "Policy Statement: School Start Times for Adolescents." *Pediatrics* 134, no. 3 (September 2014): 1697.

American Psychological Association. *Stress in America: Are Teens Adopting Adults' Stress Habits?* Washington, DC: February 11, 2014. https://www.apa.org/news/press/releases/stress/2013/stress-report.pdf.

Bacigalupe, Gonzalo. "Newton Suicides: Is High-Achiever School Culture Breaking Our Kids?" WBUR, February 17, 2014. http://commonhealth.wbur.org/2014/02/newton-suicide-stress.

———. "Teen Suicides in Privileged Suburb: We Have to Keep Talking." WBUR, February 21, 2014. http://commonhealth.wbur.org/2014/02/teen-suicide-suburb.

Barker, Jane E., Andrei D. Semenov, Laura Michaelson, Lindsay S. Provan, Hannah R. Snyder, and Yuko Munakata. "Less-structured time in children's daily lives predicts self-directed executive functioning." *Frontiers in Psychology* 5, no. 593 (June 17, 2014).

Benn, Melissa. "Education's culture of overwork is turning children and teachers into ghosts." *Guardian,* April 16, 2014. http://www.theguardian.com/commentisfree/2014/apr/16/culture-overwork-teachers-children-ghosts-schools.

Berliner, David. "Why giving standardized tests to young children is 'really dumb.'" *Washington Post,* July 19, 2011. http://www.washingtonpost.com/blogs/answer-sheet/post/why-giving-standardized-tests-to-young-children-is-really-dumb/2011/07/18/gIQAB7OnMI_blog.html.

Bhatia, Aatish. "Active Learning Leads to Higher Grades and Fewer Failing Students in Science, Math, and Engineering." *Wired,* May 12, 2014. http://www.wired.com/2014/05/empzeal-active-learning/.

Bronson, Po. "Snooze or Lose." *New York,* October 7, 2007. http://nymag.com/news/features/38951/.

Bronson, Po, and Ashley Merryman. "The Creativity Crisis." *Newsweek,* July 7, 2010. http://www.newsweek.com/creativity-crisis-74665.

Bruni, Frank. "Best, Brightest—and Saddest?" *New York Times*, April 11, 2015. http://www
.nytimes.com/2015/04/12/opinion/sunday/frank-bruni-best-brightest-and-saddest.html.

Bryant, Jeff. "Lani Guinier on our Ivy League meritocracy lie: 'You don't want only those
people who do well on the SAT.'" *Salon*, February 4, 2015. http://www.salon.com/
2015/02/04/lani_guinier_on_our_ivy_league_meritocracy_lie_you_dont_want_only
_those_people_who_do_well_on_the_sat/.

Burd, Stephen, and Rachel Fishman. "Ten Ways Colleges Work You Over." *Washington
Monthly*, September/October 2014. http://www.washingtonmonthly.com/magazine/
septemberoctober_2014/features/ten_ways_colleges_work_you_ove051760.php.

Canady, Robert Lynn, and Michael D. Rettig. "The Power of Innovative Scheduling." *Educational Leadership* 53, no. 3 (November 1995): 4–10.

Childress, Herb. "17 Reasons Why Football Is Better Than High School." *North Coast Journal
Weekly*, September 24, 1998. http://www.northcoastjournal.com/092498/cover0924.html.

Cooperative Institutional Research Program. *The American Freshman: National Norms Fall
2014*. Higher Education Research Institute at UCLA, February 2015. http://www.heri
.ucla.edu/briefs/TheAmericanFreshman2014-Brief.pdf.

Darling-Hammond, Linda. "Beyond the Bubble Test: Why We Need Performance Assessments." *Huffington Post*, July 15, 2014. http://www.huffingtonpost.com/linda-darlingham
mond/beyond-the-bubble-test-wh_b_5588990.html.

Davis, Joshua. "How a Radical New Teaching Method Could Unleash a Generation of Geniuses." *Wired*, October 15, 2013. http://www.wired.com/2013/10/free-thinkers/.

Divecha, Diana, and Robin Stern. "American Teens Are Stressed and Bored. It's Time to Talk
About Feelings." *Time*, April 10, 2015. http://time.com/3774596/american-teens-emotions/.

Dobbs, David. "Beautiful Brains." *National Geographic*, October 2011. http://ngm.national
geographic.com/2011/10/teenage-brains/dobbs-text.

Drew, Christopher. "Why Science Majors Change Their Minds (It's Just So Darn Hard)."
New York Times, November 4, 2011. http://www.nytimes.com/2011/11/06/education/
edlife/why-science-majors-change-their-mind-its-just-so-darn-hard.html.

Edwards, David. "American Schools Are Training Kids for a World That Doesn't Exist." *Wired*,
October 17, 2014. http://www.wired.com/2014/10/on-learning-by-doing/.

Emanuel, Gabrielle. "Among Dartmouth's Lathes and Saws, Lessons in Creativity." NPR,
December 1, 2014. http://www.npr.org/sections/ed/2014/12/01/353286773/among
-dartmoths-lathes-and-saws-lessons-in-creativity.

Enayati, Amanda. "Is homework making your child sick?" CNN, March 21, 2014. http://
www.cnn.com/2014/03/21/health/homework-stress/index.html.

Engel, Susan. "7 things every kid should master." *Boston Globe*, February 26, 2015. http://
www.bostonglobe.com/magazine/2015/02/26/things-every-kid-should-master/uM72L
Gr63zeaStOp9zGyrJ/story.html.

Entin, Esther. "All Work and No Play: Why Your Kids Are More Anxious, Depressed." *Atlantic*,
October 12, 2011. http://www.theatlantic.com/health/archive/2011/10/all-work-and
-no-play-why-your-kids-are-more-anxious-depressed/246422/.

———. "The Case for Recess." *Atlantic*, February 27, 2012. http://www.theatlantic.com/
health/archive/2012/02/the-case-for-recess/253549/.

Farnham, Lija, Gihani Fernando, Mike Perigo, Colleen Brosman, and Paul Tough. "Rethinking How Students Succeed." *Stanford Social Innovation Review,* February 17, 2015.

Fitzsimmons, William, Marlyn E. McGrath, and Charles Ducey. "Time Out or Burn Out for the Next Generation." Harvard College, 2000 (revised 2011). https://college.harvard.edu/admissions/preparing-college/should-i-take-time.

Flanagan, Caitlin. "The Ivy Delusion: The Real Reason the Good Mothers Are So Rattled by Amy Chua." *Atlantic,* April 2011. http://www.theatlantic.com/magazine/archive/2011/04/the-ivy-delusion/308397/.

Gladwell, Malcolm. "The Order of Things: What college rankings really tell us." *New Yorker,* February 14, 2011. http://www.newyorker.com/magazine/2011/02/14/the-order-of-things.

Gordon Commission on the Future of Assessment in Education. "Shifting Paradigms: Beyond the Abstract." *Assessment, Teaching, and Learning* 2, no. 2 (April 2012).

Gray, Peter. "The Decline of Play and the Rise of Psychopathology in Children and Adolescents." *American Journal of Play* 3, no. 4 (Spring 2011). http://www.journalofplay.org/sites/www.journalofplay.org/files/pdf-articles/3-4-article-gray-decline-of-play.pdf.

Greenfeld, Karl Taro. "My Daughter's Homework Is Killing Me." *Atlantic,* October 2013. http://www.theatlantic.com/magazine/archive/2013/10/my-daughters-homework-is-killing-me/309514/.

Hamilton, Jon. "Scientists Say Child's Play Helps Build a Better Brain." NPR, August 6, 2014. http://www.npr.org/sections/ed/2014/08/06/336361277/scientists-say-childs-play-helps-build-a-better-brain.

Hanscom, Angela. "Why so many kids can't sit still in school today." *Washington Post,* July 8, 2014. http://www.washingtonpost.com/blogs/answer-sheet/wp/2014/07/08/why-so-many-kids-cant-sit-still-in-school-today/.

Hawkins, Beth. "The Pursuit of Deeper Learning." *Atlantic,* December 2, 2014. http://www.theatlantic.com/education/archive/2014/12/the-pursuit-of-deeper-learning/383308.

Hoffman, Jan. "Anxious Students Strain College Mental Health Centers." *New York Times,* May 27, 2015. http://well.blogs.nytimes.com/2015/05/27/anxious-students-strain-college-mental-health-centers/.

———. "I Know What You Did Last Math Class." *New York Times,* May 4, 2008. http://www.nytimes.com/2008/05/04/fashion/04edline.html.

———. "To Keep Teenagers Alert, Schools Let Them Sleep In." *New York Times,* March 13, 2014. http://well.blogs.nytimes.com/2014/03/13/to-keep-teenagers-alert-schools-let-them-sleep-in/.

Hu, Winnie. "New Recruit in Homework Revolt: The Principal." *New York Times,* June 15, 2011. http://www.nytimes.com/2011/06/16/education/16homework.html.

IBM. "IBM 2010 Global CEO Study: Creativity Selected as Most Crucial Factor for Future Success." News release, May 18, 2010. http://www-03.ibm.com/press/us/en/pressrelease/31670.wss.

Jones, Todd, Mike Wagner, and Jill Riepenhoff. "Children may be vulnerable in $5 billion youth-sports industry." *Columbus Dispatch,* August 31, 2010. http://www.dispatch.com/content/stories/local/2010/08/27/day1-children-may-be-vulnerable-in-5-billion-youth-sports-industry.html.

Kamenetz, Anya. "Testing: How Much Is Too Much?" NPR, November 17, 2014. http://
    www.npr.org/sections/ed/2014/11/17/362339421/testing-how-much-is-too-much.
————. "Want your kids to opt out of standardized tests? The Constitution may be with you."
    Washington Post, January 9, 2015. http://www.washingtonpost.com/opinions/want-your
    -kids-to-opt-out-of-standardized-tests-the-constitution-may-be-with-you/2015/01/09/
    bea151b4–973a-11e4–8005–1924ede3e54a_story.html.
————. "What Schools Could Use Instead of Standardized Tests." NPR, January 6, 2015.
    http://www.npr.org/sections/ed/2015/01/06/371659141/what-schools-could-use-instead
    -of-standardized-tests.
Kohn, Alfie. "Why Self-Discipline Is Overrated: The (Troubling) Theory and Practice of
    Control from Within." *Phi Delta Kappan,* November 2008. http://www.alfiekohn.org/
    article/self-discipline-overrated/.
Kohn, David. "Let the Kids Learn Through Play." *New York Times,* May 16, 2015. http://www
    .nytimes.com/2015/05/17/opinion/sunday/let-the-kids-learn-through-play.html.
Kolker, Robert. "Cheating Upwards." *New York,* September 16, 2012. http://nymag.com/
    news/features/cheating-2012–9/.
Kreider, Tim. "The 'Busy' Trap." *New York Times,* June 30, 2012. http://opinionator.blogs
    .nytimes.com/2012/06/30/the-busy-trap/.
Lahey, Jessica. "Teach Kids to Daydream: Mental downtime makes people more creative
    and less anxious." *Atlantic,* October 16, 2013. http://www.theatlantic.com/education/
    archive/2013/10/teach-kids-to-daydream/280615/.
Lazarín, Melissa. *Testing Overload in America's Schools.* Washington, DC: Center for Ameri-
    can Progress, October 2014. https://cdn.americanprogress.org/wp-content/uploads
    /2014/10/LazarinOvertestingReport.pdf.
Lifshitz, Jessica. "An Open Letter to My Students: I Am Sorry for What I Am About to Do
    to You." *Huffington Post,* March 5, 2015. http://www.huffingtonpost.com/jessica-lifshitz/
    an-open-letter-to-my-students-parcc_b_6808060.html.
Luthar, Suniya S., Samuel H. Barkin, and Elizabeth J. Crossman. " 'I can, therefore I must':
    fragility in the upper-middle classes." *Development and Psychopathology* 25, no. 4, pt. 2 (No-
    vember 2013): 1529–49.
Machado, Amanda. "Should Schools Teach Kids to Meditate?" *Atlantic,* January 27, 2014.
    http://www.theatlantic.com/education/archive/2014/01/should-schools-teach-kids-to
    -meditate/283229/.
McMillan, Rebecca L., Scott Barry Kaufman, and Jerome L. Singer. "Ode to positive construc-
    tive daydreaming." *Frontiers in Psychology* 4, no. 626 (September 23, 2013).
Merrow, John. "What Happens in Great Schools." *Taking Note,* November 7, 2014. http://
    takingnote.learningmatters.tv/?p=7311.
Miller, Claire Cain. "The 24/7 Work Culture's Toll on Families and Gender Equality." *New
    York Times,* May 28, 2015. http://www.nytimes.com/2015/05/31/upshot/the-24–7
    -work-cultures-toll-on-families-and-gender-equality.html.
Mitchell, Jeff. "Harvard-or-Walmart Syndrome." JeffMitchellAssociates.com. http://www.jeff
    mitchellassociates.com/Jeff/harvardorwalmart3.pdf.
National Association for College Admission Counseling (NACAC). *Report of the Com-*

mission on the Use of Standardized Tests in Undergraduate Admission. Arlington, VA: September 2008. http://www.nacacnet.org/research/PublicationsResources/Marketplace/Documents/TestingComission_FinalReport.pdf.

Noguchi, Sharon. "Teen health: Depression, anxiety and social phobias rising in kids, educators say." *San Jose Mercury News,* February 5, 2014. http://www.mercurynews.com/health/ci_25074044/teen-health-depression-anxiety-and-social-phobias-rising.

O'Brien, Keith. "Why have homework? Beneath a pillar of our education system lies a troubling uncertainty." *Boston Globe,* September 17, 2011. https://www.bostonglobe.com/ideas/2011/09/17/why-have-homework/oSYVu211Wz7TXa14cziH5I/story.html.

Organization for Economic Cooperation and Development (OECD). "Does homework perpetuate inequities in education?" *PISA in Focus,* December 2014.

Pappano, Laura. "Is Your First Grader College Ready?" *New York Times,* February 4, 2015. http://www.nytimes.com/2015/02/08/education/edlife/is-your-first-grader-college-ready.html.

Partanen, Anu. "What Americans Keep Ignoring About Finland's School Success." *Atlantic,* December 29, 2011. http://www.theatlantic.com/national/archive/2011/12/what-americans-keep-ignoring-about-finlands-school-success/250564/.

Pérez-Peña, Richard, and Daniel E. Slotnik. "Gaming the College Rankings." *New York Times,* January 31, 2012. http://www.nytimes.com/2012/02/01/education/gaming-the-college-rankings.html.

Ripley, Amanda. "Bored to Death: To learn just how bored kids are in school, look at Twitter." *New Republic,* December 16, 2013. http://www.newrepublic.com/article/115928/twitter-shows-epidemic-school-boredom.

Rivero, Lisa. "High School Years: College Prep or Life Prep?" *Psychology Today,* April 11, 2012. https://www.psychologytoday.com/blog/creative-synthesis/201204/high-school-years-college-prep-or-life-prep.

Rosen, Lawrence. "Buzzed: Energy Drinks + Stimulants = PEDs of Choice?" *Huffington Post,* January 30, 2013. http://www.huffingtonpost.com/lawrence-rosen-md/kids-energy-drinks_b_2581525.html.

Ryan, Richard M., and Edward L. Deci. "Intrinsic and Extrinsic Motivations: Classic Definitions and New Directions." *Contemporary Educational Psychology* 25, no. 1 (January 2000): 54–67.

Safi, Omid. "The Disease of Being Busy." *On Being,* November 6, 2014. http://onbeing.org/blog/the-disease-of-being-busy/7023.

Sahlberg, Pasi. "Finland's Educational Success is No Miracle." *Education Week,* January 2012. http://pasisahlberg.com/finlands-educational-success-is-no-miracle/.

———. "Teach for Finland? Why it won't happen." *Washington Post,* February 12, 2015. http://www.washingtonpost.com/blogs/answer-sheet/wp/2015/02/12/teach-for-finland-why-it-wont-happen/.

Schulte, Brigid. "In McLean, a crusade to get people to back off in the parenting arms race." *Washington Post,* March 23, 2014. http://www.washingtonpost.com/lifestyle/style/in-mclean-a-crusade-to-get-people-to-back-off-in-the-parenting-arms-race/2014/03/23/9259c6a2-a552-11e3-a5fa-55f0c77bf39c_story.html.

Schwartz, Barry. "Top Colleges Should Select Randomly from a Pool of 'Good Enough.'"

Chronicle of Higher Education, February 25, 2005. http://chronicle.com/article/Top-Col leges-Should-Select/14215/.

Schwartz, Katrina. "Does The Grit Narrative Blame Students For School's Shortcomings?" KQED *MindShift,* May 5, 2015. http://ww2.kqed.org/mindshift/2015/05/05/does-the -grit-narrative-blame-students-for-schools-shortcomings/.

———. "Harvard Wants to Know: How Does the Act of Making Shape Kids' Brains?" KQED *MindShift,* November 7, 2012. http://ww2.kqed.org/mindshift/2012/11/07/harvard -wants-to-know-how-does-making-shape-kids-brains/.

Schwartz, Tony. "Escalating Demands at Work Hurt Employees and Companies." *New York Times,* June 5, 2015. http://www.nytimes.com/2015/06/06/business/dealbook/excessive -demands-at-work-create-a-humanitarian-crisis.html.

Schwarz, Alan. "Risky Rise of the Good-Grade Pill." *New York Times,* June 9, 2012. http:// www.nytimes.com/2012/06/10/education/seeking-academic-edge-teenagers-abuse-stimu lants.html.

Shankar, Sri Sri Ravi. "Rethink. Redefine. Success." *Huffington Post,* March 5, 2012. http:// www.huffingtonpost.com/sri-sri-ravi-shankar/teen-suicide_b_1319009.html.

Shonkoff, Jack P., and Andrew S. Garner. "The Lifelong Effects of Early Childhood Adversity and Toxic Stress." *Pediatrics* 129, no. 1 (January 2012): 232–46.

Singh, Maanvi. "Why Emotional Learning May Be As Important As The ABCs." NPR, December 31, 2014. http://www.npr.org/sections/ed/2014/12/31/356187871/why-emo tional-literacy-may-be-as-important-as-learning-the-a-b-c-s.

Slaughter, Anne-Marie. "Rebellion of an Innovation Mom." CNN, June 5, 2011. http://global publicsquare.blogs.cnn.com/2011/06/05/rebellion-of-the-innovation-mom/.

Stipek, Deborah. "Relationships Matter." *Educational Leadership* 64, no. 1 (September 2006): 46–49.

Tierney, John. "Your Annual Reminder to Ignore the *U.S. News & World Report* College Rankings." *Atlantic,* September 10, 2013. http://www.theatlantic.com/education/archive/ 2013/09/your-annual-reminder-to-ignore-the-em-us-news-world-report-em-college -rankings/279103/.

Turker, Ron J. "All Played Out." *New York Times,* July 27, 2014. http://nyti.ms/X4hKxb.

Turner, Cory. "Kids and Screen Time: Cutting Through the Static." NPR, September 30, 2014. http://www.npr.org/sections/ed/2014/09/30/351521488/kids-and-screen-time -cutting-through-the-static.

Wagner, Tony. "Educating the Next Steve Jobs." *Wall Street Journal,* April 13, 2012. http:// www.wsj.com/articles/SB10001424052702304444604577337790086673050.

Walworth, Carolyn. "Paly student tells of school stress: 'Students are gasping for air.'" *Almanac,* March 26, 2015. http://www.almanacnews.com/news/2015/03/26/guest-opinion -on-school-stress-students-are-gasping-for-air.

Weissbourd, Rick, Stephanie Jones, Trisha Ross Anderson, Jennifer Kahn, and Mark Russell. *The Children We Mean to Raise: The Real Messages Adults Are Sending About Values.* Cambridge, MA: Making Caring Common Project, Harvard Graduate School of Education, Summer 2014. http://sites.gse.harvard.edu/sites/default/files/making-caring-common/ files/mcc_report_the_children_we_mean_to_raise_0.pdf.

Willingham, Daniel T. "How Knowledge Helps: It Speeds and Strengthens Reading Comprehension, Learning—and Thinking." *American Educator,* Spring 2006. http://www.aft.org/periodical/american-educator/spring-2006/how-knowledge-helps.

Wong, Alia. "In 2014, One Size Didn't Fit All." *Atlantic,* December 23, 2014. http://www.theatlantic.com/education/archive/2014/12/in-2014-one-size-didnt-fit-all/384001/.

Zinshteyn, Mikhail. "Should the U.S. Make Standardized Tests Harder?" *Atlantic,* November 24, 2014. http://www.theatlantic.com/education/archive/2014/11/should-the-us-make-standardized-tests-harder/383084/.

Lectures

Achor, Shawn. "The happy secret to better work." TEDxBloomington, May 2011. http://www.ted.com/talks/shawn_achor_the_happy_secret_to_better_work?language=en.

Brown, Brené. "The power of vulnerability." TEDxHouston, June 2010. https://www.ted.com/talks/brene_brown_on_vulnerability?language=en.

Heckman, James. "Cognitive Skills Are Not Enough." Address to policy and business leaders in Chicago, Illinois, December 16, 2010. http://heckmanequation.org/content/resource/cognitive-skills-are-not-enough.

Pausch, Randy. "Last Lecture: Really Achieving Your Childhood Dreams." Presented at Carnegie Mellon, September 18, 2007. https://www.youtube.com/watch?v=ji5_MqicxSo.

Robinson, Ken. "Do schools kill creativity?" TED Talk, February 2006. http://www.ted.com/talks/ken_robinson_says_schools_kill_creativity?language=en.

Rose, Todd. "The Myth of Average." TEDxSonomaCounty, June 2013. http://tedxtalks.ted.com/video/The-Myth-of-Average-Todd-Rose-a.

Index

About the Authors

Vicki Abeles is an ex–Wall Street lawyer turned filmmaker, author, and education advocate. Her first feature documentary, *Race to Nowhere*, hit a nerve with its vivid portrayal of the pressure-cooker culture dominating America's schools. Her second film, *Beyond Measure,* about the groundbreaking leaders transforming schools for the better, premiered in 2015. She is also the founder of a nonprofit, grassroots organization that guides communities as they redefine student success and promote the health, learning, and wellness of the whole child. She lives in the San Francisco area with her family.

Grace Rubenstein is a multimedia journalist specializing in health, education, and immigration. Her stories—told variously in words, photos, audio, and video—have appeared in TheAtlantic.com and the *New York Times*. She is the multimedia editor at TED Books and a regular contributor at KQED public radio. Her five-year stint as a staff writer and producer at *Edutopia*, the publication of the George Lucas Educational Foundation, took her into innovative schools around the country. She is a fourth-generation San Franciscan.